"The long and short of *Voices and Vie*
provides especially for students a wonderful map of what some major thinkers are saying about the apostle Paul. Witherington and Myers cover big names—K. Stendahl, E. P. Sanders, James D. G. Dunn, N. T. Wright, J. C. Beker, B. Gaventa, J. Barclay, S. Chester—and do so with admirable thoroughness for those needing introduction to their thoughts. As such, this book is long on presenting what is going on in Pauline scholarship. The short is that this is not an extensive evaluation but more like footnotes and commentary. Students reading this book will want to pick up the volumes discussed, and others as well, and delve in for themselves, having been given a worthy map of the terrain."

Scot McKnight, professor of New Testament at Northern Seminary

"To reuse Ben Witherington's own pun in a different context, there has been an appalling amount of Pauline scholarship since he surveyed the landscape in his 1998 IVP book, *The Paul Quest*. A huge percentage of it has focused on Paul's theology and specifically issues arising out of the 'New Perspective on Paul.' Here Witherington and his younger colleague, Jason Myers, deftly delve more selectively but in more detail into the key viewpoints of the most significant thinkers from E. P. Sanders to today. They prove most helpful guides, offering insightful critique as well as thorough summaries, providing a welcome map for navigating a tricky hedge maze of scholarship!"

Craig L. Blomberg, distinguished professor of New Testament at Denver Seminary

"The academic study of the apostle is a world unto itself—a world in which it would be very easy to get lost without guidance. Witherington and Myers know the terrain well and offer much insight into the major trends, debates, and crosscurrents of the last two decades. Whether you are a new explorer to Pauline studies or a seasoned traveler, *Voices and Views on Paul* has much to offer in the big picture as well as the finer details."

Nijay K. Gupta, professor of New Testament at Northern Seminary

"*Voices and Views on Paul* is an invaluable resource for teachers and students of Paul. It feels as if it is a much-needed volume, bringing clarity and insight to the complexities of Pauline scholarship of the last sixty years, and taking the reader through the major developments in thinking in a way that is masterfully comprehensive and succinct at the same time. What is particularly helpful about this volume is that it not only provides excellent summaries of the work of key players and movements, but it also offers generous, insightful, and balanced critique. One is able to hear the voices of Ben Witherington and Jason Myers in a way that is pitched just right in order to give readers a handle on the strengths and weaknesses of different perspectives, while at the same time giving everyone a fair hearing. This is very nicely done. It should be on every reading list."

Lucy Peppiatt, principal, Westminster Theological Centre, UK, author of *Rediscovering Scripture's Vision for Women*

"Negotiating the nettle of Pauline studies is not for the faint-hearted or feeble-minded. In *Voices and Views on Paul,* Ben Witherington III and Jason A. Myers succeed in making leading Anglophone scholars and their seminal works on the apostle more accessible and enjoyable. Like its predecessor—the award-winning *The Paul Quest*—this volume will prove invaluable for those who are seeking a suitable entrée into the fascinating, demanding world that is contemporary Pauline scholarship."

Todd D. Still, Charles J. and Eleanor McLerran DeLancey Dean and William M. Hinson Professor of Christian Scriptures, Truett Seminary of Baylor University

"The scholarly study of the apostle Paul is a jungle of exotic 'perspectives,' but thankfully Ben Witherington and Jason Myers provide something of a Pauline safari tour to help identify and understand the many species of Pauline scholarship. A terrific guide for students who are entering into the confusing world of New Testament studies."

Michael F. Bird, academic dean and lecturer in theology at Ridley College, Melbourne, Australia

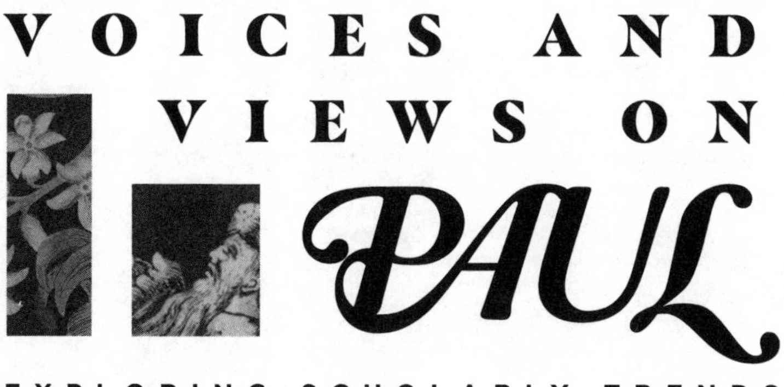

VOICES AND VIEWS ON PAUL

EXPLORING SCHOLARLY TRENDS

BEN WITHERINGTON III
and JASON A. MYERS

Academic
An imprint of InterVarsity Press
Downers Grove, Illinois

InterVarsity Press
P.O. Box 1400, Downers Grove, IL 60515-1426
ivpress.com
email@ivpress.com

InterVarsity Press® is the book-publishing division of InterVarsity Christian Fellowship/USA®, a movement of students and faculty active on campus at hundreds of universities, colleges, and schools of nursing in the United States of America, and a member movement of the International Fellowship of Evangelical Students. For information about local and regional activities, visit intervarsity.org.

Cover design and image montage: David Fassett
Interior design: Daniel van Loon
Images: © sedmak/iStock/Getty Images Plus

ISBN 978-0-8308-5231-4 (print)
ISBN 978-0-8308-7344-9 (digital)

Printed in the United States of America ♾

InterVarsity Press is committed to ecological stewardship and to the conservation of natural resources in all our operations. This book was printed using sustainably sourced paper.

Library of Congress Cataloging-in-Publication Data
A catalog record for this book is available from the Library of Congress.

P 25 24 23 22 21 20 19 18 17 16 15 14 13 12 11 10 9 8 7 6 5 4 3 2 1
Y 38 37 36 35 34 33 32 31 30 29 28 27 26 25 24 23 22 21 20

CONTENTS

To

Kingsley Barrett

(in memento mori),

and

Andrew Lincoln

and

Gordon Fee,

who taught me Paul, and taught me well.

Ben Witherington III

~

To

Lisa

and our long-awaited gift from God,

Augustine Matthew.

Jason Myers

PREFACE

A great deal of Pauline water, indeed a veritable flood of Pauline water, has passed under the bridge since the first edition of *The Paul Quest* appeared in 1998 and then won a biblical studies book of the year award from *Christianity Today* in 1999.[1] Some very major—and some would say seminal and game-changing—studies on Paul began to appear in 1998, starting with J. D. G. Dunn's synthesis volume, *The Theology of Paul the Apostle,* followed by a whole series of books on Paul or his thought world by N. T. Wright, climaxing in 2013 with Wright's magnum opus *Paul and the Faithfulness of God.* This was then unexpectedly followed by a capstone work by E. P. Sanders titled *Paul: The Apostle's Life, Letters, and Thought,* in 2015, and perhaps the most important study on Paul's theology of grace in a generation, by John Barclay, titled *Paul and the Gift,* which also appeared in 2015.

What characterizes all these works is that they are very large books indeed, the smallest one being Barclay's, which is a mere 670-plus pages, with Wright's volumes clocking in at a hefty 1,700-plus pages. Yes, there have also been a variety of other seminal, more specialized studies on Paul in the last twenty years, but none more *influential* than these on the field, and it should be noted that they all come from the pens of those who either are British New Testament scholars or spent considerable time, as Sanders did (at Oxford), teaching at British institutions and

[1]Ben Witherington III, *The Paul Quest: The Renewed Search for the Jew of Tarsus* (Downers Grove, IL: InterVarsity Press, 1998).

imbibing the Pauline air from that side of the pond. But it should not be overlooked that the more apocalyptic reading of Paul's thought by Ernst Käsemann (see especially his Romans commentary) has borne major fruit in America in Lou Martyn's landmark Galatians commentary and then in various works by his doctoral student Beverly Gaventa.[2] Also, some of the scholars associated with the "new perspective on Paul," such as Richard Hays and N. T. Wright, have been especially influential in advocating the reading of the Pauline phrase *pistis Christou* (literally "faith of Christ") to refer to Christ's own faith and faithfulness to God.

Thus it is that the course of Pauline studies in the last twenty years dictates a different approach to the study of Paul than was undertaken in the first *Paul Quest* book, where I (Ben) focused on three different aspects of the Pauline personality—Paul the Jew, Paul the Roman citizen, and Paul the follower of Christ. In this study, we must focus on the interface between Pauline thought and the Pauline mission, with special attention to the former, because that is where the balance of the discussion has been—taking up topics such as the faith of Christ, or justification, or grace. We will do this by focusing carefully on the contributions of these major works, and related seminal studies, assessing both how they have advanced our understanding of Paul and his thought world, and how they may have gone awry in the course of the deep and helpful probing that characterizes these works. We will consider the new perspective(s) on Paul, the apocalyptic Paul of Martyn and Gaventa (and others), the misreading of Paul's concepts of righteousness and grace, and much more. We have no illusions that we can cover the whole Pauline waterfront of the last twenty years—there's simply too much water! But what we can do is assess some of the major studies and contributions that have been and are likely to continue to

[2]Ernst Käsemann, *Perspectives on Paul* (Philadelphia: Fortress, 1969); Käsemann, *Romans* (Grand Rapids: Eerdmans, 1980); J. Louis Martyn, *Theological Issues in the Letters of Paul* (Nashville: Abingdon, 1997); Martyn, *Galatians* (New Haven, CT: Yale University Press, 2004); Beverly Roberts Gaventa, *Our Mother Saint Paul* (Louisville, KY: Westminster John Knox, 2007).

be the most influential for our understanding of the first great Christian theologian and missionary—Paul the apostle to the Gentiles.

As for the division of labor, Ben will be taking on the chapters on Wright and Barclay, while Jason will contribute the chapters on the new perspective in general, on Sanders, on Dunn, and on the apocalyptic Paul. In the final conclusions, we will raise and try to answer some questions about what fresh light all these discussions shed on Paul the man, his mission, and his thought world.

ACKNOWLEDGMENTS

To my editors Dan Reid and Michael Thomson, for all their encouragement over many years as I kept writing about Paul.

—Ben Witherington III

My love of Paul was inspired by my first teacher of Paul, Dr. Chris Miller. Under him, I devoured Galatians and Romans in spring 2006. Sitting on a back porch pouring over Paul's letters piqued my interest in what these ancient letters might have to say for today. I can honestly say this book would never had happened without his introducing me, in many ways for the first time, to the apostle Paul. Likewise, Dr. Gary Meadors instilled the virtue of a love for research and understanding the history of ideas. Finally, Dr. Ben Witherington has graciously guided me towards some formative readings of Paul and graciously gave me the opportunity to write this book with him. To all my teachers, I am grateful for your generosity toward me and investment in me.

Further thanks are in order to Tyndale House in Cambridge, England, where several of my chapters took form over the years. The generous hospitality of Tyndale provided much-needed space for research. From wandering the stacks to conversations over tea, I'm grateful for my time there.

I'd also like to thank our editors Dan Reid, who first commissioned this project, and Anna Gissing, who brought it to completion!

Finally, none of my work is possible without the generous support of Lisa. She has given me much freedom to research and write that has been so valuable to allow this book to come to fruition. This book is a gift to her and our son, Augustine Matthew.

—Jason A. Myers

ABBREVIATIONS

BJ — Dunn, James D. G. *Christianity in the Making*. Vol. 2, *Beginning from Jerusalem*. Grand Rapids: Eerdmans, 2008.

NPP — Dunn, James D. G. *The New Perspective on Paul: Whence, What, and Whither*. Rev. ed. Grand Rapids, Eerdmans, 2005.

OMSP — Gaventa, Beverly Roberts. *Our Mother Saint Paul*. Louisville: Westminster John Knox, 2007.

PALLT — Sanders, E. P. *Paul: The Apostle's Life, Letters, and Thought*. Minneapolis: Fortress, 2016.

PFG — Wright, N. T. *Paul and the Faithfulness of God*. 2 vols. Christian Origins and the Question of God 4. Minneapolis: Fortress, 2013.

PLJP — Sanders, E. P. *Paul, the Law, and the Jewish People*. Minneapolis: Fortress, 1983.

PPJ — Sanders, E. P. *Paul and Palstinian Judaism*. Philadelphia: Fortress, 1977.

TPA — Dunn, James D. G. *The Theology of the Paul the Apostle*. Grand Rapids: Eerdmans, 1998.

one

RETROSPECTIVE

THE NEW PERSPECTIVE ON PAUL

When John wrote, "Behold, I am making all things New!" (Rev 21:5), one wonders whether this applies to Pauline theology.

Anonymous

Since the initial publication of *The Paul Quest* in 1998, Pauline scholars have continued churning out book after book on the apostle Paul. There has been an explosion of resources from a variety of fields in the guild. While the first Paul quest book was concerned with issues relating to Paul's identity and thought, little space could be devoted to the history of interpretation of Paul, which has shaped how we know what we know. One of the larger developments in Pauline scholarship in the last thirty years is the so-called new perspective on Paul; at this time of writing, however, even this phrase is out of touch in many ways with the current state of Pauline studies.

First, the new perspective is no longer new. The phrase was coined by James Dunn in 1983 and is now thirty-seven years old. Second, the term *perspective* is a bit misleading, as there is no singular view on Paul within the new perspective on Paul. The term *perspectives* may be a bit more appropriate, as it represents a variety of persons and issues, some of whom seldom agree with one another. These perspectives will be unpacked in due course. Third, we now have new terms, such as "beyond the new perspective," that build on, extend, and truly go beyond the new perspective

on Paul. For these reasons and more, a book such as this is needed in order to keep pace with the flurry of publications on Paul over the past twenty years since the initial publication of *The Paul Quest*. However, in order to know where Pauline studies is headed, one must have an appropriate knowledge of where Pauline studies has come from.[1] Hence this retrospective is in order.

WHERE TO BEGIN?

Any work on Paul has to pick a starting point, this work being no exception. The Pauline volcano had been bubbling up for some time before the eruption that was the new perspective on Paul. Although it might seem obvious to start a retrospect on the new perspective on Paul with E. P. Sanders or James Dunn, this would be a mistake and set off the conversation within the wrong context and on the wrong track. In order to understand the context of Sanders, Dunn, Wright, and others, we must take a step back and investigate some of the forerunners who led the way to those scholars' seminal works. For the purposes of the current project we will begin with Krister Stendahl.[2]

THE GREAT-GRANDFATHER OF THE NEW PERSPECTIVE ON PAUL: KRISTER STENDAHL

The work of Krister Stendahl marked a noted shift in Pauline studies.[3] In 1963 he published "The Apostle Paul and the Introspective Conscience of the West," which anticipated much of later Pauline

[1]The student of Paul is greatly aided with this topic by the addition of key resources such as Magnus Zetterholm, *Approaches to Paul: A Student's Guide to Recent Scholarship* (Minneapolis: Fortress, 2009); N. T. Wright, *Paul and His Recent Interpreters* (Minneapolis: Fortress, 2013).

[2]Some early notable objections were made by C. G. Montefiore and George Foot Moore. Likewise, W. D. Davies's classic work on Paul, *Paul and Rabbinic Judaism: Some Rabbinic Elements in Pauline Theology* (Minneapolis: Fortress, 1980), argued that nearly every aspect of Pauline thought that others (including the history of religion school) thought derived from Hellenism could be found with equal explanatory power within Judaism. Davies argued that Paul was, like Philo, a Jew espousing a message in Hellenistic terms but still firmly rooted in Judaism.

[3]I (Ben) can attest to his influence, as I took Romans with Stendahl at Harvard Divinity School in 1975. At that point, he was working on a Romans (or Galatians?) commentary, which sadly never emerged due to his health issues.

studies emphases by almost twenty years.[4] However, even here, Stendahl's work had its own predecessors.[5] His influential work was first given as a lecture in 1960, published in Swedish in 1961, and then in English two years later. One of the primary features of Stendahl's work is his emphasis on the uniqueness of Paul's historical context and the differences between his time and ours. Stendahl argues that one of the most basic issues of Paul had gone unnoticed, and this issue shaped Paul's thought to a greater extent than any other.

According to Stendahl, the missing link in Pauline studies was the relationship between Jews and Gentiles. At the heart of Stendahl's concern is that Paul's letters have been homogenized to reveal an abstract theological outline rather than attention being devoted to the particular issues that Paul addressed. It is to this primary issue of Paul being an *apostle to the Gentiles,* in a specific historical situation, that Stendahl directs his entire attention. Stendahl raises the important correction that Paul's teaching had been detached from his mission and task, to be the apostle to the Gentiles. One can see how this sort of emphasis could even lead to some of the later Jewish perspectives on Paul that have insisted that not only is Paul the apostle to the Gentiles, but that what he says about circumcision, Sabbath, and other boundary issues are strictly applicable only to Gentile followers of Jesus. In other words, Paul is not addressing the issues of "Jew and Gentile united in Christ." He is addressing Gentile Christians only.[6]

---

[4]Krister Stendahl, "The Apostle Paul and the Introspective Conscience of the West," *Harvard Theological Review* 56 (1963): 199-215. Stendahl, himself an ordained Lutheran clergyman, was especially concerned to jettison the old Lutheran readings of Paul and place Paul more appropriately in his early Jewish context, without the caricature of Judaism as a religion of works-righteousness or legalism, emphases we hear again and again in Sanders, Dunn, and others who have contributed to the new perspective on Paul.

[5]Stendahl notes in his introduction to *Paul Among Jews and Gentiles* that at the time of his lecture "Paul and the Introspective Conscience of the West" he was highly influenced by the work of Johannes Munck, and indeed many of the views espoused in Stendahl between 1960 and 1963 are found in Munck's work *Paul and the Salvation of Mankind* (Louisville: John Knox, 1954).

[6]See for instance the recent discussions in Paula Fredriksen, *Paul: The Pagan's Apostle* (New Haven, CT: Yale University Press, 2017), and Mark Nanos and Magnus Zetterholm, eds., *Paul Within Judaism: Restoring the First-Century Context to the Apostle* (Minneapolis: Fortress, 2015), which show the whole spectrum, ranging from the assertion that Paul never left Judaism behind to the idea that

One of the first pillars Stendahl attempts to demolish in a typical reading of Paul deals with the man himself. Here Stendahl picks up the typical interpretation of Paul's Damascus road experience as involving a *conversion* (Acts 9:1-9; 22:4-16; 26:9-16; Gal 1:11-17). Stendahl highlights the continuity both before and after this event to argue that rather than a *conversion* of Paul, what we have is a new *call* for Paul. Paul receives a new assignment from God: a move from persecutor to proclaimer. Stendahl draws attention to the allusions from the Old Testament in Paul's experience, specifically to Jeremiah and Isaiah, that appear in these accounts. Stendahl surmises that what we have in these accounts is a prophetic call of Paul, like that of Jeremiah or Isaiah.

Stendahl's approach is certainly helpful for understanding Paul. One feature of his nuanced and attentive reading of Paul is our language in describing "how Paul met Jesus." He argues that the term *conversion* has too much baggage in the modern context to do justice to the experience of Paul and is perhaps too strong of a term to describe Paul's change. Certainly, it is not the same as someone changing from a polytheistic religion to Christianity. The change for Paul is not necessarily in his conception of Yahweh but in his understanding of Jesus as Messiah. To this degree, Stendahl rightly draws attention to the problems with the word *conversion* when used of Paul's Damascus road experience. The issue is the new thing Paul embraces, not the old thing he leaves behind, because he does not leave behind his faith in the God of the Old Testament.

Paul's experience as a call rather than a conversion has several corollaries in terms of understanding Paul's message. First, what is specifically revealed to Paul is not the doctrine of justification but that Gentiles can enter the people of God without becoming Jewish. In this regard, Stendahl also anticipated by many decades the recent attempts

---

Paul is simply dealing with pagans, not critiquing Judaism. The real burden of the essays in this latter volume is that the new perspective on Paul didn't go far enough in emphasizing Paul's continuity with Judaism.

by Jewish New Testament scholars to reclaim Paul as an observant Jew simply focused on bringing Gentiles to biblical faith.[7] On Stendahl's view, what accompanied Paul's new vocation was a new understanding of the law. Paul's call radically shaped his understanding of the law in the program and outworking of God in salvation history. The theological payoff for this, according to Stendahl, is that the epicenter of Paul's thought about God, salvation, and the law springs from his new vocation as *apostle to the Gentiles*.

A second corollary of Stendahl's emphasis on call rather than conversion is directed specifically against the Lutheran reading of Paul that views him as a conflicted individual before his "conversion." Stendahl rightly stresses that we have no evidence from the New Testament that Paul ever experienced a situation similar to Martin Luther. There were no pangs of conscience, no inner turmoil or despair. Rather, the New Testament evidence from Acts and Paul's letters points in the opposite direction. Paul had no issues with following the law, something he did remarkably well according to Philippians 3, calling himself "as for righteousness based on the law, faultless."

It is a fruitful exercise for the student of Paul to entertain a thought experiment concerning what changed, theologically speaking, for Paul pre- and post-Damascus. The obvious answer is that his understanding of Jesus took a 180-degree turn. Paul went from understanding Jesus as a false messiah bent on leading the nation astray to being the savior of Israel. There is perhaps no word better than *conversion* to speak of how Paul changed his mind on Jesus. However, after his messianic revolution, one can wonder whether much else changed. He certainly didn't stop being a monotheist, and his canon of Scripture seemed to stay the same as well. One might argue that his *interpretation* of that Scripture changed, but not the texts themselves. Likewise, his focus on the moral and ethical impetus of the Hebrew Scriptures is present both before and after Damascus. Again, one ought to take time to think through, rather

[7]See especially Nanos and Zetterholm, *Paul Within Judaism*.

than just assume, that *everything* changed for Paul. This is perhaps the greatest pedagogical help that Stendahl provided.

While there is much that can and should be commended about Stendahl's emphasis on call rather than conversion, there is criticism that needs to be raised. The Paul we meet in both Acts and his letters is Paul the persecutor, one who oversaw the murder of fellow Jews who in his mind had apostatized by following Jesus as Messiah and had now put the whole nation at risk. What Stendahl's argument assumes, although not explicitly, is that Paul's call to persecute apostates was acceptable and Paul merely had a transfer between theological departments. This, however, raises the precise issue that Paul had radically misunderstood his calling by God; indeed, the Damascus experience is when Paul realizes that his call had been radically pointed in the wrong direction. Perhaps we can begin to speak of a conversion of Paul's call? Might this adjudicate the two different approaches? It would seem that this notion stresses the appropriate point of Stendahl's argument, in that it eliminates the theological baggage of conversion in the soteriological sense. However, it gives due weight to the radicalness in Paul's change of thought concerning the person of Jesus and the people of God.

Likewise, when we encounter Paul's story in Luke's narrative, he has placed it right in the middle of a triple conversion narrative: the Ethiopian eunuch (Acts 8:26-40), Saul/Paul (Acts 9), and Cornelius (Acts 10). Paul's story is preceded by the conversion of the Ethiopian eunuch and followed by the conversion of Cornelius and his household. Now, we should separate how Luke has presented Paul's account versus Paul's own description, but it is worth noting at least how one first-century representative—Luke—understood the event.

Stendahl's work came to exercise a profound influence on numerous people associated with the new perspective on Paul, as will be seen below. A proper understanding of Stendahl's work reveals a profound shaping of the subsequent conversation. If nothing else, his arguments provided some of the first cracks in the traditional perspective on Paul as an advocate of grace rather than law, justification by faith rather than works-righteousness. In other words, his arguments showed that Paul was not Luther's predecessor.

(RE)VIEWING JUDAISM: E. P. SANDERS

Our next figure is E. P. Sanders, who typically leads the list in a discussion of the origin(s) of the new perspective on Paul. His epochal work, *Paul and Palestinian Judaism*, challenged many common assumptions in New Testament scholarship and secondarily in Pauline studies. His book is a massive attempt to offer a critical rereading of the relevant primary Jewish (including later rabbinical) sources to construct an historical portrait of first-century Judaism as a backdrop for the study of the historical Jesus and Paul. However, as seen above, Sanders's work has its predecessors, and thus his contribution to the discussion did not appear out of nowhere. Contrary to the popular opinion of those most critical of the new perspective on Paul, his attempt was not the first attempt to reevaluate either first-century Judaism or Paul. This endeavor, in part, had already been put on the map by Albert Schweitzer, furthered to a large degree by W. D. Davies almost twenty years prior, and echoed in theory by Stendahl ten years before Sanders's own work.[8] There was also the extensive work of Martin Hengel, who came to very different conclusions from Sanders on these seminal issues.[9] Sanders merely represents the most influential and extensive attempt to read Paul against a historical reconstruction of first-century Judaism.

In 1977, Sanders delivered his now-famous work. *Paul and Palestinian Judaism* offers a critical rereading of the primary evidence of Jewish literature between 200 BCE and 200 CE and an alternative

---

[8]Albert Schweitzer, *The Mysticism of Paul the Apostle* (Baltimore: Johns Hopkins University Press, 1998); W. D. Davies, *Paul and Rabbinic Judaism* (Philadelphia: Fortress, 1948). As noted in chap. 2, Sanders is quite aware of this and specifically notes the work of W. D. Davies as an influence on his own work. Davies was Sanders's doctoral adviser at Duke University.

[9]See Hengel's classic two-volume work *Judaism and Hellenism* (Philadelphia: Fortress, 1981) and various subsequent works, such as *Paul Between Damascus and Antioch* (Louisville: Westminster John Knox, 1997).

portrayal of Judaism. Sanders argues that previous scholarship was indebted to a critical misreading of the primary evidence by approaching it from systematic categories and relying heavily on the flawed compendiums of Hermann Strack and Paul Billerbeck.[10] The assumptions of New Testament scholars about Judaism were built on the few scholars who had profoundly misunderstood the data. Sanders aimed to offer a new methodology and to compare the two religions of Judaism and Christianity by the features of "getting in" and "staying in." He argues that the key error of previous scholarship is that it had not read the data in light of the covenant. The covenant is key to understanding the reward-and-punishment language of Second Temple Judaism. Thus, Sanders coins the term *covenantal nomism*. Listed below are the primary implications of this term:

1. God has chosen Israel and given the law. This law implies
2. God's promise to maintain the election and the requirement to obey.
3. God rewards obedience and punishes transgression.
4. The law provides a means for atonement, and atonement results in maintenance or reestablishment of the covenantal relationship.
5. All those who are maintained in the covenant by obedience, atonement, and God's mercy belong to the group that will be saved.[11]

Key to Sanders's proposal is that both God's choosing of Israel and salvation were predicated on God's mercy. Sanders holds that what was not previously understood was that the first and last points were considered within Judaism to be by God's mercy rather than by human achievement. It is this notion of *covenantal nomism* that Sanders says

[10]Hermann Strack and Paul Billerbeck, *Kommentar zum Neuen Testament aus Talmud und Midrasch*, 6 vols. (München: Beck, 1922–1961). The irony of this was not lost on Sanders's various critics, because he seemed to be arguing on the basis of some of the same theological categories that Judaism was after all a religion of grace that practiced "covenantal nomism," and his very categories—getting in and staying in—reflected Christian theological discussions.

[11]Adapted from *PPJ*.

characterized the Judaism(s) in the period of Jesus and Paul. He maintains that this form of Judaism was prevalent before the destruction of the temple in 70 CE and was not marked by hypocrisy but balanced both grace and works. There was strong pushback from scholars that this is too sweeping a generalization, since there is also evidence in early Judaism of what later was called works-righteousness in regard to both getting in and staying in.[12]

With this paradigm in place, Sanders finally turns to address the implications for the study of Paul and his message. Sanders holds that there are two convictions or presuppositions that guide the entirety of Paul's thought: (1) "Jesus Christ is Lord, in that God has provided salvation of all who believe . . . and that he [Jesus] will soon return to bring all things to an end," and (2) "Paul was called to be the Apostle to the Gentiles"; these two convictions go hand in hand (one can see the agreement with Stendahl's argument at this point).[13] In Sanders's reconstruction the entire world, both Jews and Gentiles, now stands in need of a savior precisely because of what God has provided in Christ.

Sanders views Paul's argument as running from solution to plight; others had traditionally argued that Paul's argument runs from plight to solution (from sin to salvation). Rather, Sanders stresses that Paul starts with the solution—God has acted in Christ—and then goes on to explain why humanity needed to be saved in this way. In terms of theological categories, justification is for Paul a term of "getting in," whereas in Judaism it was a term of "staying in." This was the fundamental difference between Paul and Judaism. Although Paul and Judaism agree on final salvation and judgment, Paul had misunderstood Judaism by distorting three important aspects of Judaism, election, covenant, and Torah. According to Sanders, Paul had transformed and to some extent transcended them.

---

[12]On which see D. A. Carson, Peter T. O'Brien, and Mark A. Seifrid, eds., *Justification and Variegated Nomism*, 2 vols. (Grand Rapids: Baker, 2001–2004).
[13]*PPJ*, 441-42.

Ultimately, what Sanders concludes is that what Paul found wrong with Judaism was that it was not Christianity. Many have remarked that Sanders's landmark book, *Paul and Palestinian Judaism,* ought actually to be titled *Judaism (and also Paul),* as a majority of his work is consumed with the reconstruction of first-century Judaism, with a rather short appendix on Paul. Such a lackluster conclusion on Paul did not satisfy many and set the stage for what became known as the new perspective on Paul. As became clear in the further discussions that critiqued Sanders's work, Sanders was too indebted to certain older liberal Protestant readings of Paul, for example those of Schweitzer, and had not done justice to the detailed work of scholars such as Hengel, who also sought to situate Paul firmly within the context of early Judaism. Much later, in 2015, Sanders sought to redress the balance by focusing clearly and in detail on Paul in *Paul: The Apostle's Life, Letters, and Thought,* which we will discuss in chapter two. In a very real sense, though this work was published in 2015, it reflects Sanders's much earlier work and thoughts about Paul, being chiefly his Pauline lecture material he used at Oxford and then Duke for many years before his retirement.

A NEW NAME FOR A NEW MOVEMENT: JAMES D. G. DUNN

While many appreciated (and some didn't) Sanders's reconstruction of the Judaism of Jesus' and Paul's day, not all were satisfied with his conclusion on Paul. Such was the impetus for the work of James Dunn. He argued that the portrayal of Paul that Sanders offered was no better than what more traditional readings had given. So, in 1983, in his T. W. Manson Memorial Lecture, Dunn argued that what was needed was "a new perspective on Paul" that carried forward Sanders's conclusions on Judaism and more accurately placed Paul *within* Judaism.[14]

Dunn argues that when it came to justification, Paul and mainstream Judaism were in agreement. In terms of early Christianity, Dunn argues

[14]This 1983 lecture is most conveniently found in *NPP*.

that the dividing line was not between those who believed in Jesus as Messiah and those who didn't, but rather between those who saw the role of the law as temporary and those who did not. Thus, the problem was eschatological, not soteriological. According to Dunn, Paul had no objections to the law but only to "works of the law," which Dunn argues was Paul's term for the boundary-defining elements of the law that most set Jews apart from Gentiles—circumcision, Sabbath keeping, and food laws. In the subsequent years following his 1983 lecture, he clarified that the phrase "works of the law" refers to those things that mark the Jews out as *distinctive* within Gentile contexts and not necessarily *anything* that the law requires. In Dunn's new perspective, one should focus on the social function of the Mosaic law and see justification as the overcoming of the barrier of the law that separated Jews and Gentiles. Paul, then, was not working against legalism but against Jewish particularism or Jewish nationalism and against defining the covenant in ethnic terms. However, scholars develop ideas over time. In some of his most recent works, Dunn has stepped back from his overly limited definition of "works of the law." He now agrees, with some of his critics, that the phrase could refer to anything the Mosaic law requires.[15] We will have occasion in chapter four to probe and critique Dunn's approach in depth.

It is worth noting at this point the confluence of work being done in the late 1970s on both sides of the pond that was influential in what became the new perspective on Paul. In 1977 E. P. Sanders issued his groundbreaking work. At about the same time, in 1978, N. T. Wright published his soon-to-be-influential article "The Paul of History and the Apostle of Faith."[16] Although the term "new perspective on Paul" was not coined until 1983, with Dunn's Manson lecture, the ground was already being laid, and in fact Wright can be partially credited for coming up with the descriptor "new perspective on Paul."

---

[15]See the third volume in his Christianity in the Making series, which emerged in 2015.

[16]This essay of Wright's is now most easily found in his *Pauline Perspectives: Essays on Paul, 1978–2013* (Minneapolis: Fortress, 2013), 3-20.

(RE)DRAWING THE MAP: N. T. WRIGHT

N. T. Wright's contribution to the developing new perspective on Paul include numerous journal articles and books, but one of the earliest forays was his 1978 article "The Paul of History and the Apostle of Faith," along with his exegetically detailed study *The Climax of the Covenant: Christ and the Law in Pauline Theology* (1991).[17] In an echoing of the concerns of Stendahl and with a titular nod to Martin Kähler, Wright argues that Paul must be understood within a Jewish eschatological backdrop. The core of Paul's thought can be summarized as follows: Paul was a faithful Jew, a Pharisee, who came to believe that Jesus had been raised from the dead and vindicated by Israel's God. This was the Copernican revolution that caused Paul to reformulate Jewish theology (election, covenant, monotheism, and law) in light of God's surprising action in Christ. Paul's reflection on Torah is not determined by his views on sin but rather by the Hebrew Bible itself. Wright argues that Paul's view of the law is shaped by his reading of Genesis 15; Deuteronomy 30; Jeremiah 31; Isaiah 40–55; and Habakkuk. Paul came to see that the temporary role and the plans of the law were accomplished in the person of Jesus. Thus, Paul reshaped the main elements of Judaism around the figure of Jesus, and every aspect of Paul's theology is rooted in the Judaism within which Paul *remained*. This reading of Paul in light of certain key parts of the Old Testament, especially Deuteronomy 27–30, has characterized Wright's work from the beginning. We will examine and critique his views in detail in chapter three, with attention given to Wright's magnum opus, *Paul and the Faithfulness of God*, which emerged in two volumes in 2013.

Here it is important to point out a few of the distinctive themes of Wright's work:

1. the idea of Christ (and, within the context of Christ, the church) as Israel or the true Israelite who fulfills the mission Israel was meant to fulfill of being a light to the nations;

---

[17]N. T. Wright, *The Climax of the Covenant: Christ and the Law in Pauline Theology* (Minneapolis: Fortress, 1991).

2. the notion that God's people were still in exile when Jesus and Paul said and did what they said and did;
3. that therefore, according to Wright, Jesus' coming amounted to "the return of Yahweh to Zion to redeem his people from exile";
4. the notion that the new covenant is the fulfillment of the Mosaic one, such that there is covenantal *continuity* between the various covenants; and therefore
5. the larger picture of creation, fall, and various acts of redemption should be seen within the context of covenantal theology; and so
6. God's righteousness refers at least in part to God's covenant faithfulness to his people through Christ; and
7. Christ's own faithfulness to fulfill God's mission for him, including faithfulness to be obedient even unto death on the cross. This latter is what the phrase *pistis Christou* refers to.

Here is not the place to go into a detailed critique of Wright's distinctive emphases, but what can be said is that they are permutations of a rather traditional Reformed approach to Paul and covenantal theology, apart from the exile idea and the new way of reading "the faith of Christ" (*pistis Christou*) phrase. Not many have followed Wright on (2) and (3) above (though see the new response book titled *Exile: A Conversation with N. T. Wright*, edited by James Scott and published in 2017), and (1) above has led to Wright's being accused of supersessionism, the idea that the church has superseded Israel as God's people, a notion that has great difficulties explaining Romans 9–11, where Israel seems clearly to mean non-Christian Jews.[18]

As has already been noted about the new perspective on Paul, it involves *various* perspectives even on the issue of *pistis Christou*, which Dunn and John Barclay both still think refers to "faith in Christ." Sanders thinks the phrase mostly means "faith in Christ," but perhaps in one or

[18]James M. Scott, ed., *Exile: A Conversation with N. T. Wright* (Downers Grove, IL: InterVarsity Press, 2017).

two instances refers to the "the faith Christ had," and only Wright and Richard B. Hays have strongly and persistently argued for the phrase meaning "the faithfulness of Christ" wherever one finds it in Paul. What *is* shared in common by these various scholars is an inclination to see "works of the law" as a phrase that largely critiques narrow Jewish nationalism, including the requirement of even Gentiles having to pass through the boundary markers of circumcision, Sabbath keeping, and accepting food laws to be full-fledged members of the God's people. Some of these scholars, particularly Dunn, have a disinclination to affirm that Paul was instigating a parting of the ways with Judaism. Others, particularly Wright, do not see a reference in Romans 9–11 to a future for non-Christian Israel apart from the ongoing life of the church.

In short, the new perspective on Paul not only does not involve a single perspective, but it also does not involve a total consensus about the things it does seem to generally advocate, for instance, that the old Lutheran perspective that caricatured early Judaism as legalistic and a works-righteousness religion is entirely wrong and that covenantal nomism is the only right way to characterize early Judaism. It turns out that there were just as many views in early Judaism about some of these things as there are today among Pauline scholars. Before we look at the contributions of these various scholars in detail, it will be beneficial to consider briefly one or two attempts to push beyond the new perspective.

The first of these has been undertaken by Garwood Anderson in a book that, not accidentally, is titled *Paul's New Perspective: Charting a Soteriological Journey*.[19] From the outset, Anderson laments the tendencies toward globalizing one's claims about Paul and the ensuing tendency toward polemics against other points of view. He puts it this way:

> The TPP [Traditional Perspective on Paul] and the NPP readings of Paul become *exclusive* paradigms for reading Paul only by the willfulness of their proponents and at some unfortunate loss to the fullness of the texts' witness.

[19]Garwood Anderson, *Paul's New Perspective: Charting a Soteriological Journey* (Downers Grove, IL: IVP Academic, 2016).

> Neither position is adequate in itself because both are "true" accounts of Paul, becoming false only to the extent that they become exclusive accounts of Paul.[20]

Anderson's both/and approach to things is interesting, even refreshing, and one of the key insights that comes from it is that "certain articulations of Paul's gospel are truer of some periods than of others and . . . to a substantial degree it is the claims made with regard to the whole that force false disjunctions and fund facile conciliations."[21] By the latter he is referring to the tendency of the contributors to moderate their version of the new perspective on Paul only in places where their essential particular thrust is not compromised or endangered. So, for example, with Wright, while he does his best in *Paul and the Faithfulness of God* to take a both/and approach at points, he is not about to give up on his approach in terms of exile, or that Jesus is Israel, or that Jesus is God returning to Zion to deliver his people from exile, or in terms of prospective covenant renewal and salvation history as opposed to a retrospective and apocalyptic-intrusion approach that sees the new covenant as not merely an example of covenant renewal.

In fact, much depends on the order in which we line up the chronology of Paul's letters, and even more on how many letters we are prepared to attribute to Paul. For example, if Galatians is a very early letter of Paul, written after his first missionary journey to south Galatia and prior to the council referred to in Acts 15, which is to say before the status of Gentiles in Christ and the basis of their admission to the Jesus movement was sorted out, then the letter should not be so readily identified with the perspectives of Paul we find in Romans.[22] All of these Pauline scholars work with some sort of development model of the progression of Paul's thought, and so the chronology matters greatly in many cases. Anderson carefully charts

---

[20]Anderson, *Paul's New Perspective*, 91.

[21]Anderson, *Paul's New Perspective*, 116.

[22]On this see the new biography of Paul by N. T. Wright, which was forthcoming when this study was completed but which HarperOne granted me (Ben) a chance to read through in fall 2017: N. T. Wright, *Paul: A Biography* (New York: HarperOne, 2018).

how taking into account the disputed and even the later Paulines also adds to our understanding of Paul, even if he did not write some of these letters himself.[23]

The second volume that attempts to move the needle past the new perspective on Paul in some ways is the omnibus volume *God and the Faithfulness of Paul.*[24] The discussion here is vigorous and focused on the work of Wright, not on all the contributors to the new perspective on Paul, and, interestingly, it gives space for Wright to respond and rebut where he feels necessary. But some of the critique is telling. For example, Jörg Frey draws attention to how the degree of polemics against an apocalyptic reading of Paul reflects the fact that Wright sees a danger in it to his covenantal continuity schema.

> In Wright's work apocalyptic ideas are tamed, put in a safe place within the covenantal order to prevent them from endangering the great synthesis of Pauline, or rather Wrightian, thought. . . . For Wright's sophisticated synthesis of everything in and around Paul, with everything so well-integrated into the divine master-plan of salvation-history or the all-embracing covenant, apocalyptic indeed might be the rock that finally breaks the impressive image (cf. Dan. 2.34).[25]

Equally telling is the critique of Larry Hurtado of the suggestion that the theme of Yahweh's return to Zion should be used as a way of viewing the first coming of Christ, his earthly ministry, and his death and resurrection. As Hurtado says, "Despite Wright's urgings, however, it is not clear that the theme of YHWH's return was appropriated initially to interpret Jesus' ministry, death, and resurrection. Instead, the identifiable NT instances of the appropriation of the theme present Jesus's *parousia* as effectively being YHWH's eschatological return/

[23]On the possibility that Luke wrote the Pastoral Epistles on behalf of Paul while Paul was still alive, though in the case of 2 Timothy while Paul was incarcerated in Rome awaiting execution, see Ben Witherington III, *Letters and Homilies for Hellenized Christians*, vol. 1 (Downers Grove, IL: InterVarsity Press, 2014).

[24]Christoph Helig, J. Thomas Hewitt, and Michael F. Bird, eds., *God and the Faithfulness of Paul* (Minneapolis: Fortress, 2017).

[25]Jörg Frey, "Demythologizing Apocalyptic?," in Helig, Hewitt, and Bird, *God and the Faithfulness of Paul*, 527, but the whole essay should be consulted (489-531).

manifestation."[26] The real problem in fact goes back to the embracing of the overrealized approach to Pauline eschatology, advocated by G. B. Caird, Wright's *doktorvater* at Oxford.

In other words, there is a tendency (1) to retroject future eschatological talk back into the events that already transpired during the ministry of Jesus, and (2) to change the parousia talk about a visible second coming from heaven to language about the "manifestation" of God in Christ. The problem with this approach is highlighted in texts such as 1 Corinthians 15, where Paul says that it will only be after Christ's return that the dead in Christ will be raised and the work of putting God's enemies down will be finished. Those enemies are not already entirely vanquished just because Christ's D-Day offensive against them has been successful and the turning point in the war with the powers and principalities has happened. No, V-E or final victory day is still seen as future, and meanwhile the powers of darkness are still wreaking havoc in the world.[27] Ephesians 6:10-20 captures this reality quite nicely. It is why some of the more apocalyptic warnings of Paul have such bite. Christians live betwixt and between when it comes to the eschatological endgame.

Armed with this sort of review and sneak preview, we are now ready to dive into the deep Pauline waters that have been stirred up by scholarly discussion in the last twenty years. We will do so by considering in some detail the major contributions of the aforementioned scholars made during the new perspective era, which some think is already in the rearview mirror. We shall see whether any of the waves stirred up by these scholars can be surfed successfully all the way to the Pauline beach, the Pauline resting point.

---

[26]Larry Hurtado, "YHWH'S Return to Zion," in Helig, Hewitt, and Bird, *God and the Faithfulness of Paul*, 434.

[27]The language of analogy, of D-Day and V-E Day, comes ultimately from Oscar Cullmann.

two

THE SANDERS REVOLUTION

It is little exaggeration to say that no book in the last century has challenged contemporary biblical scholarship as much as the work of E. P. Sanders and his *Paul and Palestinian Judaism*. First appearing in 1977, the work has continued to be equally championed and criticized in subsequent Pauline research. *Paul and Palestinian Judaism* levels a critical challenged to common assumptions previously—and somewhat still—held in New Testament scholarship. Sanders's work is a massive attempt to offer a critical rereading of the primary Jewish and rabbinical sources in order to construct an accurate portrait of first-century Judaism and thus provide a backdrop for the study of the historical Jesus, Paul, and early Christianity. More recently, Sanders has also contributed the culmination of his years of thought on Paul in his *Paul: The Apostle's Life, Letters, and Thought*. These works function as bookends to Sanders's career and will serve as the primary texts for Sanders's understanding of Paul and his impact on Pauline studies.

As commonplace as some of Sanders's conclusions have become in New Testament studies, this was not always the case. To set the stage just a bit, we need to remember the time prior to the work of Sanders. Before Sanders, many New Testament scholars assumed a very negative portrait of Judaism as a works-oriented religion that provided a stark contrast to a pristine Christianity. Paul emerged both from and out of this negative portraiture. Paul was often conceived as having

a tormented conscience that eventually gave up in despair from working his way to God and turned to Christianity. Judaism was presented as the antithesis of Christianity. According to Sanders, much of this pejorative portrait of Judaism was built on several misreadings of Jewish texts and the later rabbinical works that were anachronistically read back into first-century Judaism. Sanders sets out to sketch two alternative portraits. First, he attempts to show how previous scholarship had *constructed* this negative portrait. Second, he then seeks to *deconstruct* that negative image of Judaism in the New Testament guild, by pulling a reformational turning of the tables—*ad fontes*—and going back to the Second Temple texts themselves to construct an alternative portrait.

PAUL AND PALESTINIAN JUDAISM

Reassessing first-century Judaism. The first concern of Sanders in *Paul and Palestinian Judaism* is to marshal as much evidence as possible of poor and inadequate representations of Judaism by New Testament scholars. The book starts off by showing how the history of scholarship on the representation of first-century Judaism had propagated a series of misunderstandings built on the readings and research of a few scholars. The three main scholars on whom Sander argues this image of Judaism was built are Ferdinand Weber, Wilhelm Bousset, and Paul Billerbeck. Their work had influenced a generation of scholars and influenced the scholar who came to influence twentieth-century scholarship the most, Rudolf Bultmann. Since Weber, Bousset, and Billerbeck exercised such a profound influence on the field of New Testament scholarship, it is helpful here to sketch a rough summary of their views. Such an attempt to display their main lines of thought will contextualize not only the work of E. P. Sanders but also subsequent perspectives on Paul. Without an adequate understanding of the conversation partners of Sanders and New Testament scholarship before Sanders's work, one will miss the scope and purpose for his own enterprise.

A central feature of Weber's description of Judaism is his acceptance and rejection of Israel's covenant status.[1] To summarize a longer argument, Weber accepts that humanity was separated from God but that the covenant on Mount Sinai with Israel removed the sin of Adam and placed Israel in covenant relationship with God. However, as Sanders notes, and this is key, "the restoration . . . is brief."[2] Weber quizzically turns to the golden calf incident of Exodus 32 and argues that as a result of this episode Israel lost its newly restored status. We have then a "second fall," which removed the covenant status of Israel. The response to this fall, Weber concludes, was that the means of acquiring salvation were not Torah and temple, but law and sacrifice. Thus the way back to God is now manifold, through a series of commandment fulfillment, good works, and sacrifices as atonement for sin. As Sanders reflects, several problems arise from this interpretation, not least that the Hebrew Scriptures do not seem to place as much of an emphasis on the golden-calf incident as Weber proposes. More problematic is Weber's view that, with the covenant now broken, individual Israelites must pursue their relationship with God on other, *meritorious* grounds. The brief summary of Weber's view is that thus Israel must now *earn* its relationship with God.

Critique of Weber came quickly, even as it went largely unheard and unheeded. Even in 1921, G. F. Moore objected to Weber's work:

> The fundamental criticism to be made of Weber's "System" is precisely that it is a system of theology, and not an ancient Jewish system but a modern German system. This is far more than a mere matter of disposition, the ordering of the materials under certain heads taken from Christian dogmatics; the system brings its logic with it and imposes it upon the materials.[3]

Sadly, Moore's critique fell on deaf ears. Sanders argued that it was Weber's view above, accepted by and promulgated by Bousset, that ultimately filtered down to his most famous student, Rudolf Bultmann.

---

[1]Ferdinand Weber, *Jüdische Theologie auf Grund des Talmud und verwandter Schriften* (Leipzig: Dörffling & Franke, 1897).

[2]*PPJ*, 37-38.

[3]G. F. Moore, "Christian Writers on Judaism," *Harvard Theological Review* 14 (1921): 229.

One can trace the influence from Weber to Bousset to Bultmann through New Testament studies in the twentieth century. Boussett adapted Weber's view in one important way. Even though he largely takes over Weber's view wholesale, he adds the emphasis that "the idea that God is remote and inaccessible became a dominating theory," according to Sanders.[4] One can immediately see how Weber and Bousett's views set the stage for the next century's worth of discussion on Second Temple Judaism and the Mosaic law. In light of an absent God, the law was now seen as a means of returning to God.

Sanders regards one other figure as important before Rudolf Bultmann, and that is Billerbeck.[5] He promoted Weber's view of Jewish salvation sketched out above and offered to a generation of scholarship a sourcebook of rabbinic literature to parallel New Testament passages. Sanders notes, however, that Billerbeck's presentation of the evidence was selective and gave the impression that when one quoted Billerbeck's work one was directly quoting rabbinic sources. Part and parcel of Billerbeck's work was his thesis that God gave Israel the Torah so it could earn merit and reward, which God keeps track of, and in the end one's merits must outweigh one's transgressions. Sanders argues that what Billerbeck found wrong with Judaism is that it was a religion of self-redemption.[6]

When Sanders turns to discuss Rudolf Bultmann, he begins with the startling comment that in his view "Bultmann had no substantial independent access to the literature of 'late Judaism,' and particularly not to Rabbinic sources." He goes on to argue that Bultmann is entirely dependent on Emil Schürer, Bousset, and Moore. Even more shocking is Sanders's charge that Bultmann cites Moore's work alongside Schürer and Bousset, apparently unaware that their works are at odds with one another.[7]

---

[4]*PPJ*, 39.

[5]Hermann Strack and Paul Billerbeck, *Kommentar zum Neuen Testament aus Talmud und Midrasch*, 6 vols. (München: Beck, 1922–1961).

[6]*PPJ*, 43.

[7]*PPJ*, 43-44.

A primary critique that Sanders makes of Bultmann is that he simply repeated the conclusions of Weber, dismissed opposing voices, and lent enormous credibility to the work of his teacher Bousset, which was then used by subsequent scholarship. Such negative estimations of Bultmann's work of course cohere with Sanders's overall strategy, indicated early on in his work, to return to the Second Temple and rabbinic sources. Bultmann may come under extra scrutiny by Sanders since Bultmann represents the antithesis of his own project.

It was the immense project of Bultmann that then influenced further generations of New Testament scholarship and thus shaped views on Paul. In the paradigm inherited, Paul stood diametrically opposed to the Jewish faith that had sought to earn favor from an absent God and was based on merit to obtain eternal life. Paul, by contrast, gave up on this legalistic system and proposed that it was faith in Jesus, apart from legalistic works, that guaranteed eternal life. One of the enduring images of Paul and the Judaism of his day had been erected and did not face serious challenges for quite some time.

This looming edifice of ancient Judaism, constructed on an insufficient foundation, Sanders sets out to dismantle. One key piece of the deconstruction work is to begin at the methodological level. If Weber and others had imposed a system that was incompatible with these Jewish texts, how might one go about reading those texts from *within*? Do the sources themselves offer any coherent set of assumptions, positions, themes, or starting points?

Sanders seeks to offer a different methodology. He attempts to compare religions as a whole, in contrast to the previous generation, which isolated specific themes or topics. He defines this as a "pattern of religion," or in other words how participants in a religion perceive it to function. Sanders goes on to admit that this would generally be aligned with the category often titled "soteriology." The two primary questions guiding his study are how to "get in" and how to "stay in." He then attempts to survey the history of Jewish religion from 200 BCE to 200 CE by way of its extant literature and to draw conclusions about

Judaism from this period.[8] He also seeks to answer the question of the relationship between this historical reconstruction of first-century Judaism and the "religion" of Paul to see whether they had the same type of religion.[9]

It should be noted again that Sanders was certainly not the first to attempt such a task, contrary to the popular opinion of the neo-Reformed movement.[10] What Sanders represents is the most poignant and *extensive* attempt to read Paul against a historical reconstruction of first-century Judaism. However, as stressed above, this endeavor in part had already been put on the map by Schweitzer, furthered to a large degree by Moore and Davies, and echoed in theory by Krister Stendahl before Sanders's own work.[11] One might also add that both Dunn and Wright were separately working on their own readings of Paul at roughly the same time.

The majority of Sanders's work focuses on an in-depth—one might add even painstaking, yet needed—analysis of Jewish literature from 200 BCE to 200 CE. The nearly 400 pages dedicated to this first task nearly eclipse his second task, of comparing Jewish literature with Pauline literature and thought, to which 120 pages are devoted. Regardless of the balance of material, Sanders offers an overwhelming effort at historical reconstruction that had previously not been undertaken. The sheer magnitude and scope of his task are worthy of appreciation.

---

[8]*PPJ*, 17-18.

[9]*PPJ*, 19.

[10]A portrait one might encounter in, e.g., D. A. Carson, Peter T. O'Brien, and Mark A. Seifrid, eds., *Justification and Variegated Nomism: The Complexities of Second Temple Judaism* (Grand Rapids: Baker, 2001).

[11]Krister Stendahl, *Paul Among Jews and Gentiles* (Minneapolis: Fortress, 1976); W. D. Davies, *Paul and Rabbinic Judaism: Some Rabbinic Elements in Pauline Theology* (Philadelphia: Fortress, 1948). Sanders is quite aware of this historical context and specifically notes the work of W. D. Davies, who was his *doktorvator* at Duke University. Sanders critically interacts with the work of his predecessor early on in his work. Sanders's critique of Davies is that he provides in essence a study of motifs prevalent in both Paul and rabbinic Judaism. Davies's primary objective is to show how certain patterns of thought, motifs, and ideas are already prevalent in Jewish literature, and this is primarily an inductive rather than a deductive approach. In the end, Sanders believes this does not do justice to either source, as it does not take into account the larger framework of either religion.

Central to the work of Sanders, yet missing from other studies, is an understanding of the relationship between law and covenant in the Judaism(s) of the first century.[12] According to Sanders, it was Christian scholarship that argued that the Judaism that developed after the exilic period lost the concept of the covenant as established by God's grace and replaced it with a merit-based legal observance. Sanders adamantly disagrees with such a conception of a misplaced grace in understanding the covenant; rather, a grace-based covenant structure is evidenced throughout the Second Temple material. This is one of the "universal" features of all the literature Sanders surveys, and he argues it must be kept in mind when reading the Second Temple literature.

Throughout the Old Testament and Second Temple literature, there are commands to obey and instructions regarding obedience. How then might obedience function within a framework of grace? Sanders argues that when the issue of obedience arises it must be understood that obedience "maintains one's position in the covenant, but it does not earn God's grace."[13] Stated more plainly, obedience is not a means of getting in but staying in the covenant. Possible exceptions to these patterns may be shown in some texts from the Second Temple period, such as Ben Sirach and 4 Ezra. Sanders responds to those exceptional cases by arguing that in the case of Ben Sirach the issue is one of *assumption*. If Ben Sirach is speaking mainly to Israelites, his audience is already in the covenant, and thus this a priori discussion about getting in or staying never needed to be raised.

The work of 4 Ezra presents the most perplexing case for Sanders's approach. According to Sanders, it is 4 Ezra that represents "the closest approach to legalistic works-righteousness that can be found in the literature of the period." Sanders attempts to mitigate this challenge by attributing this emphasis to the extremely pessimistic view of the author on the human condition. Or, as Sanders notes, 4 Ezra views sin as an "inescapable power" and says that "human inability to avoid sin is

[12] *PPJ*, 419.
[13] *PPJ*, 420.

considered to lead to damnation."[14] Thus perfection is demanded in 4 Ezra. This negative view of the human condition seemingly overshadows the role of the covenant and God's forgiveness and grace.

One might notice the counterintuitive point made indirectly by Sanders's work. If, as the traditional view of a legalistic Judaism argues, pride or boasting in human ability by achievement through works of the law runs counter to grace, then we arrive at exactly the opposite point in 4 Ezra. The covenant is not eclipsed by human pride but by human weakness. The critics of Sanders and of the seeming Achilles' heel that 4 Ezra presents to his framework have not fully appreciated this point. Likewise, balance is needed in weighing the Second Temple evidence. If a majority of authors and works do not envisage this pattern of 4 Ezra, then 4 Ezra may appear to be the exception rather than the rule.

Sanders's Copernican revolution is summarized in the phrase "covenantal nomism." Listed below are the primary features of this term:

> (1) God has chosen Israel and (2) given the law. This law implies (3) God's promise to maintain the election and (4) the requirement to obey. (5) God rewards obedience and punishes transgression. (6) The law provides means for atonement, and atonement results in (7) maintenance or re-establishment of the covenantal relationship. (8) All those who are maintained in the covenant by obedience, atonement, and God's mercy belong to the group which will be saved.[15]

Sanders argues that points (1) and (8) were not thought to be accomplished through human achievement or performance but squarely by the mercy of God. It is this notion of covenantal nomism that Sanders says characterized the Judaism(s) in the period of Jesus and Paul. He maintains that this form of Judaism was prevalent before the destruction of the temple in 70 CE and was not marked by hypocrisy; rather, it kept "grace and works in the right perspective."[16]

---

[14] *PPJ*, 418.
[15] *PPJ*, 422.
[16] *PPJ*, 422, 427.

Reassessing Paul's theology and thought. After 429 pages of historical-critical work on Second Temple Jewish texts and with the major planks of his argument in place, Sanders *finally* begins his work on Paul. At the onset, Sanders posits that Paul was a coherent but not systematic theologian.[17] Part of Sanders's critique is that Paul has been viewed through systematic lenses, and this inherently distorts the picture of Paul that emerges. Sanders's preferred term is that Paul is a "coherent thinker." By coherent he means Paul was a theologian who spent time reflecting on his gospel and that his letters express his desire to express that gospel in specific circumstances. He notes that in the "theology of Paul" there is a "pronounced soteriology." Such a conversation about the coherence of Paul's thought enters into the fray of debate surrounding the quest in Pauline studies to find the elusive center of Paul's thought.

In the quest for Paul, much of the debate has focused on sifting through Paul's letters to find a primary theme or image from which Paul theologizes. The proposals have been endless and many are only in the eye of the Pauline beholder. Topics range from the classic doctrine of justification by faith, to participation in Christ, to the faithfulness/righteousness of God. Nearly every major Pauline scholar in the nineteenth to twentieth centuries sought to make their own contribution to the complex puzzle of Paul's thought. The quest begins earnestly with the work of Albert Schweitzer.

Sanders begins his appraisal of Schweitzer's project with initial agreement. Sanders admits some aspects are entirely central for Paul, namely, eschatology, and in robust agreement notes that if eschatology is reduced to a mere addendum to Paul's thought, then his thought is entirely misunderstood. By recentering eschatology in Paul's thought, Schweitzer shifted the course of Pauline studies. Sanders, in agreement with Schweitzer and some subsequent Pauline interpreters, argues the center of Pauline thought is being in Christ.[18]

---

[17] *PPJ*, 433.
[18] *PPJ*, 441.

Sanders holds that there are two convictions that guide the entirety of Paul's thought: "(1) Jesus Christ is Lord, in that God has provided salvation of all who believe . . . and that he [Jesus] will soon return to bring all things to an end" and "(2) Paul was called to be the Apostle to the Gentiles." These two convictions go hand in hand. He offers these two issues as the underlying center of Paul's thought. Contrary to previous reconstructions, Sanders argues that for Paul the solution preceded the plight. The entire world, both Jew and Gentile, stands in need of a savior precisely because this is what God has provided in Christ. This of course contrasts with the approach of the Bultmann school, which saw humanity's need, that is, its plight, preceding God's action in Christ. In a poignant quip, Sanders remarks, "Paul did not start from man's need, but from God's deed."[19] As confirmation of this point, Sanders appeals to the content of Paul's statements in 1 Corinthians 15, where the common Christian belief is the death and resurrection of Christ. He goes on to argue that Paul did not begin with the misdeeds and sins of humankind but with the action of God in Christ, and in particular his death and resurrection. This allows Sanders to decenter anthropology as the controlling motif of Paul's thought.

In a clear response to the traditional ways of reading Paul, Sanders argues that anthropology is "only the implication of his theology, Christology, and soteriology."[20] This not only flows from Sanders's argument of solution to plight but also directly reverses the approach of Bultmann. Sanders attempts to strike a balance between Bultmann and Schweitzer by denying the anthropological starting point of Bultmann but affirming that individuals are "affected differently" by their belief in Jesus as Messiah, thus reining in Schweitzer's mystical and cosmic approach. Although this does not negate the cosmic significance, it raises the importance of the individual's belief within the cosmic scope of God's action. However, one wonders whether this goes far enough beyond a traditional reading. Sanders's reading is still ultimately

[19]*PPJ*, 441-42, 444.

[20]*PPJ*, 446.

individualistic at some level, and later movements within the new perspective stress the communal aspect of Paul's thought to a much greater degree.

Pauline soteriology. As Sanders turns to discuss Paul's soteriological framework, he proposes two fundamental convictions of Paul. First, in the near future those who believe will receive "full salvation," while those who do not believe will be destroyed. Second, the Spirit is the present sign of that guarantee for those who believe.[21] The future element of Paul's salvation language is well attested both within his letters and within the interpretive tradition surrounding the apostle. Although there is debate surrounding which specific elements are future oriented, there is general agreement that Paul believes Jesus *will* come back, the faithful *will* be saved, and creation *will* be returned to God. Further as Sanders points out, the verbs for "to save" for Paul are also future tense, with one exception (Rom 8:24), and likewise the resurrection is a future event (1 Cor 15; Rom 6:5; Phil 3:11).

What then do we make of the present experience of salvation, or what impact is there in the present? This brings us to Sanders's second fundamental conviction for Paul: the role of the Spirit. Sanders unequivocally states, "There is no ambiguity about the Spirit. It is the present possession of the Christians and their guarantee of salvation." After assembling a litany of texts, primarily from 1 Corinthians, that discuss cleanliness and holiness, Sanders concludes that "we have described a soteriology of cleansing, awaiting the coming salvation in a pure state, possession of the Spirit as the guarantee of future salvation and the provision of repentance for the repair of relapses."[22]

A problem presents itself to students and scholars of Paul. One wonders whether this is sufficient to cover the terrain of the Pauline corpus. The primary argument put forth thus far is solely dependent on one letter of Paul, directed to a uniquely problematic community. Further difficulty arises in Sanders's emphasis that Paul's concern for

[21]*PPJ*, 447.
[22]*PPJ*, 450, 452.

cleanliness is connected to Paul's role as the apostle to the Gentiles and Paul's view that the Gentiles were morally suspect. Paul seems to find moral impurity within non-Gentile groups as well. If Romans 2:1-4 is any indication, we might give weight to Paul's phrase "because you, the judge, are doing the very same things." Paul's critique of moral impurity is at home with both groups; he is in a sense an equal-opportunity critic. Second, the Spirit language in Paul is connected to far more than cleansing language alone. Paul connects Spirit language to transformation and new creation. Not enough texts are surveyed, and the limited scope of Sanders's inquiry produces limited results. In a critical manner, the framework that Sanders has applied to the evidence has produced the very same result that it sought to find—the same critique Sanders makes of previous analyses of early Judaism.

Also central to Paul's theological framework and unique to Paul, according to Sanders, is his emphasis on the Spirit, participation, and present salvation. Paul's nuance is that he "deepened the idea of the *possession* of the Spirit as a *guarantee* so that it became *participation* in one Spirit," and such a distinctiveness is clearly indicative for Sanders, so much so that he argues that here "lies the heart of his soteriology and Christology."[23] Sanders's evaluation reveals that it is the theme of participation that is key for Paul and thus in sync to some degree with Schweitzer's reading of Paul.

In his discussion of participatory language, Sanders correctly notes that this should not be limited to one specific term but is a dominant theme of Paul, appearing in two contexts, "controversy and moral exhortation," or paraenesis and in polemic.[24] Sanders provides four main areas that reveal the core of Paul's participatory language, which are (1) members of Christ's body/the body of Christ, (2) one Spirit, (3) "in Christ" language, and (4) servants of the Lord.[25]

[23]*PPJ*, 453.

[24]*PPJ*, 456.

[25]He agrees with Schweitzer that there was no separation of soteriology and eschatological expectation; however, he does maintain, in distinction to Schweitzer, that there was a mixing of mystical and forensic terminology.

Sanders turns from the discussion of Paul's soteriological framework to discuss this terminology of how one gets in or "transfers" into this group. Sanders enumerates five key points in Paul's terminology of transfer: (1) participation in Christ's death, (2) freedom, (3) transformation/new creation, (4) reconciliation, and (5) justification and righteousness. Out of the five areas proposed by Sanders, he spends the most time discussing (1) (approximately 4.5 pages) and (5) (a mere two pages). Sadly too little space is devoted to the latter category.

Sanders's first point about terminology is that the language about "dying with Christ" is for Paul a description of entering into the group. While not negating that the death of Christ was atoning *for* the believer, it also becomes for Paul entrance language. Sanders maintains that not all the references to Christ's death are fully explained with the past referent of atonement for sin but that participation is also a keen emphasis. He notes the importance of passages such as 2 Corinthians 5:14; Romans 14:8; and 1 Thessalonians 5:10, which highlight that the purpose of Christ's death was to declare him Lord, and this provides assurance for future salvation. Sanders draws the conclusion that Paul, "in thinking of the significance of Christ's death, was thinking more in terms of a change of lordship."[26] As he notes later, transfer into the group takes place by means of a participation in Christ's death.

Sanders's fifth and final category for Paul's transfer language focuses on the terms *justification* and *righteousness*. He concludes, "Being justified refers to being cleansed of or forgiven for past transgressions and is an intermediate step between the former state of being an enemy of God and a transgressor and the future state of being glorified. The meaning is equivalent to 'reconciled.'"[27] But is this necessarily the case? Might Sanders be collapsing terminology in on itself so that what is left over is terms that are indistinguishable? Certainly the terms *reconciliation* and *justification* are related to each other, but are they identical? Or might there be a more precise nuance to Paul's discussion? Like the

[26]*PPJ*, 465-66.
[27]*PPJ*, 471-2.

spokes of a wheel, justification and reconciliation each contribute something unique to Paul's multifaceted understanding of salvation.

In complete antithesis to Bultmann's structure, which ran from humanity's plight and onto salvation, Sanders's outline situates the plight of humanity after his discussion of soteriology. Sanders fully applies his insight that solution preceded plight and reiterates that "for Paul, the conviction of universal solution preceded the conviction of a universal plight."[28] As Bultmann's primary sparring partner, Sanders seeks to undermine the looming edifice of his opponent's project. Sanders regards it as backwards to view Paul's doctrine of salvation as springing out of his understanding of universal sin. To put it succinctly, we ought to allow Sanders to speak for himself: "Paul's logic seems to run like this: in Christ God has acted to save the world; therefore the world must be in need of salvation; but God also gave the law; if Christ is given for salvation, it must follow that the law could not have been; is the law then against the purpose of God which has been revealed in Christ?"[29] He rejects Bultmann's premise that it was the tragedy of human sin and self-righteousness that led away from God as a "starting point" for Paul's understanding of salvation. One question that arises from a rather persuasive accounting of the evidence is the "necessity" issue. Why was it necessary for God to provide a Messiah? One need not race to old conclusions about the notions of seeking human merit or self-aggrandizing caricatures of first-century Judaism(s). On implicit if not explicit grounds, the very necessity of the act of salvation and provision speaks to some sort of plight, however construed. Such a matter is not considered deeply enough by Sanders's framework, and he has encountered strong pushback on this point, not least by Wright, among others.[30]

The law, plight, and possible solutions. To Sanders the greatest proof of his reading of Paul and the "solution to plight" framework is Paul's

---

[28]*PPJ*, 474.

[29]*PPJ*, 475.

[30]N. T. Wright, *The Climax of the Covenant: Christ and the Law in Pauline Theology* (Minneapolis: Fortress, 1991), 258-67.

attitude toward the law. An understanding of the law will illuminate both plight and solution. Sanders frames the question starkly by asking: "Why did Paul think that those who accepted the law were excluded from being saved by Christ?" Sanders argues against Schweitzer's reading that the messianic age had abolished the law, noting, somewhat peculiarly, that Paul never appeals to this as *the* reason for the abolishment of the law.[31] Such a reading is downright puzzling to maintain and foolish in light of Galatians 3:25. To be clear, Galatians 3:25 is not enigmatic but rather straightforward. The law was operative until the Messiah came. Paul, in a classic coming-of-age story, might not agree with Sanders's language of abrogation, but fulfillment is certainly in order.

Part of the confirmation that Paul is looking at a coming-of-age scenario is the direction of his argument in Galatians 3:29–4:6 and Paul's discussion of heirs and offspring. Further, as many commentators have noted, the term *paidagōgos* infers a temporal argument. The *paidagōgos* in Greco-Roman culture was not a lifetime appointment but rather a temporary assignment for specific purposes. Paul utilizes such common moral imagery of his day to make precisely the opposite point of Sanders, namely, that the law was not eternal.

One can name something as temporary without resorting to disparaging comments about the law. In working with students, I usually give the analogy of the relationship between engagement and marriage. Engagement is a wonderful period in the life of any relationship, a moment of celebration and joy. However, it's never meant to be permanent but to lead to its intended goal of marriage. Likewise, once one is married, one typically does not denigrate one's engagement period as being a burden or as some atrocious phase one merely had to get through. Rather, in light of a wedding ceremony, engagement simply pales in comparison to the wedding event. In an analogous way, if the law was meant to lead, prepare for, or anticipate the Messiah, in Paul's mind this has happened—despite the disagreement of some of his

[31]*PPJ*, 475-76, 480.

contemporaries. Likewise, Paul can speak of the fulfillment of the law without negative connotations.

Paul's view on the temporary nature of the law most likely set him at odds with various Second Temple Jewish groups. Certainly Paul would have faced and did indeed face violent pushback against such an idea in the first century. So Sanders's insight is partly correct that Paul did not come to his conclusion based on a "pre-existing Jewish view." The concern in this section is that Sanders takes too critical a view of the term *abrogated* and in his attempt to counter Schweitzer offers a tortuous interpretation of Galatians 3:25.

Against Bultmann, who saw the law as not only leading to sin but given with the *intention* of doing so, Sanders notes that what Bultmann holds as a presupposition was merely a consequence for Paul's view. Stated more directly, with the coming of Christ, *it is now sinful* to try to keep the law as a Gentile. Sanders maintains that Paul's view of the law is drastically shaped by his conviction that if, by the death and resurrection of Jesus, salvation has been given and people have received the Spirit, *then* (and this is a huge caveat), *and only then,* all other means are excluded. Sanders's view on the law can be summarized as follows: the two issues of the Gentile congregants and the exclusivism of Paul's soteriology (that is, that there is one basis of salvation for both Jew and Gentile) "dethrone the law, not a misunderstanding of it or a view predetermined by his background" (contra Schweitzer's apocalyptic view).[32] The final impact of this is rather significant. Sanders is arguing that it was Paul's Christology, not his anthropology, that determined his view of the law.

Paul's covenantal nomism. Near the end of *Paul and Palestinian Judaism,* Sanders seeks to make a comparison between the two halves of his work. He attempts to discuss whether "covenantal nomism" is present in Paul. The concise answer is that Sanders does not see the covenantal framework as helpful for explaining Paul primarily because

---

[32]*PPJ*, 482, 497.

covenantal nomism cannot explain the participatory actions of Paul's thought. As he states, "The covenantal conception could readily encompass the discussion of Christ's dying for past transgression, but it is not adequate to take into account the believer's dying with Christ and thus to the old aeon and the power of sin."[33]

Although different terminology is used, the covenantal framework might actually have room for participatory elements. Likewise, the entirety of the covenantal framework has not been appreciated. According to Sanders, the participation of believers in dying with Christ does not have a parallel in the covenantal framework. What then of the Day of Atonement? Even a cursory glance at Leviticus 16 ought to note the role of both the goat and the scapegoat as a means by which the people *participated* (at least by way of analogy) in the atonement. That is, might not the sacrificial goat represent the means by which the people died to the sins of the past year? The goat takes the place of the people, and, via metaphor, the people die with the goat and are also set free, like the proverbial scapegoat? There is room within the covenant framework of the Old Testament to see a participatory element that has been neglected by Sanders.

In his conclusion, Sanders argues that Paul represents an "essentially different type of religiousness from any found in Palestinian Jewish literature." One of the primary differences is the righteousness language that in Jewish literature indicates obedience to Torah (including notions of repentance) and implies the "maintenance of status," whereas in Paul it is a "transfer term."[34] Paul moves the righteousness language from a staying-in function to a getting-in function.

A second difference, according to Sanders, is the conception of sin. In Jewish literature sin is seen as transgression, whereas in Paul sin is thought of as a power, and one needs a change of "lordship" to be saved.[35] Here there is an obvious tie-in with the apocalyptic interpreters

---

[33]*PPJ*, 514.
[34]*PPJ*, 543-44.
[35]*PPJ*, 547.

of Paul, both in Sanders's day, as represented by Käsemann, but more substantially developed in the coming decades through the work of Martyn and others. One caution inevitably arises: If, as Sanders has argued, Paul should be situated as a Jewish thinker, then from where did the influence of sin as a cosmic power arise? The tension exists in Sanders's statement that this conception of sin appears "unique" to Paul. How do we at the same time situate Paul within the Jewish apocalyptic landscape of his day?

Further, Sanders's conception of sin does not appear to take adequate appreciation of the role of sin in the apocalyptic literature of the Second Temple period. There is clearly not time or space for a full treatment of the matter here. Hannah K. Harrington argues that in the Apocrypha and Pseudepigrapha, although the idea of sin as transgression continues, "a tendency emerges to describe sin more abstractly, *as a force or realm* that is antagonistic to both God and humanity."[36] Certainly the Qumran community and the Dead Sea Scrolls saw the world divided into two categories related to the forces of sin and darkness or righteousness and light, not to mention the "two ways" motif that dominates some of the biblical Wisdom literature. In regard to sin, even if one disagrees with the interpretation of some of the evidence, one wonders whether Paul is just tracing a trajectory to its ultimate conclusion rather than parting ways with his Jewish heritage.

Finally, regarding Paul's understanding of Judaism, Sanders offers his sharpest critique of Paul. He notes Paul "effectively" denies the aspect of covenant in the Jewish system, thus in effect "denying the basis of Judaism."[37] However, this should not lead to seeing Paul as a radical critic of Judaism or to viewing Judaism as the antithesis to Christianity. Simply stated, Sanders charges that Paul's problem with Judaism is that it is not Christianity. Thus Paul's polemic should be understood in light of the coming of Christ. In this view, neither the law nor Judaism itself

---

[36]Hannah K. Harrington, "Sin," in *The Eerdmans Dictionary of Early Judaism*, ed. John J. Collins and Daniel C. Harlow (Grand Rapids: Eerdmans, 2010), 1230.

[37]*PPJ*, 551.

has come to terms with the new work of God in Christ, and therefore they are seen as deficient from Paul's view.

Conclusion and final critique. What can we say about Sanders's epochal work on Paul, which shaped and shifted the discussion on Paul for decades to come? First, it ought to be categorically stated that the negative depictions of Judaism to which Sanders was responding needed a rousing dismissal. Truth and honesty are at the core of all historical work to present ideas fairly. A stereotype, ancient or otherwise, is unhelpful and at its core deeply unchristian. In light of this, the radical critique and dismantling of erroneous views about Judaism that arose in the history of research was utterly needed. Much praise can be heaped upon the deconstructive aspects of Sanders's work. It also appears that this has been the anchor of his work that has held sway for the last several decades. The pendulum was shifted, and in many ways there is no going back now.

Likewise, appreciation is certainly the appropriate response to the scope and vast survey of ancient Jewish sources that Sanders investigated. Sanders marshaled colossal evidence that has allowed us to see more clearly the nature of the discussion at hand. Although one might not agree with the *interpretation* of the evidence, one ought to appreciate the undertaking by Sanders. No one so clearly heralded and turned the attention of the guild toward the topic like Sanders was able to do.

Critically speaking, certainly not every aspect of Sanders's work is or has been met with resounding approval, nor should that be surprising. It is the constructive piece of the work that has run into the most resistance. The criticism even came from *within* what became the new perspective on Paul. It is often missing in discussion of Sanders that it was not just traditional scholarship on Paul and the law that critiqued Sanders. As will be shown in subsequent chapters, both Dunn and Wright marshaled their own negative evaluations of some of Sanders's proposals. The conclusion that Paul's critique of Judaism was that it was not Christianity failed to prove appealing to many, and rightly so.

PAUL, THE LAW, AND THE JEWISH PEOPLE

Six years later Sanders returned to the topic of Paul in his *Paul, the Law, and the Jewish People,* where he responds to some of the criticisms of his earlier work. Two chapters in particular, in his own words, "expand and clarify, and sometimes correct, the account of Paul's view of the law which was sketched in *Paul and Palestinian Judaism.*"[38] In the introduction to this work, he also attempts to defuse criticisms of his previous work and the intention to say something about Paul's relationship to Judaism. He claims this was not his intention in *Paul and Palestinian Judaism.* Rather, that work was focused on "getting in and staying in" and not the broader topics Pauline scholars have been interested in since its publication.

Sanders begins this work with a note of "hesitation" for the sheer fact that all the heat and light that has been directed toward this topic has resulted in little consensus on any front. The dizzying array of attempts to understand Paul and the law shows this is not an easy subject. Problematic at the outset is Sanders's statement that "the different things which Paul said about the law depend on the question asked or the problem posed . . . [and] when set alongside one another do not form a logical whole." Rather, Sanders claims that each of Paul's responses correspond to their own internal logic, springing from the problem at hand. Although he mentions that there is coherence to Paul's "central concerns" (a term he later defines as including features such as monotheism, the sending of Christ as salvation for all, that Jew and Greek are saved on the same basis, etc.), the law does not feature in Sanders's list.[39]

Several concerns and promising avenues emerge here. It is true that Paul responds to problems on the ground as in some sense dictated by his churches and uses these controversies as a means to teach his communities. However, the claim that Paul's statements about the law have their own "internal logic" is not a far cry from circular reasoning. Ancient, modern, or otherwise, no one appreciates hearing that their

---

[38]*PLJP*, ix.

[39]*PLJP*, 4-5.

logic is circular. It is better to assume that an author has a logical train of thought, hopefully clear at least to the author. Such an assumption must guide our work with other scholars, not least Paul. One point that helpfully emerges is that the law may not have been as central a feature as twentieth- and twenty-first-century scholars have made it. The occupation or preoccupation with Galatians and Romans may reveal more about modern scholarship since the Reformation than it does about Paul himself. From surveying his several other letters, it appears that Paul does not need to always talk about the law and has other concerns, as do his churches.

Moving his argument further, Sanders goes beyond his positions in *Paul and Palestinian Judaism* by agreeing with the subsequent work of J. Christiaan Beker that "it is the *christological* interpretation of the triumph of God that is the central characteristic of his [Paul's] thought."[40] Such a statement is developed from what Sanders expressed in his earlier works, but it also helps us understand some of his subsequent arguments about Paul and the law. In short, we might say that *Christology* determines *nomology*.[41] Utilizing his paradigm of "getting in" and "staying in," Sanders concludes that Paul's view of the law is determined by the category he is responding to in debate. When Paul discusses getting in, we find negative statements such as "not by works of the law." However, Sanders argues, when Paul is discussing staying in, behaving and keeping the law are mentioned.[42] Chapters one and three of *Paul, the Law, and the Jewish People* are Sanders's attempts to understand those two categories.

The first chapter of *Paul, the Law, and the Jewish People* is titled "The Law Is Not an Entrance Requirement" and addresses the negative statements about the law and the question of getting in. Sanders addresses Galatians 2–3; 5:3; Romans 3–4; 9–11; and Philippians 3:9 before offering some concluding remarks. Much of what Sanders offers in this

[40]*PLJP*, 5.
[41]Nomology of course being the study of *nomos*, the Greek word for "law."
[42]*PLJP*, 10.

updated version is not new; rather, there is expansion and further clarification of positions already taken in his previous work. His argument does become more explicit in this chapter. In concluding his exegesis on the relevant passages, Sanders writes that in Galatians Paul offers an "attack on the traditional understanding of the covenant and election."[43] The word *attack* appears frequently in this chapter. In *Paul and Palestinian Judaism,* Sanders's critique of Paul's neglect of the covenant was more latent and less direct, while in this updated work it has become more focused and explicit.

One problem with Sanders's overall argument is that there is a complete absence of Spirit language in his reconstruction of the dilemma of Paul, the law, and the Galatians. He correctly connects the scriptural proofs and argumentation of Paul from Scripture, but the missing piece is the Spirit. The confusion only mounts when one notices in Galatians that Paul's argument begins with a discussion of how the Galatians received the Spirit (Gal 3:2-5). Part of the inclusion argument that is building in Galatians is that participation in the family of Abraham can now be identified by the role of the Spirit in the life of the community. It is confusing that Sanders does not, in this discussion of entry requirements, focus on the one thing that Paul seems to emphasize as the linchpin of his argument—the Spirit. An interpreter who misses the Spirit language in Galatians (appearing eighteen times) misses a vital component of Paul's argument. To put this in perspective, the term *nomos* (law) appears twenty-five times. What should be of particular interest is Galatians 5:5, where Paul connects the terms *Spirit, faith,* and *righteousness* in a similar way to how (as Sanders highlights elsewhere) he links *law* and *righteousness* in the passages listed above.

More surprising is that when talking about the law and its inability to function as an entrance requirement, particularly in connection with righteousness, Sanders gives no attention to the later portion of

[43]*PLJP,* 46.

Galatians in terms of the Spirit and the law. In an argument laid out in several stages, Paul seems to argue that the law is not necessary because it is the Spirit who works against the "acts of the flesh" and produces the "fruit of the Spirit," which is functioning somewhat like a law in that it seeks to limit evil and produce the good (Gal 5:16-26). Further, Paul mentions that a person, aided by the Spirit, does fulfill a law, "the law of Christ" (Gal 6:2), by bearing another's burdens and love of neighbor. For Paul, it is the Spirit who makes one an adopted son of Abraham and thus accepted into the promise made beforehand and confirmed by the Spirit, not the law. Such concerns, although not noted in this chapter of Sanders, are at least relevant to why the law is not an entry requirement, though they are a theme of the following chapter, which is about law fulfillment in Paul's theology.

In his third essay, titled "The Law Should Be Fulfilled," Sanders addresses the positive statements about the law and the "staying in" question. Behind these statements for Sanders is the idea that the law is not a means of righteousness, nor is it an entry requirement. This naturally leads to the question, "What, then, is the reason for the giving of the Law? What is its function?"[44] Sanders raises an important point, one that many Pauline interpreters have missed. Many seek to dismiss or diminish the law, but Sanders rightly draws attention to how Paul had strong views of correct behavior and believed that one's life should be characterized by holiness. Paul is at times shocked with his communities' failure to live in a holy manner.[45] Sanders summarizes his views in two major points. He states that Paul rejects as "wrong or optional three laws or groups of laws: the requirement of circumcision, special days, and special food. The most obvious common denominator to these laws is the fact that they distinguish Jews from Gentiles." Second, Paul's own requirements differ from the Mosaic law in that "many of the aspects of behavior which he regarded as obligatory are not specifically

---

[44]*PLJP*, 93.

[45]Sanders cites Gal 5:14, 22; 6:2; 1 Cor 1:8; 7:19, 34; 9:21; 2 Cor 7:1; Rom 8:4; 12:2; 13:8-10; Phil 1:9-11; 2:15ff.; 1 Thess 3:13; 4:3-7; 5:23 (*PLJP*, 94).

governed by Scripture."[46] There is much disagreement with this second proposal of Sanders. It is hard to conceive of how Paul, steeped in the Hebrew Scriptures, would be able to set it aside or not be shaped by it when discussing the behavior of his communities.

There is much agreement with Sanders's first point in terms of Paul's categorical rejection of circumcision and special days for his Gentile communities. There is, however, a bit of a quibble with special food. When one turns to 1 Corinthians and Paul's discussion of food offered to idols and reads all the way through Paul's argument, one finds that Paul actually rules out eating (1) in the temple and (2) if the food is known to have been offered to an idol, the only exception being ignorance on the actual status and origin of the meat. It is interesting that in 1 Corinthians Paul does seem to lay down a new food law. Indeed, in a roundabout way, Sanders does seem to draw the conclusion—and one gets this often from Paul—that "there is an important sense in which his views of behavior function as law."[47] One also sees such a view at work in 1 Corinthians 5, where Paul commands that the person living in sexual immortality needs to be addressed and directly cites a theme of Deuteronomy (Deut 17:7; 19:19; 21:21; 22:21, 24; 24:7) with his command to "drive out the wicked person from among you." Paul's first letter to the Corinthians bears out several of Sanders's points, but one quickly notices that the more positive features of this appear in a letter where the Jew-Gentile issue is not as prevalent of a concern for Paul.

Further problems arise when Sanders concludes, "There is no systematic explanation of how those who have died to the law obey it." Again, to reiterate the point from above, Sanders has almost entirely neglected the Spirit in Paul's thought, logic, and theology, and this leads to numerous problems and introduces complexities into the situation that otherwise would not be apparent. In Sanders's chapter, the role of the Spirit receives merely one small paragraph, which is more of a statement than an explanation. Sanders seems at pains to avoid such a

---

[46]*PLJP*, 114.
[47]*PLJP*, 114.

discussion that frames this problem thusly, "Our present concern, however, is not to offer a full account of what Paul meant by 'life in the Spirit,' but to understand his treatment . . . of the law."[48] Part of the problem is, to paraphrase Paul, the builders have rejected the chief cornerstone. It is this absence that complicates a full treatment of the law by Sanders and thus renders inadequate at many levels a fuller understanding of, Paul, the law, the Spirit, and the people of God.[49]

PAUL: THE APOSTLE'S LIFE, LETTERS, AND THOUGHT

In 2016, after a period of long gestation, Sanders's long-awaited introduction to Paul emerged as *Paul: The Apostle's Life, Letters, and Thought.* Sanders himself notes that he had hoped the book would be out around 1998, but it wasn't until after retirement, near 2005, that he began serious work on the project, and approximately eighteen years later the book finally saw publication. It is worth noting this delay in publication, as Sanders admits up front that he has not kept up with the voluminous nature of the Pauline publishing machine. In this work, Sanders aims to present "the complete Paul—as complete as I can make it."[50] The book is set out in two unequal parts: the first half covering Paul's life and the features of the ancient environment in which Paul lived and moved, and a second, larger half, comprising a study of six Pauline letters (1 Thessalonians; 1–2 Corinthians; Galatians; Philippians; and Romans). Due to the incredible size of Sanders's work, this chapter will survey the relevant sections of the book as it relates to his previous work to showcase any further modifications or changes to the views sketched out in his two previous works on Paul.

In his chapter "Paul Before His Call to Be an Apostle," Sanders returns to a description of the Judaism(s) of Paul's day to contextualize the apostle to the Gentiles. He begins with a description of the Pharisaic

---

48 *PLJP*, 99, 104, 114.

49 The last line evokes the title of Gordon's Fee's work on Paul and the Spirit, *Paul, the Spirit, and the People of God* (Grand Rapids: Baker, 1996).

50 *PALLT*, xiv, xv.

movement. After giving a short history of the movement and its origins (as best as can be known), he moves to a description of the characteristics of Pharisaism. He starts by confronting two caricatures of the Pharisees in popular Christian thought and even within New Testament studies: (1) the Pharisees were obsessed with the minute trivia of the law, and (2) they had the ability/power to make other Jews follow their teaching. Sanders thinks both points are completely wrong.[51] In response to the first charge, he argues that the trivia wasn't trivia and gives the example of Pharisaic debates over calendar dates by posing the interesting parallel experience of trying to change the date of Easter or Christmas for Christians. The second observation, about the *zeal* of the Pharisees, he thinks is overplayed. He notes that several groups were *more* zealous than the Pharisees (e.g., the Essenes) and that it wasn't the Pharisees who were in charge of the revolt against Rome. He concludes that a better word to describe the Pharisees is *precise* and uses both Luke and Josephus to prove his point. However, the word *zeal* is interesting, for it is a term that Paul uses for his pre-Jesus days and is connected to violence. Certainly one should conclude that the Pharisees had more zeal than, say, the *ʿam hā-ʾāreṣ* (people of the land) who chose not to be part of any identifiable group in the first century. *Zeal* is a comparative term at its core, so it is only within the context of other Jewish groups that we can begin to place Paul and his Pharisaic past.

In "Pharisaic Soteriology," Sanders returns to a distinct topic in his other works. He begins with a peculiar analogy that is roughly summarized as "(1) Christianity developed into a religion of dogmas / beliefs; (2) Christian scholars come from dogmatic backgrounds; (3) Christian scholars apply their dogmatic categories onto ancient religions; (4) ancient religions were not dogmatic; (5) therefore it's a category error to seek out dogmas in ancient religions as they had no 'required beliefs.'"[52] Two problems quickly arise from the assumed framework Sanders chooses to employ. First, is it as clear as Sanders

---

[51]*PALLT*, 32.
[52]*PALLT*, 44.

seems to make it out to be? Take, for example, the idea of monotheism. Certainly it was not just a belief but also a practice within the first century. It does seem to be an example of a "rare Jewish dogma," a term that Sanders a little later on chooses to use when he discusses the notion of God as being "just, righteous, and fair." There couldn't be various beliefs on monotheism; one was either a monotheist or not. If not, one would no longer be considered Jewish. Interestingly, in a discussion of *common* Jewish beliefs, Sanders does not mention monotheism.

This brings us to our second problem: terminology matters. Although it may not be dogma, most groups and especially Judaism in the first century were interested in group boundaries. Look at Qumran. Considering who's in and who's out need not be a negative thing and in some sense is required for any group identification. Of course in the ancient world this was a mixture of both belief and practice, but certainly not at the expense of belief. An example will prove helpful. Take the Maccabean Revolt and Matthias, who killed a Hellenistic Jew for attempting to sacrifice to an idol. It appears there was in Matthias's view a requirement/belief that Jews not sacrifice to idols, and this informed his practice. Boundaries mattered and do matter, and beliefs help inform and demarcate boundaries.

Sanders is correct that we ought to note the diversity of belief within the Judaism(s) of the first century, but it does not suffice to say one group stressed dogma over flexibility without retreating to the old stereotypes. Early Christianity was certainly concerned with both belief and practice and was a movement that sprang out of the same social matrix of the Judaism(s) Sanders seeks to reconstruct.

Sanders on Galatians. About halfway through the work, Sanders turns to discuss Galatians in Paul's life and thought. His treatment of Galatians spans four parts, though only parts two through four are of concern for our purposes. In part two he discusses the problems in Galatia to which Paul responds in the letter. Sanders rightly identifies, and its bears repeating and memorizing, that "most of Galatians is one long argument, consisting of many parts," and therefore we ought to be cautious about taking any one part and making it the whole without reading to the end of the argument.[53] In terms of his interpretive framework presented above, our concerns are focused on the interpretation of Galatians 2:14–3:29, and other relevant sections will be included as appropriate.

Sanders begins his explanation of Galatians 2:14-16 with a linguistic lesson on the translation difficulties that are presented to the interpreter with the terms *justify*, *righteous*, and *faith*, which confront the interpreter at every turn in the span of a few verses.[54] His discussion is worth the attention of every reader. Much of the following section is dedicated to a detailed analysis of the relevant terms and arguments in Paul's unfolding argument. Sanders discusses, among other things, the role and character of Abraham, Jewish interpretive practices, quotations from the Old Testament, and the modes of argumentation Paul uses.

Most important for our purposes here is Sanders's treatment of the *purpose* of the law in Galatians 3:19a. Sanders postulates that it is Paul's discussion of the law's "curse" that prompts his discussion of the law's purpose. To this end, Sanders briefly summarizes Paul's use of *hina* (meaning "in order that," "so that") in Galatians to show that God's salvation-historical plan is wrapped up in this discussion of law, though in this section Sanders appears to be too dependent on Romans to explain Galatians, a point he readily admits. One of the leading questions of this section identified by Sanders is "Why then the law?" connected to an interpretive question of "Why did Paul oppose the law?" To the first question, Sanders concludes the answer is to keep people in bondage until Christ. To the second question, Sanders answers, "God intends to save people in another way."[55]

Both solutions are entirely lackluster in argumentative force, if not downright arbitrary in their theological import. Regarding especially

---

[53]*PALLT*, 473. In terms of the relationship between the book of Acts and Galatians, Sanders does not see Acts 11 or Acts 15 as being the event described in Gal 2 (*PALLT*, 464).

[54]*PALLT*, 503-14.

[55]*PALLT*, 530-33, 536.

the second solution, in its worst form, God seems capricious to set up a system that in the end he just replaces with another way. Certainly this is unsatisfactory. The scenario envisioned is that plan A, using the law, did not work, that is, "make alive" (or "impart life"; Gal 3:21); therefore, God sent his son as plan B.

Second, both solutions proposed by Sanders and his interpretation of Paul's positions in Galatians 2:14–3:29 operate on the assumption that the law "saves." In an odd turn of events, Sanders has assumed a point in his interpretation of Paul that his previous work dismantled. Sanders's Paul needs his own new perspective. Sanders assumes that Paul thought the law saved, or at least his opponents did. Are his opponents Second Temple Jews? Doesn't *Paul and Palestinian Judaism* argue that Second Temple Jews did not hold such a view? We are faced with a conundrum: either Paul got his opponents wrong, or Sanders's assumptions about Paul's opponents and Paul's arguments are wrong. Sanders's interpretation of Paul here in this section makes Paul's logic bear characteristics similar to a traditional reading.

Ultimately, what Sanders's reading misses in Galatians is the *temporal* argument. *Now* that God has sent his Son and Spirit, the law has fulfilled its very good and perfect purpose and it *no longer* remains necessary for Gentiles to be circumcised. Paul will marshal an argument using his opponents' favorite character, Abraham, to offer a subversive (re)reading of the story, which places the law in a *temporary* role until the coming of the Messiah. However it is an *interpretive* move to claim that temporary equals negative. It is an *interpretive* move to claim "guardian" equals bondage. These conclusions need not necessarily be negative. One can begin to see the seeds of Paul's thought germinating about positive views of law, which will find fuller expression and maturation in Romans. Namely, the laws are the "words of God" (Rom 3:2) and they are "holy, righteous and good" (Rom 7:12). The topics of law, righteousness, faith, and the Gentiles reoccur in Paul's later letter to the Romans, to which we now turn.

Sanders on Romans. As Sanders returns to Romans, he picks up on several themes further developed from his previous works. Sanders argues that Paul returns to and even reuses some of his previous arguments from Galatians in the writing of Romans, as Paul is "most strongly concerned with the issue of Galatians: the status of Gentiles in the people of the God of Israel. Consequently, he is still thinking about the difficult issue of the role of the Jewish law in the divine economy."[56] While it is true that there is overlap between Galatians and Romans on the issue of Jews and Gentiles and their relationship to the law, it is not as clear as Sanders would like to conclude that the same issue is present in Rome as was in Galatia. Although we have similar arguments with Abraham and the issue of circumcision, the argument appears in a slightly different context in Romans. The shifting context is represented in Romans by the extended discourse in Romans 9–11 on the nature of Israel, its membership, identity, and purpose in the plans of God. Such a discussion indicates that the issue in Rome, though similar to that in Galatia, is probably addressing the inverse issue. Namely, whereas in Galatia the temptation was conversion to Judaism, in Rome it appears that there was Gentile arrogance and disdain for the Jewish roots of the Jesus movement. Paul offers an autocorrect on the hubris of Gentile privilege and reorients the Roman communities to a proper understanding of the issues. So although on the surface Romans and Galatians deal with similar issues, Paul is addressing them from a different viewpoint.

In his discussion of the main theme of Romans, Sanders returns again to the solution-and-plight framework of Paul's thought. Sanders retraces his main conclusion that the solution provided in Christ, what he calls "God's great plan," necessitated a "single problem," one that Paul identifies as Sin with a capital *S*. Sanders argues that this solution to plight characterizes at least Romans 1–7. Surprisingly, however, he goes on to state that though Paul's thought moved from

---

[56]*PALLT*, 617.

solution to plight, in Romans we meet the opposite: his thought runs from plight to solution.[57] Confusion abounds at this point in reading Sanders, for one wonders why in Romans (of all his letters), this striking feature of Paul's thought would not be on display. If we take Sanders's conclusions seriously, even his argument on the development of thought in Paul's theology, why would we not find such a central element of Paul's thinking here in Romans? Further, if Paul is reusing some arguments from Galatians, as mentioned above, why does Paul not reuse that framework? The evidence might suggest the opposite conclusion, but Sanders does not pursue or advance any elaborate argument to suggest why Paul shifted on this supposed central issue.

In turning to a discussion of Romans 7, we enter not only a complex discussion within the interpretation of Romans but also another glance at Sanders's view of the law. Sanders returns to his discussions of the "two dispensations" of election/law and faith in Christ, and the fact that Paul could not denigrate the old dispensation since it too was given by God. Sanders maintains that Paul "had a problem reconciling the two divine dispensations."[58] Sanders notes Romans 2 and Romans 9–11 as signs of Paul's difficulty. In what is a very convoluted argument, Sanders outlines the following parts of Paul's thought that display the complexity apparent in Romans 7. They are as follows:

1. Mild position: Sometimes Paul says that faith in Christ is a new age just "more glorious" than the old.
2. Mediating position: At other times, Paul says the law was being "done away with" and can be equated with "nothing," as he states in Philippians 3:7-8.
3. Negative position: Finally, Paul shifts form a "useless" position for the law to the law being "a positive *evil*."[59]

[57] *PALLT*, 622.
[58] *PALLT*, 640.
[59] *PALLT*, 641; italics original.

4. Conclusion: Paul is in knots over this contrast, and "since God gave the law, Paul will have to retract or modify the negative position above."

Given these assumptions on Paul and the law, Sanders's conclusion about Paul's view of the law is that Paul's views are inconsistent, even contradictory. Sanders has maintained this position for a while now, and it remains unpersuasive. To make matters somewhat more difficult, this complexity is irreducible, as attempts to reconcile the election of Israel, the giving of the law, and universal salvation lead Sanders to conclude that it "cannot be done."[60] Someone please tell Paul and the subsequent tradition of interpretation! The problem is certainly in the eye of the beholder. We must always be cautious of the problems we introduce as interpreters of Paul that are often projected onto him.

In part two of his section on Romans, Sanders turns to discuss the all-important and underlying issue of Romans 9–11. These chapters are the foundation for much of Romans, and in the last century their value and importance has been rightly recognized as central to the message of Romans. Sanders maintains his past conclusions on the matter when he concludes that in the midst of Romans 10:1-4, what Paul finds wrong "with the Jews is that they are not Christians; what is wrong with Judaism is that it does not accept Christianity." Such a conclusion rests on the faulty assumption that Paul was, in Sanders's words, "facing a problem to which there is no solution, given his basic premises, that God chose Israel and that he saves only through Christ."[61] Such a conclusion does not seem to represent the apparent turmoil that Paul faced, indeed the anguish that is described in Romans 9:3. Again we are faced with the issue of a priori assumptions, which is all the more shocking given the use of the Old Testament in Romans 9–11. It seems Sanders has confused the problem with the solution. It certainly is problematic that on the surface it appears that God has rejected Israel in favor of an

---

[60]*PALLT*, 641.
[61]*PALLT*, 676, 681.

arbitrary election of the Gentiles, but this is precisely the charge that Paul is *responding to and not his conclusion*. Paul appears at pains to find a better remedy for the inherent problem facing his first-century communities. Romans 9–11 is how Paul works out that resolution, and surprisingly his argument comes from the Old Testament itself and the story of God throughout Israel's history, not in spite of it.

Finally, one must take issue with the carelessness with which Sanders posits Judaism *versus* Christianity, as it lacks any of the depth of nuance of the first-century realities and in many ways retrojects future caricatures into first-century realities. This irony should be noted. Although we may speak of a nascent Christianity, we have not yet come to the parting of the ways. Certainly Romans seems to envision a scenario with a Gentile majority, but in light of other realities, this is not the norm for first-century house churches, although certainly a sign of things to come. One notes in Sanders's portrayal of dogmatic versions of Christianity that, although he is at pains to say that Paul is not a theologian like Aquinas who seeks to set out dogmas, he nevertheless argues a conclusion based on the reality of Christianity having a fully orbed system, which is nowhere near the picture we get from the letters of Paul. One cannot have it both ways.

CONCLUSION

A scholar should not be judged on whether one agrees with that scholar's conclusions but whether one is stimulated to think deeper about the subject. Such a characterization marks the person and work of E. P. Sanders. Over his career, Sanders has continued to offer thought-provoking ideas and books that prompt further reflection and careful responses, even when one doesn't always agree with him. Sanders has done just this on historical, theological, and ethical issues raised by Paul's letters and thought.

For example, there is widespread agreement that Paul is not a systematic theologian, nor is he constructing a systematic theology. This does not mean that Paul is not *theological,* as he most certainly is in this regard. When interpreting Paul, there is a balance that must be struck between the problems that Paul responds to in his letters and the thought process behind those letters. *Sometimes* Paul is responding spontaneously to an issue that is brought up by the community. However, this does not mean that Paul's letters are carelessly written ad hoc. Sometimes Sanders creates new problems by suggesting this.

Although there are serious theological weaknesses in *Paul: The Apostle's Life, Letters, and Thought,* one must be fair about the numerous strengths. One example is his critique of a typical Lutheran reading of Romans 7. From our viewpoint, Romans 7 is not a description of the Christian life. His discussion of Romans 7 showcases the weakness in reading it as either an autobiography or as a description of the Christian life. Paul argues that Christians have been set free from the bondage of sin. Romans 7:14-25 is a Christian take on pre-Christian existence.

A major shortcoming is Sanders's failure to interact with major Pauline studies of the last twenty years in any significant way. Although Sanders does explain this, it is certainly an issue with the book regardless. A Pauline interpreter also faces the difficulty of what to do with the book of Acts, as scholarly opinion is divided. To this end Sanders makes many assumptions about Acts that are incorrect from our viewpoint. One glaring issue is that Sanders nowhere discusses the faint possibility that Luke may have been a travel companion of Paul during the segments of his last two missionary trips and may have gotten some of his information about Paul's early years from Paul himself. There is only silence from Sanders on this possibility. Even if he adamantly disagrees, an argument needs to be put forth.

As we have noted along the way, too often Sanders reads into the silences of Paul's letters things he should not. One example suffices. Just because Paul doesn't say as much in Romans about "being absent from the body and present with the Lord" as he did in 2 Corinthians 3–5 doesn't mean Paul has changed his mind on that subject. Paul can speak about similar issues in different ways and doesn't need to say everything about a subject each time he encounters it. Second Corinthians 3–5 doesn't lack future eschatology. It speaks, for instance, of Christ being the Judge on judgment day. It would have been more helpful to discuss how Paul holds both otherworldly and future afterlife ideas together, affirming both.

What of Sanders's discussion of righteousness by faith? Here we think he is quite helpful, and he is right to critique the imputed-righteousness idea again and again. Paul is not talking about a legal fiction; he is talking about a real change, not just in status but also in condition at conversion. It is Abraham's faith that is reckoned as Abraham's righteousness. Nothing is said about imputing Christ's righteousness to the believer. In fact, the whole language of credits and debts, of reckoning, is not legal language. It is business language, the kind Paul the tentmaker knew well. Paul was not a trained lawyer, unlike John Calvin.

Despite the lack of substantive interaction with the Pauline scholarship of the last twenty years, *Paul: The Apostle's Life, Letters, and Thought* is an important book that nicely sums up many of Sanders's views on Paul, gives us lots of stimulating exegesis, and shows us that his thought about Paul has not changed much from the late seventies until now. Few if any scholars have done as a good a job of refuting Christian caricatures of early Judaism and Paul's views on the Jewish law as Sanders. For this and many other excellent contributions to our understanding of Paul and early Judaism, we owe Sanders a great debt.

three

CLIMBING THE WRIGHT MOUNTAIN

Tom would have written a shorter book . . . but he didn't have the time.

RICHARD HAYS

While the impact of the voluminous writings of N. T. Wright is not as *broad* as the impact of the work of E. P. Sanders from 1977 to the present, nevertheless, in conservative Protestant and Catholic contexts no one has left a larger imprint on discussions about Paul than Wright, beginning already with various earlier works such as *The Climax of the Covenant* (1991), *Justification: God's Plan and Paul's Vision* (2009), and many articles (see *Pauline Perspectives: Essays on Paul from 1978–2013* for his articles).[1] But it is safe to say that *Paul and the Faithfulness of God* (two volumes, 2013), weighing in at some fifteen hundred pages and coming as it does with a companion volume reviewing the recent discussions by Pauline scholars in *Paul and His Recent Interpreters* (2015), reflects the fullest and most seasoned expression of Wright's thoughts on matters Pauline. Most recently he has published a biography of the apostle to the Gentiles as well.[2]

[1]N. T. Wright, *The Climax of the Covenant: Christ and the Law in Pauline Theology* (Minneapolis: Fortress, 1991); Wright, *Justification: God's Plan and Paul's Vision* (Downers Grove, IL: InterVarsity Press, 2009); Wright, *Pauline Perspectives: Essays on Paul from 1978–2013* (Minneapolis: Fortress, 2013). Some of the material in this chapter appeared first in another form on my Patheos blog, The Bible and Culture, January 11–October 8, 2014. See www.patheos.com/blogs/bibleandculture/2014/01/11/wrights-paul-and-the-faithfulness-of-god-part-one.

[2]N. T. Wright, *Paul: A Biography* (New York: HarperOne, 2018).

We will concentrate on an analysis and critique of *Paul and the Faithfulness of God,* because that work conveniently sums up many of his major themes, arguments, and lines of approach to Paul and his thought world. There is a further reason to do so, because there is now also a very large and detailed response volume to that work by many scholars all in one volume, titled *God and the Faithfulness of Paul* (edited by Christoph Helig, J. Thomas Hewitt, and Michael F. Bird, 2017, eight hundred–plus pages), not to mention a response from a variety of scholars to Wright's major thesis about "the return of Yahweh to Zion and the return from exile."[3]

One thing should be stressed from the outset. Wright is a global, big-picture thinker, and no analysis of his work can be satisfactory unless one takes into account the macro level of his presentation as well as the particulars of his exegesis. By macro level I mean not only the intellectual framework in which he presents Paul's thought and praxis but also the contextual factors and assumptions that guide his exegesis of particular texts. This chapter, then, is dealing more with the bird's-eye view or big-picture view of Wright's presentation of Paul, which provides the keys for understanding his exegesis of crucial Pauline texts.

THE IMPERIAL CULT

In a broad sense, Paul operated in a context where the Roman Empire was everywhere he turned, or worked, or visited, or lived. So, it is natural to ask the question how Paul viewed the empire, and perhaps most importantly to ask how he viewed the growing imperial cult, which involved the worship of recent or current historical figures—the emperor and his ancestors, including both Augustus and Livia. It can be said from the outset that Wright has nuanced some of his earlier, bolder statements about Paul's reacting to the imperial cult, though he is still prepared to use his choice aphorism—for Paul, Christ is the reality, of

[3]Christoph Hellig, J. Thomas Hewitt, and Michael F. Bird, eds., *God and the Faithfulness of Paul* (Minneapolis: Fortress, 2017); James M. Scott, ed., *Exile: A Conversation with N. T. Wright* (Downers Grove, IL: InterVarsity Press, 2017).

which the emperor is but the parody. But even the more nuanced approach produces notable and strong critiques, for instance in John Barclay's essay "Why the Roman Empire Was Insignificant to Paul."[4]

In the wake of many recent imperial cult studies, including studies of the evidence that the New Testament reflects a critique of the imperial cult, chapter five of *Paul and the Faithfulness of God* is in some ways the most crucial chapter in Wright's first volume of this two-volume work. It is a pity that his book went to press shortly before the appearance of *Jesus Is Lord, Caesar Is Not* (edited by Scot McKnight and Joseph Modica, 2013), as it would be interesting to see his reaction to a certain amount of pushback against the reading of imperial cult critique into many places in the New Testament, including a plethora in Paul's letters.[5] The McKnight and Modica book largely concludes (through the voices of some twelve scholars, counting the editors) that anti-imperial rhetoric is *not* a major emphasis of the New Testament writers, nor was it a key purpose of the New Testament writers to oppose Rome in what they wrote. Indeed, some of the authors stress that the real opposition in the New Testament is not between God's kingdom and the emperor's but rather God's rule and Satan's (though Satan might well be involved in the governmental structures in various ways). I would also commend as well reading Christopher Bryan's fine book *Render to Caesar* (2005) for a critique of the imperial-cult theory of interpretation of the New Testament.[6] What, then, does Wright say about the matter?

In the first place, Wright gives a review of Roman history, what led up to its being the empire, and the laudatory attempts by Virgil and others to explain the whole history of Rome as leading up to the climax in Augustus and a new golden age, call this Roman eschatology or

[4]John Barclay, "Why the Roman Empire Was Insignificant to Paul," in *Pauline Churches and Diaspora Jews* (Tubingen: Mohr, 2011), 363-87. We now also have Seyoon Kim's "Paul and the Roman Empire," in Hellig, Hewitt, and Bird, *God and the Faithfulness of Paul*, 277-308.

[5]Scot McKnight and Joseph B. Modica, eds., *Jesus Is Lord, Caesar Is Not: Evaluating Empire in New Testament Studies* (Downers Grove, IL: InterVarsity Press, 2012).

[6]Christopher Bryan, *Render to Caesar: Jesus, the Early Church, and the Roman Superpower* (Oxford: Oxford University Press, 2005).

teleology. The point of this is to suggest that perhaps this story of the Roman good news and king and kingdom influenced the way Paul told the story of Christ and kingdom, or served as a counterpoint thereto. Wright argues,

> Though the components of this great narrative are so radically different from the great single story in which the Apostle believed himself to be living, the overall shape, and indeed the very idea of there being such an overall shape to a centuries long story, would I think have been recognized at once. . . . There is every reason to suppose that an intelligent boy growing up in Tarsus, or for that matter in Jerusalem, would know at least its main themes, if not its finer details.[7]

Not surprisingly, this chapter proves to be one of the longest in the whole work. It is rather crucial to the picture of Paul and his thought world that Wright is attempting to draw up.

Much of chapter five is spent demonstrating the evidence for and growth of the imperial cult during the first century AD. Of this there is no lack of evidence. What we cannot directly tell from the archaeological remains is *the effect* this specific cult had on the mentality of Jews and Christians living in the Roman Empire. We know of course of the repugnance felt by Jews and Christians about idolatry of any and all sorts. We also hear the lament of Plutarch that "nowadays Olympus is over-crowded." Yet there is sometimes more specific evidence, such as that found in Wisdom of Solomon 14:17-21, that there was an especial repugnance of the Jews to the worship of a king or an emperor. This is of particular interest to us because one would imagine the exact same revulsion when it became clear to non-Christian Jews that a crucified manual worker from Nazareth was being worshiped as well. Jews did not anticipate the Messiah being worshiped, much less a crucified messianic figure. The question becomes, Is there *enough* evidence in the remains, and perhaps in the New Testament, to justify the suggestion that Christians were regularly contrasting Jesus with the emperor, with

---

[7]*PFG*, 306-7.

the former being the divine reality of which the latter was just a parody? Wright does not try to answer the question in regard to the New Testament in this chapter but rather is content to build up an impressive picture of the proliferation of the imperial cult in the eastern and the western empire. He is well aware that the evidence is complex.

Wright cites the study of S. R. F. Price, which concludes in part: "The religion of place was now restructured around a person. But it is misleading to categorize this as 'the imperial cult.' The term arbitrarily separates honors to the emperor from the full range of his religious activities, and it assumes that there was a single institution of his cult throughout the empire."[8] On the same page in a note it is stressed that there were a series of different cults sharing a common focus in the worship of the emperor, his family, or his predecessors, but operating in various ways in various locales (sometimes combined with the cults of other gods, such as Demeter; sometimes just a special altar, rather than a constructed temple). Wright notes that Price and his colleagues say that Romanization was often more advanced even in its religion by the establishing of Roman colony cities than by the establishment of the imperial cult itself.

Wright is content to say that so long as one recognizes that there was no single uniform reality that corresponded to the phrase "imperial cult," it is still an important factor to consider in evaluating the New Testament. This is a more nuanced view than in some of his previous writings. *The challenge is to get the balance right between too much minimizing of the impact of the pluriform imperial cult and too much hyperbole about its effect on New Testament writers.* Were these writers really often or always looking over their shoulders and writing over against the imperial cult? I would say they occasionally seem to have been doing this, but not as extensively as most of the enthusiasts for this approach to the New Testament have suggested (see again the volume edited by McKnight and Modica). I will give one example.

[8] *PFG*, 313, quoting S. R. F. Price, "The Place of Religion: Rome in the Early Empire," in *Cambridge Ancient History*, ed. A. K. Bowman, E. Champlin, and A. Lintott (Cambridge: Cambridge University Press, 1996), 10:812-47.

It is not an easy thing to decide when a phrase such as "the ruler (s) of this world" refers to Caesar and/or other human figures and when it refers to Satan and his minions. Sometimes it seems more likely to be the former (see, e.g., 1 Cor 2:6-8, where we hear about rulers who crucified Jesus), sometimes more likely the latter (Col 1:16ff., where names used for ranks of angels appear and seem to refer to heavenly beings). Then too, one can make a case for satanic influence on human institutions, indeed on the emperor himself (see, e.g., Mr. 666 in Rev 13:18). On the whole, however, when one reads a text such as Ephesians 6:10ff. it seems clear that the major emphasis is that Christians are not busy fighting off the emperor cult devotees or the idea of the Roman Empire, but rather the powers of darkness and the kingdom of night. Satan is specifically mentioned.

The narrative in the New Testament is more like the Lord of the Rings and less like a movie about Caligula. I think that Wright has made as strong a case as can be made for a strong influence of the rising tide of imperial cult across the empire; the question still remains of the degree to which the New Testament, and in this case the Pauline corpus, is a response to that rising tide. One can see, for example, how a bad emperor, a crazy emperor, a persecuting emperor such as Nero or Domitian or Caligula might well call forth a written, even if veiled, response from Christians. I think we do see this, for example, in 2 Thessalonians 2 or Revelation and a few other places.

Wright quotes S. J. Friesen, "The discourse of imperial cults was committed to preventing the imagination from imagining the end of the world," to which he adds, "No, declared Paul: God has fixed a day on which he will have the world brought to justice."[9] In other words, imperial eschatology would have been a target for critique, not just imperial cult writ large. Yet Christians absolutely did not go in for the sort of violent response to Rome that we find in the two Jewish revolts in AD 66 and again in the second century with Bar Kokhba. This can

[9]*PFG*, 342, quoting S. J. Friesen, *Imperial Cult and the Apocalypse of John: Reading Revelation in the Ruins* (Oxford: Oxford University Press, 2001), 130.

partly be attributed to imbibing Jesus' ethic of nonviolence (see Mt 5–7 and compare Rom 12–13), but there is something else at work as well. Christians saw the real enemy as not made of flesh and blood but rather as spiritual forces, including "the ruler of the kingdom of the air" (Eph 2:2). This is why, despite troubles from human officials, we still have texts such as Romans 13, or instructions to pray for kings and rulers and in 1 Peter to honor the emperor.

When it comes to the enemies of God's people, they are no longer the pagans but rather the powers and principalities, the spiritual forces and Satan. The fight is not against flesh and blood, and it is not against the Romans or any other conqueror. The fight is against the devil's tools and lures—sin and death. The battle is fought with life, forgiveness, love, good news, faith, not with literal weapons (see Eph 6:10ff.). Zeal has been totally redirected in the life and writings of Paul, but there is still plenty of zeal. Listen for a moment to John Barclay's critique of Wright's approach to this matter.

Barclay points out that for Paul the new creation created by the Christ event stands over against the god of this age, which is to say cosmic satanic powers, not over against the Roman Empire, and Paul does not see the empire as one of those powers or even necessarily the agent of those powers.[10] Further, the demonic powers operate across all levels of existence—individual, social, political, and cosmic. Yes, the Roman Empire can be co-opted by powers greater than itself, influenced by the lies and delusions of Satan because it is part of "this present evil age," but no, this particular empire is not seen as somehow different from other previous anti-God empires in terms of either its idolatry or immorality (after all, many ancient Near Eastern empires had rulers with a taste for being worshiped as some kind of deity). So Barclay concludes that Paul "relegates it to the rank of a dependent and

[10]One tendency of the strong advocates of reading the New Testament in light of the imperial cult and its rhetoric (e.g., Warren Carter) is to blend together the cosmic with the mundane when it comes to the references to powers and principalities. The problem with this is that there are specific denials at key points that the Christian struggle is *not with flesh and blood.*

derivative entity, denied a distinguishable name or significant role in the story of the world."[11] It can be an agent or force for good and for justice (Rom 13), and it can also be an agent of evil and wickedness.[12]

Lest one think, in light of Wright's strong conviction that Paul *is* in some measure critiquing the imperial cult, that Wright is actually an advocate of Paul being seen as something of a subversive or a political revolutionary in general, the following should lay such concerns to rest. He says:

> Yet I believe in the last analysis Paul did affirm the goodness, the God-givenness, of human structures of authority, even while at the same time undermining, through central aspects of his theology, the hubris, idolatry, blasphemy and other wickednesses which, as a Jew, never mind as a follower of Jesus, he associated with the arrogance and swagger of Rome. To say that a particular police force is riddled with corruption, racism, or collusion with organized crime is not say "therefore we should have no police force." . . . The answer to corrupt authorities is not anarchy. Paul, once again as a good creational monotheist, would not suggest such a thing; that is what is underneath his strong affirmations, so shocking to some liberal democrats, never mind Anabaptists, in Rom. 13.1-7. . . . Creational monotheism entails a strong statement about the God-givenness of human structures, even while at the same time also indicating that the one God will hold the office-holders to account.[13]

Wright is an honest scholar, and so despite his proclivity to read between the Pauline lines and find more of a critique of the imperial cult than may be there, he also admits: "The fact that some cities were being redesigned to highlight the imperial architecture produced, so far as we

---

[11]Barclay, "Why the Roman Empire Was Insignificant to Paul," 384.

[12]Wright, while seeming to agree with Barclay's critique (see *PFG*, 1285-88) to some degree, doubles down by suggesting that Paul sees Rome as especially significant, being "the . . . focused instantiation of what 'the powers' were all about" (1318). Not only does Paul never say something like this about the Roman Empire by name, but he says something like the opposite of this while Nero was ruling in the late AD 50s in Rom 13. As Kim, "Paul and the Roman Empire," 281-88, points out, it is a mistake to turn Paul's view into something identical to the critique we find in John of Patmos's Revelation. Paul does not say or suggest that Caesar or the empire at the time when he was writing his letters was either *necessarily* and *inherently* the chief agent of Satan or the fourth beast of Dan 7.

[13]*PFG*, 381.

know, no written comment from him. Nor did he explicitly mention the coins with their basically blasphemous inscriptions: Caesar as Pontifex Maximus and Divi Filius."[14] Exactly so. This is because Paul thinks the real enemy is of a supernatural sort, just as he thinks that the real solution is the coming kingdom of God, not power politics. While it is true that the story Paul is telling of Christ is a story that *indirectly* challenges the imperial rhetoric of the *Aeneid* and other sources, it is not a directly reactionary story but a positive story told on the basis of first principles and biblical accounts. Furthermore, the story Paul is telling, he is quite convinced, will have an inevitable historical conclusion when Christ returns. In that sense, the story the emperor is now telling is temporal, temporary, and ultimately irrelevant. Empires rise and empires fall in this present evil age, but the age to come is already breaking into the present, making obsolete the rhetoric of human empire. *Because Paul has such faith in God's future on earth, he only feels the need to critique the emperor or empire at the point of its idolatry and corruption, not as an institution in itself.*[15]

I entirely agree with the major thrust of the rest of Wright's chapter five. What is central to Paul's worldview is not merely Christ but "the fact of a new community, a community which transcended the boundaries of class, ethnic origin, location, and (not least) gender, by all of which the pagan world in general, and the imperial world in particular,

---

[14]*PFG*, 383.

[15]It should be noted as well that Paul's letters are *insider* literature, meant to be read aloud by a Christian to a group of Christians. They were not broadsides for public display or proclamation. That being the case, there was no reason for Paul to pull his punches and be vague about a critique of the Roman Empire if he saw it as *necessarily* "the evil empire" in thrall to the Dark Lord, Satan himself. Yes, he can allude to the false claims of the current rulers pretending to offer "peace and safety" (see 1 Thess 5:3), but those hyperbolic claims are just seen as typical of megalomaniac human rulers in general. The Roman Empire is not viewed as a special case or the final full expression of the evil empire. Rather than Paul seeing the emperor and the Roman Empire at its worst as a parody of Christ and his kingdom, Paul sees them as a rerun of previous fallen human rulers and empires that have already risen and fallen. In other words, this is nothing new, and after all "this world in its present form is passing away" (1 Cor 7:31), so why waste time and energy polemicizing about or against it? That would be reductionism, for the real problem is at the cosmic level, not at the political level. Caesar is not "the god of this world" in Paul's thought (see, e.g., Rom 16:20).

set so much store."[16] Paul is content to focus on Christ and his people and to turn the world upside down not by focusing on the world but by building this positive, new, inclusive community.

So when Paul says Jesus is the risen Lord, this is a historical claim and only indirectly a critique of all other so-called lords, including of course the emperor. Since in 1 Corinthians 8 Paul does not single out the emperor as the foil for his Christian Shema but rather says there are many gods and many lords in the pagan world, in contrast to the one God the Father, and the one Lord Jesus Christ, the focus of his polemic is on *any kind of idolatry*, not just the imperial claims and forms. In short, he does not seem to be just contrasting Christ as the reality of which the emperor is the parody, though that is true enough as well. Wright is correct that Paul is arguing that

> because there is only one God, there should only be one human family, a family united by faith in Christ, and whatever boundary markers that prevent slave and free, male and female, Jew and Gentile from being united, they have to go! Paul is trying to foster union and unity in Christ, and this involves some pretty radical social implications for institutions like slavery and patriarchy, not to mention implications for the boundary rituals of Judaism.[17]

PAUL'S NARRATIVE THOUGHT WORLD AND COVENANTAL THEOLOGY

In chapter seven, Wright takes on the pushback against narratival analysis of Paul's letters. He does so not just because he knows that human beings make sense of what happens to them by telling stories but because Rudolf Bultmann was wrong:

> The main problem with Bultmann's [demythologizing] proposal, in addition to the muddling of the different senses of "myth" [which does not necessarily refer to a fictional story], is that when he insisted that we should strip the early Christian world of its "mythology" he meant not only that

[16] *PFG*, 383.
[17] *PFG*, 384.

> we should express the existential challenge of the Gospel without its pre-Enlightenment scientific assumptions but also that we should reconceptualize the Gospel in a *non-narratival form*, reducing it to the pure existential challenge of every moment, in which one is called to hear God's word *now* rather than think in terms of the . . . sad time stretching before and after.[18]

As Wright correctly shows, even Bultmann could not do without narrative in describing Paul's gospel; in fact, he remythologized the Pauline gospel.

Here it is worth remembering that Paul's symbolic universe (the big, taken-for-granted ideas such as God) is configured in stories, out of which he does his theologizing into specific situations. While Paul's "theology" usually refers to our construal and combining and sorting and sifting of the theologizing we find Paul doing in his letters, Paul himself is *not* constructing a theology in his letters. He is theologizing and ethicizing in response to specific situations in the congregations he is addressing.[19]

Wright goes on to point out that Bultmann's new narrative—consisting of (1) humans being unaware of the divine spark hidden in a clod of earth, (2) the arrival of revelation or even the Revealer who raises a person's consciousness, and (3) that human going on to live in tune with the inner divine spark abandoning the concerns of the clod of earth—*is essentially a summary of Gnosticism*! This is correct. Among other things, it involves a radical de-Judaizing of the story. Did Paul recast the message of the gospel in non-Jewish forms? Wright responds in the negative.

Wright says it all boils down to this question: Were the early Christians aware that they were living within a narrative that was larger than that of their own sin, salvation, and spirituality, or not?[20] He suggests

---

[18]*PFG*, 457. Wright's critique of Bultmann is all the more germane now that there is something of a renaissance in Bultmann studies and a reappreciation of Bultmann's work. See the various essays in Bruce W. Longenecker and Mikeal C. Parsons, eds., *Beyond Bultmann: Reckoning a New Testament Theology* (Waco, TX: Baylor University Press, 2014).

[19]See Ben Witherington III, *The Indelible Image*, 2 vols. (Downers Grove, IL: InterVarsity Press, 2009–2010).

[20]*PFG*, 460.

that this question is really what the whole new perspective debate was all about—was the old Jewish story taken over, modified, or abandoned by Paul? Did he ditch everything about his previous worldview—symbols, stories, praxis—and start afresh, or not? Sometimes the term *apocalyptic* is used to indicate the breaking in or interrupting and re-routing of the old stories by means of heavenly invasion of a vision or a person. Wright wants to retain the word *apocalyptic* as something radically new, but within the larger historical framework of Jewish narrative. This is where one can see the real debate between a narrative theologian such as Wright and others who are not. It leads to questions such as, How new is the new covenant? How much discontinuity is there between the Mosaic covenant and the new covenant? Is Paul mainly appropriating the story of Moses and Israel, or the earlier story of the patriarchs, as the precursor to the story of Jesus? What Wright is guarding against is Lou Martyn's type of use of the term *apocalyptic* to suggest radical discontinuity with the previous Jewish story.

Wright pushes back against the pushback by J. C. Beker and Francis Watson, who suggest that Paul's gospel is *not* narratival in character and does not amount to seeing the gospel as the climax of Israel's story or the story of salvation history.[21] He admits that the story is not always on the surface of the letters, but the story in his view is fundamental and undergirds the whole. Worldview is what one looks *through*, not *at*, in Paul's letters. Wright explains the difference between poetic sequence, which is what the text says on the surface when it proceeds from one thing to the next, and referential sequence, which is what the surface story or sequence is really about, what it is getting at, and worldview, which undergirds both of the other two.

Now, worldview can as easily be expressed in symbol and praxis as in a story, so a focus on the Pauline narratives, which are the basis for the theologizing and ethicizing into specific situations, does not mean that symbols and praxis should be ignored. Indeed not. But notice, for

---

[21]*PFG*, 462.

example, that a praxis such as the Lord's Supper implies a story, as does baptism, for that matter. Wright's point is that "without the story, we cannot be sure we have discerned the meaning of the symbolic praxis."[22]

As Wright goes on to say, much depends on what one means by apocalyptic when it comes to Paul and his stories. If by apocalyptic, says Wright, one means something that enters the story unexpectedly and gives it a new direction, shedding new light on the meaning of it all, or even brings the story to a climax, that is one thing. If one means by apocalyptic something that brings the story tellingly to a halt altogether, like a fire alarm that goes off in the middle of a play, forcing an evacuation and no finish to the play, then that is quite another.[23]

For the record, it is worth pointing out that when Paul uses the term *mysterion* he seems almost always to be talking about a surprising or unexpected ending or reversal of expectations at the end of the story: for example (1) the *mysterion* about the resurrection mentioned in 1 Corinthians 15; or (2) the *mysterion* about what will happen with Israel and the Gentiles (the order in which they come into the eschatological people of God), and when all Israel will be saved; or (3) the marriage of Christ and his church and when that will transpire. In other words, it seems clear enough that when Paul begins to talk about apocalyptic secrets, it does have to do with the main story, indeed to do with the climax or end of the main story he has been telling all along.

Wright thinks in terms of five stories that are crucial to understanding Paul, and he stresses that these narratives shed fresh light on the exegesis of many passages. The outer story, as he calls it, is about God and creation, but in fact it is also about the fall, or else there would be no story. "God created the universe" is not a story any more than "The cat sat on the mat." It is when a sin, a fall, enters the creation story that we begin to have a plot, not just an announcement of an accomplishment. There is now a present evil age, and Jesus must intercede and bring the age to close and thereby inaugurating a new creation for the original

---

[22]*PFG*, 467.
[23]*PFG*, 473.

design and story to be properly fulfilled. One is rescued out of the evil age, but not out of the world. This is not a Gnostic story about matter being evil and spirit good. It's about redemption of creature and creation.[24] Through the death and resurrection of Jesus, the old, fallen order, indeed the fallen world, has been crucified, the form of the old world is thus passing away, and the new has broken into the midst of the increasingly obsolete old.

Under the heading of the large plot about God and creation comes a theme that crops up some seven times in Paul's letters—the dominion of God, or God taking back his creation from the powers of darkness. In other words, God is not just interested in saving humans; he's interested in the renewal of his whole creation (see Rom 8). Thus, Wright stresses that the larger outer story about God and creation is a story about judgment. Judgment is to be seen as a positive thing. Passing judgment is seen as a good thing—it restores equilibrium to creation by countering and judging the world, the flesh, and the devil. The term *basileia* can refer to the current saving reign of God in a person or community's life, but with a future verb it regularly refers to the realm of God, when he will retake the earth through Jesus, and "the kingdoms of this world become the kingdoms of our God and of his Christ." Meanwhile we pray, "thy kingdom come," indicating it has not yet fully done so. "Judgment is what happens when the creator says 'No' to all that stands out against his good, positive, purposes for his world, in order to say 'Yes' to that world itself, in all its fullness"[25]

Within the larger outer plot are three subplots: Wright lists (1) humans—their vocation, failure, rescue, reinstatement; (2) Israel, the people called to be light to the world; and (3) Jesus the Jewish Messiah, who must succeed where Israel failed in being the light of the world. The human plot is related to the outer plot, because humans were given the task of stewardship of creation in the first place. If humans fail to do this, then God's plan for creation and its caretaking is thwarted.

[24]*PFG*, 476-79.
[25]*PFG*, 481, 483.

Enter the story first of Israel, then of Christ (and, I would add, finally of those in Christ—Christians). Just as the creation story involves all of creation (not just humans), so the fall story involves all of creation (see Rom 8), and thus the redemption story also involves all of creation, not just humans.

Wright suggests that human beings in God's image are "both about reflecting God into the world (purpose) and about receiving and returning divine love (the relationship)."[26] The book of Revelation speaks of this in terms of the priesthood of all believers. The goal is not for Christ to reign on earth on our behalf, but through him to restore the creational task of those created in his image to rule on earth with and through Christ, hence the references to our judging even angels and the like when Christ returns. Creation is set free when God's children are glorified, empowered to do their creational task once more (Rom 8:21). The glory of God's children refers to the glorious reign of God's children (see Rom 5:17). Creation will not share this glory of the saints. When the saints are glorified by resurrection, then the creation will also be set free from disease, decay, and death.

Wright's discussion of Paul's anthropological terms, though intended to be telegraphic at this point, sounds far too Bultmannian for me, though I am sure Wright would not fully agree with this assessment.[27] It is simply not true that flesh, body, spirit, mind, heart, and will are simply *different ways* of talking about the whole person. Robert Gundry, in an important monograph, shows that Bultmann's famous dictum, "man does not have a *soma* [body]; he is a *soma*," is essentially wrong. The *sōma* is the outer physical component of the human being, contrasted most basically with the human spirit. This is why Paul in 2 Corinthians 5 can talk about being absent from the *sōma* (i.e., our individual bodies) and present with the Lord when we die. Of course, we are psychosomatic wholes; all these facets of who we are are intertwined in various ways. Wright, on the other hand, is right on target

[26]*PFG*, 487.
[27]*PFG*, 490ff.

when he says that Paul can and does use all these terms, including *flesh* (*sarx*) in a positive way. Paul is neither a Gnostic nor committed to some sort of cosmic dualism between matter and spirit.

Wright is correct that all these parts or aspects of the human being can be corrupted and need to be redeemed. Sometimes by "flesh" or "flesh and blood" Paul refers to the body as subject to corruption and thus not to be redeemed. What is redeemed is the person in a new or renewed resurrection body, not made of something that cannot inherit the kingdom (namely, corruptible flesh and blood).

Wright is also right to protest skipping directly from the story of the fall to the story of Christ, which occurs in so much of Protestant theology, bypassing most of the Old Testament and its stories. So he says, "The vital narrative element, the crucial turn in the road . . . almost all exegetes miss is [that] the creator's plan was to call Abraham and his family," which he equates with "the story of Israel."[28] This, however, is not quite correct either. The story of Abraham and the big three patriarchs precedes the story of Israel being formed as a people, of Moses as their leader, of the Sinai covenant, and so on. Indeed, we only begin to get a story of anyone or anything called "Israel" *when Jacob gets a name change*. This is not the same thing as the story of Abraham, which Paul certainly does refer to, always in a positive manner. This is quite unlike, for example, what we hear about "Jacob and his impiety," which the Redeemer must come forth from Zion to turn back (Rom 11). In other words, the story of Abraham is one thing; the story and subsequent tale of Israel is related to and dependent on the story of Abraham in various ways, but it is *a subsequent story*. Abraham, it should be noted, already lived in the Promised Land. He did not need to be rescued from bondage in Egypt. His story is not a story of exodus and Sinai, frankly. Nor is it the story of the Mosaic covenant, which Paul deliberately contrasts with the Abrahamic covenant in Galatians 4. Paul, when he reflects on the story of Abraham in Romans 4 and refers to Abraham

[28] *PFG*, 494.

our father, does so because he knows that Abraham was first a pagan before he placed his trust in Yahweh. So in fact he can be the father in faith of both Gentiles and Jews, just as Paul will go on to suggest that the eschatological order of redemption will be the full number of Gentiles first, and then "all Israel will be saved" (Rom 11:25-32).

Here I would say that Wright, for all his insightful analyses of the subplots, has one too few subplots—we need a subplot about Abraham, and we need another subplot about Israel. Put another way, God's people then and now need to emulate Abraham's trust in God and being reckoned in right standing because of it. But God's people also needed to be rescued out from under the effects of the Mosaic law and its covenant, and Paul says that is precisely what Christ came to do—to rescue those under the law out from under the law (Gal 4).

This makes the story of Israel under the Mosaic covenant a story that gives us a holding pattern, an interim arrangement, a temporary covenant until the Jewish Messiah could come. This is the radical reading or rereading of the story by Paul, and how very different it is from those who wanted to retroject the Mosaic covenant not only back into the Abrahamic one but even back into the covenant and commandment given to Adam. No, says Paul in Galatians 4—Hagar, Mount Sinai, the present Jerusalem, and bondage go together, and by contrast there is Sarah, the heavenly Jerusalem, the covenant of promise, and freedom. Thus, Paul says, "we" (i.e., Jew and Gentile in Christ) are the children of promise, like Isaac. Notice that this is not like either Esau or those who were later under the *paidagōgos*, the Mosaic covenant. Followers of Christ not only don't have to keep the badges of the Mosaic covenant (circumcision, food laws, Sabbath) but aren't under the Mosaic covenant at all.

This of course is not Wright's view of things, and I would say it is in some ways the most fundamental mistake he makes in his otherwise brilliant reading of Paul. Jesus is not Israel; he is Israel's Messiah, and as Paul says, he is "the seed of Abraham," not the Israel of God. The question to be asked is, *In what way is the plot advanced between Abraham and Christ?* What we see is various preliminary and only partially successful attempts by God to redeem and create a people, before, during, and after the exile. Had there been true success, Christ need not have come or died or risen and so on. This is why the true eschatological people of God are Jew and Gentile united in Christ, not outside that locus. There could be no such people had the radical rescuer not come and effected the rescue, starting with the lost sheep of Israel. It is breathtaking indeed when Paul says things to his largely Gentile converts in Galatia such as "we are the children of Abraham" or in Romans when he speaks of Abraham "our father."

A more cogent point comes when Wright stresses that Israel was entrusted with the oracles of God to share them with the nations. He is absolutely correct that vocation is one thing, salvation another. I would add that election to a specific vocation is not the same thing as election unto salvation of this or that individual person. Cyrus was "anointed" and chosen to set God's people free, but that had nothing to do with his individual salvation.[29]

If Jesus is the seed of Abraham, the true Jew who fulfills the destiny of Abraham's people to be a light to the nations, then indeed the whole story from after Abraham until Christ has been mostly a series of unfortunate incidents, of ups and downs without any full salvation coming to light or any full vocation being accomplished, on the way to the birth of the Messiah. Christ is the last Adam, bringing the human story to its climax and fulfillment; he is the seed of Abraham, bringing the covenant of promise to its fulfillment; he is also the true Jew, assuming the vocation that Israel failed at and which he alone completes. But neither he nor the church is Israel, whose fate must await the return of Christ, according to Romans 11.

THE STORIES IN THE SACRAMENTS: EXODUS OR ELSE?

Wright analyzes things under three major headings—stories, symbols, and praxis—and he sees all three as telling stories, or at least grounded in stories. There is agreement with Wright about this and with the

[29]*PFG*, 496. On this whole issue see Ben Witherington III, *Biblical Theology: The Convergence of the Canon* (Cambridge: Cambridge University Press, 2019).

conclusion that the stories being told in the sacraments are Jewish to the core. They are not really drawing on the mystery religions (and here the critique of Udo Schnelle and others by A. J. M. Wedderburn I think is accurate, fatal, and final). The central point he wants to make is that baptism is about "us," about who the community is, not chiefly about "me," who I am.[30]

What is not really adequately discussed by Wright (anywhere to my knowledge) is the difference between what Paul says about water baptism itself in, say, 1 Corinthians 1, and what he says about the work of the Spirit, in which he uses the language of water baptism but in fact is not talking about the ritual! He is talking about the activity of the Holy Spirit in 1 Corinthians 12:13 ("we were all baptized by one Spirit . . .") and in Galatians 3:27 ("for all of you who were baptized into Christ clothed yourselves with Christ"). This has to be contrasted with what he says in Romans 6 and in Colossians about baptism being a burial with Christ, or in Colossians a circumcision. He is right that there is this parallel with the circumcision ritual in the Mosaic covenant, though baptism is a gender-inclusive symbol.

Circumcision is a cutting-off ritual, a sign of the oath curse (if you don't keep the commandments you will be cut off). Similarly, baptism is a symbol of the burial of the old self, the putting off of the flesh, in order that one might rise to newness of life. Baptism no more entails resurrection or rising to new life (for then the mystery-religions case might have some teeth) than Jesus' death in itself entails his resurrection. Baptism is about being cut off from the old world, the old self, and joining a new community—it's an entrance ritual.

At one juncture in the discussion Wright points to 1 Corinthians 10.[31] Alas, for Paul is using the analogy with the exodus generation to warn the Corinthians that the sacraments do *not* work magically and do not serve as some sort of protection from future apostasy or harm. Anyway, there was no "baptism" into Moses—the Israelites crossed the Red Sea

---

[30]*PFG*, 421.
[31]*PFG*, 418-27.

without getting wet. The point of the analogy is in regard to spiritual benefit, not in regard to ritual praxis, otherwise Christians would need a much drier ritual of baptism! But even if one allows that the story of the exodus and Sinai adventures undergirds the story of baptism, then the point to be made is that leaving Egypt (exodus) as a symbol of baptism does not entail entering the Promised Land; it's the leaving behind of the old bondage, not the entering into the new Promised Land. Only two Israelites in the end did the latter. In other words: (1) the water ritual of baptism symbolizes the cutting off of the flesh, the shedding of the old self; but (2) it is only the actual work of the Spirit, which may or may not be coincident with water baptism, that joins one to Christ. The symbol of the shedding of the old is one thing, the actual rising to life by means of the internal work of the Spirit quite another.

This brings us to the story of the Lord's Supper and Passover. If the Lord's Supper is a retelling and updating of the story of Passover, in light of the death and resurrection of Jesus, it should have struck us as a little odd that baptism on the one hand is connected with the exodus, but the Lord's Supper is connected with a *preexodus event*—the Passover event, and then the meal that celebrated it. Isn't this telling the story backwards? The answer, it seems, is that Paul is not really interested to simply pay it forward with the whole story of Israel, not in 1 Corinthians 1–11, not in Romans 1–11 (despite what Wright says in his Romans commentary), and not elsewhere. Paul simply selects portions of the Old Testament to draw analogies in some cases, and in other cases he does presuppose more of a narrative, but even then he does so selectively (so, e.g., when he thinks of Abraham he thinks primarily of the story of his trusting God, not of his later misadventures, and not even of his offering of his son Isaac, despite how resonant that tale is).

The point of bringing this up at this juncture is that there are two stories in the Old Testament that Wright *overuses* in his reading of the New Testament—the exodus story and the exile story. By "overusing" I mean that he sees these motifs in New Testament places where they don't exist, and they don't exist because Jew and Gentile united in Christ are *not viewed as Israel or as a replay of Israel's history*. Israel still has a story to be told about it, as Romans 11 makes clear. Its story must not be subsumed into or taken over by the story of the church.

Consider, for example, the last large portion of Wright's chapter seven (more than thirty pages), which presents us with some of the most critical and also controversial elements in his analysis. We need to bear in mind that Wright is here talking about worldview and stories that are part of the worldview, that which lies beneath and undergirds the theologizing. For example, Deuteronomy 27–30, which is so fundamental to Wright's argument, is treated as something of a long-range prophecy, not merely a narrative account, revealing the pattern of sin, judgment (which Wright calls exile), and then redemption beyond judgment on God's people.

The real controversy lies with Wright's analysis of the story of Israel and its relationship to the story of the Messiah, and not surprisingly how the Mosaic law fits into these stories hinges on whether one accepts Wright's understanding of Christ as Israel. For the record, it should be stressed that while Paul does indeed call Christ the last or eschatological Adam, he does not call Christ the last Israelite, or even true Israel. Christ is the Messiah of the Jews, and indeed he will fulfill the vocation of the Jews to be a light to the world, but the story of Israel is not simply incorporated into the story of the Messiah, or vice versa. This becomes especially clear in Romans 9–11, but one could back up to Wright's exposition of Romans 7, where he thinks the text is speaking of Israel and the law. I would suggest, rather, that it refers to Adam and those in Adam from a Christian point of view. In Romans 9–11 the Messiah comes from Israel but does not circumscribe Israel. Thus, Paul can refer to Israel after the flesh and true Israel and in neither case refer to Christ (see Rom 9–10).

Even later in Romans 11 the full number of Gentiles come in, and then Paul says, "and in like manner all Israel will be saved" (not *are being saved* but in the future *will be* saved). The quotation from the

Old Testament makes perfectly clear that the impiety of Jacob (i.e., Israel) must be turned away when the Redeemer comes forth from heavenly Zion. That is, the story of Israel is not completed in Christ's previous actions on earth. It still has a future, and that future is for Israel to be rejoined to the largely Gentile people of God, regrafted into the olive tree, to use Paul's metaphor, when the true gardener returns—Christ (not Paul).

Wright does make clear that he sees the *paidagōgos* metaphor in Galatians 4 indicating that the Torah, as Mosaic covenant law, has a temporary function in relationship to Israel. Its necessary, preliminary role is finished once Christ comes. Torah shows that Israel is the people of God but also makes clear that Israel is still in Adam, and so the law turns sin into trespass. Wright says clearly that the law is never seen as a bad thing by Paul; it's a good thing but frustrated in its purpose by sinful flesh. That, however, is not the only problem. Wright should have added that the law in no case had the power to enable a person, whether Adam or any fallen person since, to keep it, to obey it.[32]

The law could inform a person but not transform a person. The law could tell a person what to do but not enable her to do it. Wright suggests we have to read Romans 8 as a continuation of Romans 7, such that "Now that the 'sinful flesh' has been dealt with in the death of the Messiah, Torah is able at last to fulfill its original purpose—through the death of the Messiah and the power of the spirit."[33] But this is to dramatically underplay the contrast at the beginning of Romans 8, which says, "What the Mosaic Law could not (indeed, could never) do, God's Spirit has done." Wright thus wants to read the word *nomos* in Romans 8:2 as referring to the Torah, but this will not do. It won't do because already in Romans 7:13-25 we have a contrast between the "law of my mind" and "a different law ruling in my flesh." Sometimes Paul does indeed mean a "ruling principle" rather than the "Mosaic law" by *nomos*, and this is clear enough in the contrast in Romans 7:13-25. The

---

[32]*PFG*, 510-11.
[33]*PFG*, 511-12.

law of the mind may well be God's law, or more narrowly the Mosaic law (if Paul is thinking of a Jew outside Christ), but this law is being opposed by the ruling principle of human fallenness in a person's flesh. God's law is not that unruly, unholy principle.

So too in Romans 8:2 the ruling principle of the Spirit of life is something different from the good but impotent Mosaic law, and Paul makes this contrast quite clear here. In short, the attempt to take *nomos* anywhere and everywhere in Paul to mean "Torah" doesn't work, any better than trying to suggest Christ is the true Israelite or Israel. The new covenant is not the Mosaic covenant renewed. It is a new covenant connected to the one with Abraham. The story of the Mosaic covenant comes to an end in Christ himself, who fulfills its purpose, bringing it to an end, and does not extend its license to rule the life of the believer.

There is a "law of Christ," but this is the law of the new covenant and not simply a continuation of Torah. There is strong disagreement with Wright's conclusion when he says:

> This new-covenant people is "not under Torah" in the sense that it is not "Israel according to the flesh," living in the place where Torah goes on pronouncing the necessary and proper sentence of condemnation. But it "fulfills the decrees of Torah," and indeed "keeps God's commandments," insofar as it is the Deuteronomy-30 people in whom what had been impossible under Torah, because of Israel's fleshly identification with Adam, is not accomplished by the spirit.[34]

Wrong. The new-covenant people are not under Torah in any sense, if by Torah one means the Mosaic law. Nor do the people have any need to fulfill Torah's decrees, since that covenant is defunct, having been fulfilled in and by Christ and brought to an end when he inaugurated the new covenant on the cross.

God's people are not under two covenants at once, only one, and that one is the new covenant with the law of Christ, which among other things involves many mandates from Jesus not only not found in the

---

[34]*PFG*, 513.

Mosaic law but in fact superseding what the Mosaic law says, for example, about the lex talionis, "the eye for an eye" principle. Thus, while it is helpful to some degree when Wright says that "everything Paul says about Jesus belongs within one or more of the other stories . . . the story of the creator and the cosmos . . . the story of God and humankind . . . and the story of God and Israel," this deserves a yes-and-no response. The story of Jesus brings some new elements into the overarching narrative, and while it is true that Christ enables the story of God's people to carry on, as well as the story of the cosmos and humankind in general, this is not all the story of Christ does, and in some respects Christ brings the subplot of the story of Israel under the Mosaic covenant to an end. It does not continue, being once fulfilled in Christ. More helpful is Wright's remark that "Israel's Messiah brings Israel's history to its strange and unexpected conclusion, precisely so that he can then bring God's justice [or better said *mercy*] to the nations."[35]

Wright rightly stresses that the rescue operation Christ is involved in is a rescue from the present evil age, not a rescue from the world of space and time. Equally helpful is the preview of coming attractions when he stresses "that the supposed clash or conflict between two models of salvation in Paul, the forensic or the juristic on the one hand and the incorporative on the other, is also a category mistake, the result of a failure to see how his different stories actually work." A misstep happens, however, when Wright sees the story of Adam alluded to in Philippians 2:5-11 (a view Dunn argues for). Adam did not preexist, nor was he "in very nature" God. The key term here means "take advantage of," not "snatch at" something one doesn't have. To be sure, Adam did the latter, but Philippians 2:5-11 says that Christ did something else—he did not take advantage of his divine prerogatives.[36]

At the end of this important chapter, Wright explains why he does not deal with the story of the church, or Christians, in this long discussion of worldview. He says it is because that story occurs on the

---

[35]*PFG*, 517-18.
[36]*PFG*, 532-34.

surface of Paul's texts, not embedded down below. But clearly enough various of these other stories rise to the surface of the text as well, from time to time. And if, as he says, "the *ekklēsia* itself . . . constitutes the central symbol of Paul's *worldview*," then it should have been dealt with here and in these preliminary chapters.[37]

WHO, WHAT, AND WHEN?

The last chapter in volume one of *Paul and the Faithfulness of God* reviews for us Wright's answers to the who, what, when, where, why, and so on questions.[38] On the "who" question it is notable that he is perfectly comfortable saying that Paul could call any and all Christians "the Jew" as well as "the seed of Abraham" and "Israel." The middle of these three terms is clear enough; the other two are quite controversial. Wright has to concede that this doesn't quite work with the use of Israel in Romans 9–11, for example, and indeed when we look at a passage such as Galatians 1, Paul refers to *Ioudaismos* as a way of life that Paul left behind. Even in regard to his own individual identity, Paul is prepared to say in 1 Corinthians 9:20 that he has to "become like a Jew" to the Jew from time to time for mission's sake, but what this implies of course is that he is *not* simply a Jew any more, at least in terms of praxis.

We suggest there is a very good reason Paul, the apostle to the Gentiles, does not address his congregations as "the Israel of God" (and no, that is not happening in Gal 6 either). Rather, he calls them the *ekklēsia* or "assembly of God" in this place or that. The new people of God are Jew and Gentile united in Christ, not simply Jews. When he distinguishes his mission from that of Peter, he says Peter goes to the circumcision, he to the uncircumcision. He is not happy to simply call his largely Gentile converts "the circumcision," though of course the metaphor about circumcision of the heart could be applied to any convert. It is precisely because we agree with Wright that the *ekklēsia*

---

[37] *PFG*, 536, emphasis added.

[38] *PFG*, 538-69.

tou theou is central to Paul's worldview that it is important to be very careful about what we say about Paul's terminology for this new community. It is a community of already and not yet. God has not finished making it what it will be when the new creation is completed at the return of Christ.

There is a good reason for Paul's reticence when it comes to the use of what today might be called supersessionist (or even "hostile takeover") language: the story of non-Christian Israel is not finished yet and was not completed by the first coming of Jesus or his death and resurrection. Romans 11 says just this. It is a story still awaiting a better resolution, when it is enfolded into the story of the *ekklēsia* when Christ returns and "all Israel is saved." Paul's Gentile converts have been taken into the patrimony of Abraham through Christ, Abraham's seed, not into the story of Israel. Were the latter the case, the Judaizers would have had a point—Gentiles need to become Jews to be followers of the Jewish Messiah. Due attention needs to be paid to 1 Corinthians 9, where Paul even says he becomes as one under the (Mosaic) law for those who are in such a state, indicating that *this is not his normal modus operandi,* and then he goes on to talk about being under the law of Christ—clearly something else again.

Wright argues, "The people to whom Paul reckons he belongs could almost be defined as those who tell the scriptural story, the great story of God and Israel, as *their own story now fulfilled in, and transformed by, the Messiah.*"[39] But has this really taken the measure of Galatians 3:28, where Paul says that in Christ there is *neither* Jew *nor* Gentile, neither Israel nor any pagan ethnic identities? Has the *ekklēsia* really hijacked the story of Israel, or does it still have some time to play out and some future to conclude? In Paul's view, the answer to the latter is yes. Yes, the *ekklēsia* is the Messiah's people, Jew and Gentile united in Christ. Yes, there are Jews who have rejected their own Messiah and refuse to participate in the *ekklēsia,* and according to Paul have *temporarily*

[39]*PFG*, 543, emphasis original.

(underscore that word) been broken off from the people of God (with Jewish Christians being seen as the "root" in the Christian era). But as Paul clearly says, they can be grafted back in (just as the Gentiles, if unfaithful, can be broken off again). *It's a fluid situation.*

Wright's answers to the questions "What is wrong?" and "What is the solution?" are uncontroversial and have already been stated before. The problem is not just individual human sin; it is also the fallenness of all of creation that needs to be rectified. To paraphrase that great philosopher Sting—what good is a resurrected body if one is living in a decaying and dying world? As Wright stresses, the solution is the return of Christ to enact his restorative judgment, which the saints will assist with, and the spread of Christ's rule over the earth, not to mention the renewal of the earth itself in the end.

To address the issue of when, Wright quotes Philippians 3 to good effect: maturity consists in recognizing one has not yet achieved maturity, completion, perfection. The actual bodily resurrection has not happened yet for believers. The discussion of the already and the not yet in Paul is helpful in clarifying Wright's own vision of the future, as Paul outlines it. Clearly Paul was not guilty of either overrealized or underrealized eschatology. Equally clearly, he believed Christ had already inaugurated the end times, "the ends of the ages."[40]

Bringing this section to a close, there is a splendid discussion of what expectation means for Paul. Drawing on Anthony Thiselton, Wright points out,

> "Expectation" is not simply a "mental state," nor a matter of making calculations or dreaming imaginatively about the future. Expectation consists . . . of "appropriate conduct or behavior in a given situation." To expect a guest to come to tea does not mean "to imagine a guest's arrival"; it means "to put out cups, saucers, plates, to buy cake, and perhaps tidy the room and to begin to boil the kettle." For the Thessalonians to "expect" the coming of the Lord means that "they must seek holiness and work hard."[41]

---

[40] *PFG*, 552ff.
[41] *PFG*, 554.

One of the things that makes Wright such an interesting New Testament scholar is that he is not afraid to pursue lines of argument that are somewhat speculative and may or may not bear fruit. One such exploration takes place when he explores whether Paul may have thought of the present inbreaking rule of God as establishing some sort of Sabbath here and now.[42] If *now* is the day of salvation, the day that all the world has been groaning for, then *now* as well is the time when *shabbat shalom* is or should be happening, in this case through the ministry of Paul. Now is the time of the new creation.

This, however, is a yes-and-no proposition. No, the creation itself has not yet been set free; yes, there are already new creatures in Christ. No, the world has not been released, nor have human bodies become exempt from disease, decay, death, suffering, sin, and sorrow. But yes, there is something new already happening the renewal of hearts, minds, wills, emotions, the inner self of those in Christ. On the larger scale—yes, the turning point in the war versus the powers and principalities has happened in the death and resurrection and exaltation of Christ. But no, such powers have not been eliminated or prevented from continuing to do harm in this world.

It must be said that the book of Revelation suggests that the final sabbatical rest and restoration does not happen *now* but after the second coming, and indeed after the millennium and the final disposal of enemies. It is, however, interesting that the term *rest* can refer to God finally "residing" with and in the midst of his people, which John Walton suggests is in mind in the Genesis tale about six days of creation followed by God taking up residence in his temple, his creation. Wright is correct that getting the balance right between the eschatological already and the not yet is tricky—the Scylla being a pessimism grounded in seeing just how little the world looks like a new creation, and the Charybdis being the cockeyed optimism that thinks that because the resurrection has happened to Jesus that everything has already begun

---

[42]*PFG*, 557-59.

to turn up roses. "Maturity lies in the celebration of messianic time within the muddle and misery of the present age. . . . The mature mixture of times is foundational to Paul's entire worldview."[43]

Wright brings us to the end of part two by reminding us of the peculiar nature of Paul and his calling—no one else was claiming to be *the* apostle to the Gentiles, and in Wright's view this means Paul saw himself in a sense as the special agent of a Messiah who was the suffering servant of God and who had as his vocation to complete the vocation of Israel to be a light to the nations. Thus, Paul takes on this messianic vocation in his mission and sees himself living into and out of the story of the Christ, who is the light.

Wright explains why it is important: "Theology, for Paul, was quite simply essential if the worldview, especially the united and holy *ekklēsia* which was its central symbol, was to stand firm and remain in good repair." Interestingly, Wright stresses that the reason theology became so crucial for early Christians such as Paul was that they had rejected the symbols, the boundary markers of Judaism, and at the same time were not going to embrace pagan symbols and boundary distinctions either. Therefore, they needed to have deep and profound theological roots to sustain the faith. The faith could not be sustained simply by praxis or the central symbol of the church. It needed to think, to have a renewed mind and a profound grasp of what it believed, and indeed of the necessity of belief in order to be saved. This helps account for a major difference in focus between Judaism, which focused on orthopraxy and assumed as part of its worldview monotheism, and Christianity, which focused on orthodoxy and needed to define theological terms in detail. Finally, as Wright says, Paul was not interested in doing all our thinking for us but rather teasing our minds into active thought, goading us and guiding us to contribute to the task of doing theology and ethics in the Christian tradition. Or, as Wright aptly puts it—"give someone a thought, and you help them for a day; teach them to think [theologically], and you transform them for life."[44]

---

[43]*PFG*, 562.

[44]*PFG*, 566, 569.

THE AXIOMS: MONOTHEISM

The way Wright approaches the task of deciphering Paul's thought and praxis is based on the following basic assumptions (which prove that Wright completely rejects the form-critical approach to the text): (1) he assumes Pauline letters have an inner logic and a central concern, and (2) "I take it as axiomatic, on the contrary, that Paul deliberately lays out whole arguments, not just bits and pieces, miscellaneous topoi which just happen to turn up in these irrelevant 'contingent' contexts."[45] Exactly so, which is precisely why a rhetorical analysis of whole arguments in Paul's discourses is crucial. It's not enough to examine the minor rhetorical devices, the micro rhetoric, when it is the macro rhetoric, the whole arguments, that are driving the train. But, oddly, Wright does not do rhetorical analysis of Paul's letters, nor does he interact with those who have done this extensively. Instead, he is apt to draw on Ken Bailey's chiastic types of analyses, for instance of 1 Corinthians. This is passing strange.[46]

This is problematic for a host of reasons, not least that Paul's letters are oral texts, meant to be heard, not meant to be looked at and studied. Paul's audience would have involved not just elite persons who could read but also numerous nonelites who could only listen and ponder. Chiasms are not orally recognizable devices unless they are very compact indeed. But Wright and Bailey see chiasms spanning several chapters, for instance in 1 Corinthians.[47] These sorts of expansive structures would need to be seen, not heard. They are not oral and aural devices, which is precisely why the usual scholarly critique of such things is that chiasm, like beauty, tends to be in the eyes of the beholder (emphasis on *eyes*).

Another fundamental assumption of Wright is that he believes salvation is best dealt with under the heading of *election* (remembering

---

[45]*PFG*, 610.

[46]It is interesting that in his most recent book, his biography of Paul, he recognizes the fruit of extensive rhetorical analysis of Ephesians as an example of Asiatic rhetoric.

[47]See especially Kenneth Bailey's *Paul Through Mediterranean Eyes: Cultural Studies in 1 Corinthians* (Downers Grove, IL: InterVarsity Press, 2011).

that his big-ticket categories are monotheism, election, eschatology).[48] In this Wright makes clear once more that he is a scholar in the Reformed tradition, with some basic Reformed assumptions. Election has to do with vocation, not personal or individual salvation. *This is especially clear in the Old Testament, where the Christian concept of salvation meaning the gift of everlasting life from Jesus does not even surface, and yet we have plenty of discussions about election.* Agreement is found with Wright that when election is discussed it is a corporate notion—it happens in Israel in the Old Testament, and in Christ in the New. Here it's enough to point out that Wright resists the usual Protestant tendency to make soteriology the central category or lens through which we read Pauline theology.

Jewish monotheism. In identifying the main thing Paul needed to come to grips with as he was reconfiguring the central Jewish beliefs in monotheism, election, and eschatology (reconfigured on the basis of Messiah and Spirit), Wright finds himself in fundamental agreement with Wayne Meeks when he says, "For Paul himself, the central problem is not just to spell out the implications of monotheism, but to explain how the unified purpose of God through history could encompass the *novum* of a crucified Messiah."[49] Wright also continues to stress from the outset that Paul is not simply having an intramural Jewish conversation with other Jews about their Jewish worldview. Paul is in constant dialogue with the pagan world, insisting that the transforming power of the gospel upstages the philosopher's dream of and quest for a true humanity. He encourages the churches to live with a spirit and *koinōnia* that pagan religion had been striving toward but not achieving, and he believes the lordship of Christ upstages the grandiose claims to divinity of the emperor. Paul was quite capable of taking every thought captive for Christ, and so he does sometimes borrow ideas from pagan philosophy, but his basic framework and modus operandi is Jewish. "The fact

[48]*PFG*, 611.

[49]*PFG*, 612n9, quoting Wayne Meeks's classic *The First Urban Christians* (New Haven, CT: Yale University Press, 1983).

that humanness had been spoilt by idolatry did not mean that the divine plan of salvation involved the abandonment of humanness."[50]

Certainly Wright is correct that, just as the belief that there is only one God was central to early Judaism, for Paul the reformulation of what that belief *meant* is central to Pauline theology, and Wright is prepared to explain why. "When the major symbolic praxis of the Jewish worldview (circumcision, food laws, Sabbath-keeping) had been deemed 'adiaphora' . . . then theology and particularly monotheism needed to take on far more of the load in sustaining the worldview in its radically new form."[51] The key to understanding Second Temple monotheism is not a particular proposal about the inner nature of the one God, and it had nothing to do with debates about thrones or exalted angels.[52] It had never been part of the Jewish Second Temple worldview that God was the only nonhuman intelligence in the universe. "The main focus of Jewish monotheism in our period, then, looked not . . . inward, towards the analysis of the one God, but decidedly outward, to the relation of the one God to the world."[53]

"Monotheism therefore meant foundationally and scripturally the renunciation of ontological dualism. Renouncing the world itself, pretending it was a dark and gloomy place, complaining about the soul being imprisoned within a material body, or grumbling at the very existence of human rulers and power structures, was not part of this worldview."[54] There was God, and there was everything else, which the one God had created. This is what creational monotheism amounted to—a fundamental denial of dualism when it comes to all that exists.

Furthermore, creational monotheism involved a celebration of the essential goodness of all that exists. Thus,

---

[50]*PFG*, 613-14.

[51]*PFG*, 625.

[52]Here he is largely in agreement with Richard Bauckham on the former point, and in disagreement with Larry Hurtado on the latter.

[53]*PFG*, 627.

[54]*PFG*, 628.

> when they [Jews] prayed the *Shema* twice or more each day, they knew they were opposed, in heart, mind, and with the breath of life, to idols, to the making and worshpping of them, to the way of life that went with them and—not least—to the actual human beings and actual human systems whose lives revolved around "the gods of the nations," their temples and their worship.[55]

Thus, this is an exclusive kind of monotheism, not the kind that we find in the Letter of Aristeas 16, where one hears that the God Jews worship as Yahweh, you Greeks call Zeus, and so on. For Jews, a rose by any other name was in fact *not a rose*. As the story plays out in the Bible, there is only universalism through the vehicle of particularism—the world shall only be set right through faith in the one biblical God and not otherwise. There is no endorsement here of modern pluralism. God will come and establish his own singular kingdom on earth, to which all must give allegiance or else find themselves left out. Once more with feeling: "In second-Temple monotheism, the fact that there was one God, utterly supreme, the only creator and governor of all, did not rule out the possibility of . . . inhabitants of the heavenly realm, but actually tended to entail that possibility."[56] These supernatural beings just weren't gods. They were good creatures gone wrong, just like fallen humans and a fallen world. Nor did belief in the absolute goodness of God and (originally) of all his creation entail some sort of moral and material dualism, like one finds in Gnostic thought. Evil is simply a cancer in and on the good, not an independent deity, entity, reality.

Wright affirms Richard Bauckham's label—eschatological monotheism. Yahweh will be one and his name one in the end, when he establishes his rule on earth fully. Then every knee will bow and every tongue confess (as Isaiah says), whether willingly or unwillingly, whether wittingly or unwittingly. Wright argues that early Christology was not a reconfiguration of early Jewish beliefs about angelic mediators or the like. "It was a radical concretization of pre-Christian Jewish

---

[55]*PFG*, 630.
[56]*PFG*, 632.

beliefs about the one God, and particularly about what this one God had promised to *do*."[57]

Wright begins his discussion on how exactly Paul reformed and reaffirmed Jewish monotheism with a text that is a storm center of controversy: Romans 8:18-30. His translation of key phrases is interesting. Instead of the word *predestined*, he prefers "marked out in advance to be shaped according to the model of the image of the Son." He also prefers the translation "called according to his purpose," even though the word *his* is nowhere in any Greek manuscript, and as Chrysostom says, the word itself can mean "choice" as well as "purpose." Then one has to ask, Whose choice, God's or the responders'? This is indeed a viable question here because the *ous* ("those whom") in Romans 8:29a has as its antecedent "those who love God." In other words, the text reads "for those who love God, whom God foreknew, he also destined or marked out in advance." The discussion then is about *the destiny of believers*, not about how persons came to be believers in the first place. Their destiny is to be conformed to the image of the Son. Again, Paul is referring to a group of people—"those who love God, who were called according to choice/purpose." Those folks whom God foreknew would love him (making clear that God's choice was not mere fiat or arbitrary but on the basis of God's clear advance knowledge of how these people would respond), he marked out in advance. None of this is really dealt with at this juncture in the book. Wright is certainly right here that we have a clear affirmation that the God who created it all is also the God who is in the process of recreating it all. This is an expression of creational monotheism, now reconfigured to include the Son and conformity to the Son's image.[58]

But there are more implications of an affirmation of creational monotheism:

> This positive view of creation also explains the passages where Paul indicates that, even among pagans, there is a moral sense which will recognize the good behavior of the Messiah's people and from which, in turn, one can

---

[57]*PFG*, 633, emphasis original.
[58]*PFG*, 636.

> even learn by example. It is this, too, which enables Paul, exactly in line with at least one regular second-Temple viewpoint, to affirm the goodness and God-givenness of governments and authorities, even while . . . reserving the right both to remind them of their God-given duty and to hold them to account in relation to it.[59]

No idols also means there is only one true "image" of God that has ever been on earth since the fall, that is Jesus the Messiah, himself the truly human one. Those who are in the Messiah are to be renewed according to that image. What Wright does not say but could have is that this fits nicely with Paul's contention that Christ is the last Adam, remembering that the first one was also created in the image of God.[60]

Christ and monotheism. Turning more specifically to Wright's discussion of Jesus and monotheism, he is not happy either with the traditional liberal notion that high Christology is late and therefore tells us nothing about the historical Jesus or with the attempts à la Martin Hengel and company to demonstrate high Christology was thoroughly Jewish and early. Wright clearly rejects the analysis of modernity, saying: "At the same time, Romanticism constantly implied that the 'primitive' form of any movement was the genuine, inspired article, the original vision which would fade over time as people moved from charisma to committees, from adoration to administration, from spontaneous and subversive spirituality to stable structures and a salaried sacerdotalism."[61]

A note of irony is present in Wright's pronouncement that the work of Hengel, Bauckham, and Hurtado makes it "almost inconceivable that one would go back to the old days of Bousset and Bultmann (or even Dunn, Casey, and Vermes)." Obviously, he was not aware that Bart Ehrman was about to launch yet another salvo based on such assumptions, with the title *How Jesus Became God* (2015). Nonetheless, Wright is right that the idea that high Christology must be late has been so widely rejected that even Jewish scholars such as Daniel Boyarin have

---

[59]*PFG*, 639.
[60]*PFG*, 640.
[61]*PFG*, 646.

"swung round in the opposite direction, arguing that most if not all of the elements of early christology, not least the 'divinity' of the expected Messiah, were in fact present within pre-Christian Judaism itself."[62] Wright's judgment is that Boyarin has claimed much more than the early Jewish texts will support.

More importantly, Wright is correct about noticing what Paul does *not* have to argue for:

> Early Christians, already by the time of Paul, had articulated a belief in the "divinity" of Jesus far more powerfully, and indeed poetically, than anyone had previously imagined. Paul can, in fact, assume his (very "high") view of Jesus as a given. He never says, even to Corinth, "How then can some of you be saying that Jesus was simply a wonderful human being and nothing more?" Nor does christology seem to be a point of contention between him and (say) the church of Jerusalem. Despite regular assumptions and assertions, *there is no historical evidence for an early "Jewish Christianity" which (like the later "Ebionites") denied any identification between Jesus and Israel's God.*[63]

He thus concludes that Paul's view of Jesus couldn't all have come from that revelatory moment on the Damascus road.

Thus the historical question remains: What pushed Jesus' earliest followers after Easter in the direction of a high Christology? Wright is not satisfied with the older view that Jesus himself made such a thing possible and clear by the use of "Son of Man" language, suggesting some kind of equality with Israel's God, and that the early church saw the resurrection as the confirmation of Jesus' claim. He oddly says about this view, "I regard such a view as hopelessly short-circuited though not entirely misleading and mistaken."[64] He does not explain what he means by short-circuited.

Wright is more impressed with the proposal of Larry Hurtado that

> it was *the sense and experience of the personal presence of the exalted Jesus,* in the way that one might expect to experience the presence of the living God,

[62]*PFG*, 647-48.

[63]*PFG*, 648, emphasis added.

[64]*PFG*, 649.

> that led Jesus' earliest disciples first to worship him (without any sense of compromising monotheism), then to re-read Israel's scriptures in such a way as to "discover" him in passages which were about the One God.

In other words, it was "'early Christian experience' of the risen lord in their midst that compelled them to the first stirrings of what would later become trinitarian and incarnational theology."[65]

Wright thinks Hurtado is basically correct in his presentation and analysis of the phenomena, and he sees it as completely ruling out the Bousset hypothesis (namely, that when Christianity fully engaged with the pagan world it absorbed pagan notions about deities and lords and applied them to Christ). In addition, Wright points to the recent work of Chris Tilling, which demonstrates that Paul's descriptions of the relationship between the early Christians and Jesus match the scriptural descriptions of the relationship between Israel and the one God.[66] For example, see Paul's passages about Christ being married to his believers (2 Cor 11:2; Rom 7:4-6; never mind Eph 5, which relates directly to the Old Testament theme of Israel being Yahweh's bride).

But beyond a basic agreement with Hurtado, Wright finds the proposals of Richard Bauckham even more important. The major point is that you can't get to worship of Jesus as divine from what is said in early Judaism about exalted angels or mediators. For example, notice the fierce rejection of the worship of an angel in Revelation coupled with the clear worship of God and the Lamb. "Bauckham's main proposal is that the New Testament, Paul included, offered a christology of divine identity in which Jesus is included in the unique identity of this one God."[67] So Bauckham stresses that that identity concerns *who* God is, to be distinguished from divine "nature," which concerns *what* God is. Thus, he distinguishes what is going on in the New Testament from later debates about Jesus' divine and human natures. Bauckham notes, however, there is one exception to the rejection of the worship of

---

[65]*PFG*, 650, emphasis original.

[66]Chris Tilling, *Paul's Divine Christology* (Tübingen: Mohr, 2012).

[67]*PFG*, 651.

intermediary figures—namely, what is said about the Son of Man in the parables of Enoch. This is correct, and it provides a background for Jesus' use of "Son of Man" in an exalted sense, which Wright should have made more of.

Thus Bauckham concludes, "The highest possible Christology—the inclusion of Jesus in the unique divine identity—was central to the faith of the early church even before any of the New Testament writings were written, since it occurs in all of them."[68] Bauckham stresses there are three key aspects to Jewish monotheism—God is the sole creator, he will at last establish his kingdom, and he and he alone is to be worshiped. He then proceeds to demonstrate that in the New Testament Christ is portrayed as the agent of creation, the one through whom all things are reconciled and the kingdom comes, and he is to be worshiped. Wright's own proposal is to build on Bauckham but to add another component to eschatological monotheism, namely, that the God who abandoned the temple when it became corrupt had also promised to return to Jerusalem and his temple after the exile, come back to be king once more in Zion, and set his people free from bondage.

Wright's essential premise is that far from taking intermediary figures and symbols and using them as a basis to *promote* Jesus into the divine sphere, to the contrary, Paul takes images of God himself and applies them to Christ. Specifically, he takes a Jewish question (What will it look like when God returns to Zion and is once more king on the hill and frees his people?) and applies this to his analysis of the incarnation, life, death, and resurrection of Jesus. In Wright's view, all of that was the inauguration of the kingdom of God on earth. He puts the matter succinctly:

> Early Christology did not begin . . . as a strange new belief based on memories of earlier Jewish language for mediator-figures, or even on the strong sense of Jesus' personal presence during worship and prayer. . . . The former was not . . . relevant, and the latter was . . . important but secondary. The

[68]Quoted approvingly by Wright in *PFG*, 652. The most direct access to Bauckham's views is found in *Jesus and the God of Israel* (Grand Rapids: Eerdmans, 2008).

> most important thing was that in his life, death, and resurrection, Jesus had accomplished the new exodus, had done in person what Israel's God said he would do in person. He had inaugurated God's kingdom on earth as in heaven. Scholars have spent too long looking for pre-Christian Jewish ideas about human figures, angels, or other intermediaries. What matters is the pre-Christian Jewish ideas about Israel's God. *Jesus' first followers found themselves not only . . . permitted to use God-language for Jesus, but compelled to use Jesus language for the one God.*[69]

Though this analysis has some correct elements to it, nonetheless one should ask, What's wrong with this picture? There is a problem with seeing the first coming of Jesus as the fulfillment of the Yom Yahweh traditions, since Jesus does *not* in fact take on the task of judging the world of human beings during his first coming. Indeed, Mark 14:62 suggests he associates it with a later event. The problem is further exacerbated when Wright tries to associate the scene in Mark 14:62 with Daniel 7 and other related material to the exaltation of Jesus, rather than to his second coming, which is what Mark 14:62 is about.[70]

Wright then proceeds to walk through a demonstration of how the material in Sirach 24 and Wisdom of Solomon is used by Paul in his portrayal of the person and work of God's Son, God's Wisdom come in the flesh. I am in agreement with him about the influence of these traditions being used by Paul, and as he says, they have to do with God himself, not with some lesser intermediaries. Wisdom personified is the Wisdom of the one God personified. It is not a reference to a second figure in heaven alongside the one God. Less convincing is the argument that suggests that even in light of Psalm 2:7-8, "The phrase 'son of God' was not used in the pre-Christian Jewish world, so far as we know, for anyone thought to be a human embodiment of Israel's God."[71] While perhaps "human embodiment of Israel's God" is saying too much,

---

[69]*PFG*, 654-55.

[70]See now Michael S. Heiser, *Angels: What the Bible Really Says About God's Heavenly Host* (Bellingham, WA: Lexham, 2018), who makes quite clear that the language in Dan 7 is about a descent to judge the earth, not an ascent.

[71]*PFG*, 658.

nonetheless Psalm 2 seems to originally be part of a coronation ode for David the king, and we know for a fact that in the ancient Near East anointed kings were called the son of some particular deity in a special sense, sometimes even suggesting some sort of quasi-divine status and power.

Wright in this study does a better job than heretofore in showing that the exodus and liberation-from-slavery theme undergirds key passages in Paul: Galatians 4:1-11; Romans 8:1-4; 1 Corinthians 8–10.[72] This furthers his case for seeing the coming of Jesus as the return of God to his people, but what it does *not* further is his case that Jesus is seen as Israel herself as well. If Jesus is Wisdom, the rock, referred to in the Sinai wandering period (1 Cor 10, by which, Wright takes Paul to mean that God's presence was with them), he is not the people themselves wandering in the wilderness. If Jesus is the Creator and Redeemer God, he is not also God's people who were created and needed to be redeemed. In other words, the *stronger* the case for the high christological reading of Paul's Christ talk, the *weaker* the case for an ecclesiological reading of Jesus. He is correct that Jesus is not seen by Paul as a second God; "that would abrogate monotheism."[73] Paul says, "For us there is One." Wright says, "To have said, or implied, 'For us there are Two,' would have meant, 'We are simply a new, curiously restricted, form of paganism'; whereas Paul, throughout the letter [1 Corinthians is in view], is claiming to be standing on the ground of Jewish-style monotheism over against the pagan world."[74]

Another point of agreement with Wright is the view that the crucifixion is at the very heart of the revelation of the character of the one true God, "and that reflection must shine through the life of the community," for example in the commitment to self-sacrificial behavior by the strong in relationship to the weak. It is worth adding that if self-sacrifice, and more specifically self-sacrificial love, is the epitome of the

---

[72]*PFG*, 658-61.
[73]*PFG*, 666—the page number on which this comment appears seems strangely apropos.
[74]*PFG*, 666.

revelation of God's character, this presents a very different picture from the image of a narcissistic deity jealously guarding his glory and being at his core self-referential in character.[75]

Wright's treatment of the Christ hymn in Colossians 1 is very helpful, especially with his translation of *prototokos* as "and he is ahead," coupled later with the phrase "He is the start of it all," leaving out the confusing concept of birth, which has misled some to think Christ is seen as the first creature rather than on the Creator side of the ledger. Wright helpfully shows the echoes of monotheistic language from the Shema in 1 Corinthians 8:6 and elsewhere.[76]

Wright suggests that the reference in the Christ hymn in Colossians 1 to Christ being both the beginning and the image would have sent the knowledgeable reader back to Genesis 1. The question is, Were there such readers in the Colossian congregation? Wright insists on the stronger reading of the text of 2 Corinthians 5:16-19: "God was in Christ reconciling the world to himself, not merely 'through Christ' but in Christ, because Paul included Christ within the divine identity, expressed in Colossians as 'the fullness of deity dwelt in him bodily.'" Colossians 1 expresses both creational and eschatological monotheism. Christ is the head over both realms, and his intent is the redemption of creation, not rescue of humans from creation.[77]

There is an extended exposition on 2 Corinthians 3–4, and Wright takes time to unpack the differences between what is said about Moses and the people of God then (God would not show his face to Moses, and Moses had to cover his face when he appeared to the people because of their hardheartedness—they could not bear the Shekinah) and what is said of Jesus and the people of God now (the people of God now have their hearts transformed, and therefore they can look at the glory of God in the face of Jesus). In other words, 2 Corinthians 3–4 is talking about the final eschatological theophany in the person of Jesus. He has

---

[75]*PFG*, 667.
[76]*PFG*, 670-73.
[77]*PFG*, 676-80.

returned to God's people. Once again, the point to be made is that wisdom Christology is all about portraying Jesus as an expression of God, the divine identity. It is not about portraying him as Israel, the people of God who need redeeming, as does the world. Wright is "redrawing the monotheism of divine identity around Jesus."[78]

One of the more problematic aspects of Wright's exposition of a text such as Philippians 2:5-11, particularly the second half of that Christ hymn, is that he wants to have his cake and eat it too. By this I mean he thinks that the exaltation of Christ to the right hand of God and giving him God's glory with universal acclamation and the predication of Isaiah 45–46 allows this *to also be about God's eschatological return as well.* While that latter theme is in Second Isaiah, it does not necessarily crop up in Philippians 2. Exaltation Christology is not the same as parousia Christology. The real problem is that while it is sometimes true that more of the Old Testament context is alluded to when Paul cites this or that text, it is not always the case that one can take for granted that the larger Old Testament context is in play. This is a problem not only in Wright's work but also in some cases with Richard Hays and R. Wagner as well. This is a yes-and-no proposition—sometimes the larger Old Testament context is assumed and is important for understanding the point in the New Testament, sometimes it is not. As a famous Revelation 13 verse says, "this calls for wisdom."

Wright, following Dunn to some extent, attempts to suggest that an Adamic story lies in the background of the first half of Philippians 2:5-11.[79] Adam does not preexist, and he does not choose to become human, and he does not limit himself in order to do so, and frankly it is not Adam to whom the snake says, "You can become as gods," so we do not know that Adam desired godlike status. Part of the problem here is the misinterpretation of the word *morphē,* which is badly translated by the word *form*. A much better translation is "nature,"

[78] *PFG*, 680.

[79] I have given reasons in my Philippians commentary for why I find this unconvincing. See Ben Witherington III, *Paul's Letter to the Philippians* (Grand Rapids: Eerdmans, 2011).

because what the word means is an outward manifestation of what a person *already* is—not merely what he appears to be or would like to be. Jesus did not take on the mere "form" of a servant; he was indeed a servant and indeed claims that his purpose in coming was to serve (Mk 10:45). Furthermore, there is nothing in the first half of this Christ hymn about Christ or Adam exercising sovereignty over creation. The ruler-of-creation theme is absent.[80]

As we have already alluded to, one of Wright's key theses for this whole project is that there were several reasons why Jesus' first followers came to think of him as *the embodiment of the returning Yahweh*, the first having to do with messiahship, the second with their sense of his presence through the work of the Holy Spirit in their hearts. The question of course to be asked about the first of these is, Did the earliest Christians really see Jesus "at his first coming" as the return of Yahweh to his people (not at his second coming, note, but at his first coming)?

Wright stresses not merely that the resurrection demonstrated the truthfulness of Jesus' pre-Easter messianic claims but that this, joined up with the return-of-Yahweh theme and the spiritual presence of Jesus among his followers after his ascension, is the threefold cord that cannot be broken, the three things that produced high Christology. He thinks that no one of these themes, or even two of them, would be sufficient to produce such an outcome, but all three are required.

It is hard to see why one needs the return-of-Yahweh theme to explain the rise of early Christianity, especially if one insists this theme should be associated with the first coming of Jesus rather than the second to produce such a product. If Jesus is present by the Holy Spirit post-Easter and postascension, whenever and wherever the disciples gathered together, and if the Scriptures were being read messianically as a result of the resurrection and the encounters with the risen Jesus, this surely was enough to produce a divine Christology in itself—only God can be in two places at one time! One doesn't need to tack on the return of

---

[80]See Witherington, *Paul's Letter to the Philippians*.

Yahweh the judge to get there. For what it's worth, Jesus himself in Mark 14:62 associates the Son of Man coming to judge people with the second coming, not the first.

Perhaps here is a good place to discuss at more length two of the linked key elements in Wright's reconstruction of "the story," namely, the return of Yahweh to Zion and the notion that early Jews saw themselves as still in exile—views that Wright believes he can demonstrate both Jesus and Paul affirmed in regard to Jesus' first coming.[81] James Scott counts at least seventy-five or so places this twin theme shows up in *Paul and the Faithfulness of God*, distributed rather equally throughout the two volumes of the tome.[82] While the theme may not be omnipresent, it is certainly and surprisingly more present than, for example, the discussion of the divinity of Christ or the second coming. It is certainly a key to understanding Wright's reconfiguration of Israel's story, and Christ's as well.

Perhaps the first thing to be said about the theory that early Jews saw themselves as still in exile is that we should all be wary of broad generalizations such as this. A case can be made that *some* Jews viewed themselves that way, even while living in the Promised Land. Second Baruch would perhaps be a good text to point to, except that this text seems to have been written after the fall of the temple in AD 70, and much changed in early Judaism after that date. In any case, for every 2 Baruch I can point to a text such as 4 Ezra, which comes apparently from within the very same time frame but still looks forward to those kinds of consummation as in the future.

So we are not disputing the idea that some early Jews may have held views similar to what Wright affirms. That is not the issue. The issue is whether this view was *very broadly* affirmed in early Judaism, and even more crucially whether Jesus and Paul thought so. Part of the problem is that, for both Jesus and Paul, the coming of the eschatological divine

---

[81]See now the new and improved version of this thesis with more textual support in Scott, *Exile*, 19-80.

[82]Scott, *Exile*, 8n8.

saving activity or dominion of God was an *already-and-not-yet* proposition, and the *not yet* involved the sort of final judgment for example alluded to in the prophets right through to Malachi. The not yet also involved retrieving the lost sheep of Israel by the heavenly Redeemer, namely, Jesus. None of these things—not final judgment nor final return from exile, nor final retrieval of lost Israel—is associated with the first coming of Jesus either by Jesus or by Paul. In other words, this theory involves too much overrealized eschatology, not to mention too much reliance on Deuteronomy 30–31 for the whole gestalt of how Paul's thought is configured.

In his helpful essay in the aforementioned *Exile* volume, Scot McKnight makes a crucial point:

> When Jesus declares that "the kingdom *of God* has come near," we need to pause for a moment to see something very special in the "of God." This is not the kingdom of Moses or Samuel or David or Solomon or any other of the kings of Israel and Judah. This is the kingdom *of God* as it was before Samuel's fateful request and God's accommodation to Israel, and yet God rules in his Son, King Jesus, and he will be modeled on David.[83]

In other words, the coming of the kingdom of God is not the continuation of the story of Israel; it is the incursion of God's direct rule once more, which God's people gave up on when they demanded to have a king like other nations. This final eschatological rule of God involves a new covenant and a new story. Rather than the church being the extension of the story of Israel, Israel continues to have a story until Jesus returns and turns away the impiety of Jacob, and then "all Israel" (by which Paul means non-Christian Jews) will be saved.

But let's consider this from another point of view. Paul himself is not really concerned to connect Jesus with Israel or with Israel's story. Rather, Paul connects Jesus with the more universal story of Adam, for example in both 1 Corinthians 15 and Romans 5:12-21, and he connects it with the pre-Mosaic, pre-Deuteronomistic, more universal story of

---

[83]Scot McKnight, "Exiled in the Land," in Scott, *Exile*, 214.

Abraham, very clearly in Galatians 3 and Romans 4. It is not an accident that it dawned on various early Jews that Abraham was not, in the first place, born a Hebrew! He was someone both Gentiles and Jews could relate to, not on the basis of submitting to the later Mosaic covenant but on the simple basis of trusting in the God of the Bible and having that credited as righteousness and for right standing with the living God.

Moses only really shows up in Paul in order to dramatically contrast the ministry and covenant of Moses with the new covenant and the ministry of Paul in 2 Corinthians 3. Even more dramatically, the story of Sinai and the Mosaic covenant ends up in the column with Hagar the slave woman and the present Jerusalem in Galatians 4, which is contrasted with the story of Sarah (again part of the Abrahamic saga) and the new covenant and the Jerusalem which is above. In other words, Paul gives Moses short shrift because his covenant is not the new covenant and has only fading glory. The future is not *now* for non-Christian Israel in Paul's thought, not now while the full number of Gentiles are coming into the fold. It is later, when Jesus returns, judges the earth (1 Cor 15), and redeems Israel. Israel enters into this kingdom of God, this new-covenant situation, by grace through faith in Jesus and by the mercy of God. Yahweh has not yet returned to Zion for final judgment, and neither is the long-troubled history of Israel and its suffering and dispersion over yet. Paul says, Stay tuned for further developments, when the Lord Jesus returns to raise the dead and rule, bringing the kingdom on earth as it is in heaven.

In order to get clarity on Wright's argument about various Pauline texts referring to "the return of Yahweh" being associated with the incarnation of Jesus, Wright was asked to state as clearly as possible which texts in Paul *definitely* refer to the second coming. His short list sent includes the following: "clearly Phil 3.20f., 1 Thess 1.10 and 1 Thess. 4 of course, Col 3.4 . . . and I assume that Jesus' coming/appearing is the central feature of the 'big picture' passages such as Rom 8 and 1 Cor 15." This is a fair reading of these texts. Wright is not collapsing all future references to the return of Christ into references to the first coming of

Christ. Yet the discussion here leads precisely to that question of where Paul again and again associates the incarnation of Jesus with "the return of Yahweh" texts (*Yom Yahweh* texts).[84] The problem is that Galatians 4 and other texts suggest that the first coming of Jesus was to redeem Israel out from under the law, *not* to judge it for its sins. Notably, Paul has very little to say about the existing Herodian temple, which in itself is rather remarkable. What is even more remarkable is Paul's use of Isaiah 59:20-21 in Romans 11:26-27. Here Paul associates the second coming of Christ with the return of Yahweh to Zion to finally turn away the impiety of Jacob, judge its sins, and redeem it. Paul says this is when "all Israel will be saved."

The parallel of Jacob with Israel here surely rules out the notion that "Israel" in Rom 11:25 could possibly refer to the church (or even to just Jewish Christians, rather than non-Christian Jews). No, Paul's entire argument is that the full number of Gentiles will first be saved, and then in the same manner at the second coming "all Israel" will be saved, by which is meant a large number of Jews (as the phrase "all Israel" means both in various places in the Old Testament and in the Mishnah; it is not a claim that every last Israelite will be saved). Now, if this is true, and it is also true that Paul associates the return of Yahweh for judgment with Christ's return to "put everything under his feet" (1 Cor 15:27), then it seems to muddy and muddle the waters to suggest that the return of Yahweh (*Yom Yahweh*) should be associated with Christ's first coming. If Paul did this as well, then he himself would seem to have created a muddle.

Wright says that the new covenant is a "renewal" of the covenant with Abraham with the promises given to Abraham. This is not in fact how Paul views the matter—it is a matter of the fulfillment of the Abrahamic covenant in the new covenant, and in the process the bypassing of the temporary covenant, the Mosaic covenant. Covenant renewal is one thing. Covenant fulfillment is quite another. The Mosaic covenant is fulfilled

---

[84]*PFG*, 700-710.

and brought to an end/completion/goal in Christ (Rom 10:4). This does not mean it has been renewed in the new covenant. Nevertheless, Wright is quite right that Paul takes for granted the high Christology that can even call Christ *theos*. He does not argue for it; he simply asserts it and assumes his audience will agree. This does indeed suggest that high Christology, even divine Christology, existed in the minds and hearts of the earliest Christians even in the 40s, and indeed already in the Jerusalem community (hence the origin of the *marana tha* prayer or cry).

Spirit and monotheism. There are important points along the way where Wright helpfully summarizes what he is arguing for or believes, and this helps provide clarity to the discussion. For instance, we hear:

> With both christology and pneumatology it seems that the normal assumption of many [modern] writers is radically mistaken. It is not the case that the New Testament is unclear or fuzzy on these subjects, and that the early Fathers invented a high view of Jesus and the Spirit which was then wrongly read back into the early period. Rather, it seems as though the earliest Christians, precisely from within their second-Temple Jewish monotheism, leapt without difficulty straight to an identification of both Jesus and the spirit within the divine identity, which the early Fathers then struggled to recapture in the very different categories of hellenistic philosophy. As with christology, so with pneumatology. The idea of a "low" Jewish beginning, from which a gradual "ascent" was made on the dictates of Greek philosophy, is exactly wrong. The Jewish context provided the framework for a thoroughly "high" christology and pneumatology, and it was the attempt to restate that within the language of hellenistic philosophy, and without the help of key Jewish categories, that gave the impression of a difficult doctrine gradually attained.[85]

Wright then explains why it was that there was not more discussion of the Spirit's place within the Godhead in the New Testament period: "The spirit was not, for Paul and his contemporaries, a 'doctrine' or 'dogma' to be discussed, but the breath of life which put them in a position to discuss everything else—and more to the point, to worship,

[85]*PFG*, 710.

pray, love and work. We should not, then, be surprised at the relative absence of discourse, including monotheistic discourse, *about* the spirit."[86] He draws an analogy between worldview and the Spirit—the Spirit is something you look through that affects your thoughts about other things, not something you mainly look at. Life in the Spirit was the gestalt or milieu that shaped all the early Christian thoughts.[87]

Wright goes on to point out the connection between the use of temple language of the community and the individual Christian and the discourse about the Spirit. It is when the Spirit, the living presence of God, indwells something that it becomes a temple, of course, and it is this living presence that sanctifies, creates holiness or set-apartness, and that finally unifies.

He thus concludes that Paul is saying that the founding of the church is the long-awaited rebuilding of the temple and that the long-awaited indwelling of the Spirit is the return of Yahweh to Zion. "For the divine spirit to take up residence in the church is for Exodus 40 and Ezekiel 43 to find a radical, unexpected and even shocking new fulfillment."[88]

If, however, the promised *return* of God has been fulfilled in the incarnation and then by means of Pentecost, it is hard to see why it is that in passages such as 2 Thessalonians 2 Paul associates the return of God to judge the world with the second coming of Christ, not with either of the two events that have already transpired, that is, the incarnation and the ascension. It is even more difficult to make sense of all this when one realizes that God still has future plans for non-Christian Israel, as Romans 11 makes clear. It is to be saved and regrafted into the people of God when the Redeemer comes forth from heavenly Zion and turns away the impiety of Jacob (which is clearly not the church).

---

[86]*PFG*, 710, emphasis original.

[87]Here one should consult the discussion on the Spirit as a person, not a mere power or force, in Witherington, *Biblical Theology*. One should also consider the detailed study by Gordon D. Fee, *God's Empowering Presence* (Grand Rapids: Baker, 2009), which makes clear Wright has rather severely underplayed the role of the Spirit in Paul's theology, here and elsewhere, and indeed what Paul actually has to say about the Spirit.

[88]*PFG*, 711.

In other words, the judging and redemption of God's first chosen people, the establishing of God's full kingdom on earth as it is in heaven, is most commonly associated in Paul with events that have not yet transpired. It is precisely these not-yet events that raise questions about Wright's interpretation of the already. Why not say Exodus 40 and Ezekiel 43 are best seen as being fulfilled when it involves a large number of Jews and has to do with their redemption and judgment, not with the church per se? At the end of the day, when you take Wright's line of approach, Paul appears to be a person who muddies the water by indiscriminately mixing the metaphors. If you want to claim that texts such as Exodus 40 and Ezekiel 43 have both a present fulfillment in the church and a later one at the eschaton, this seems to be an attempt to have one's cake and eat it too. By and large, the promises of Yahweh's return to "Israel" are still awaiting fulfillment when Jesus returns again. This is not to say that Paul does not speak of the church and individual Christians as the eschatological temple of God where the Spirit dwells. Clearly he does. What he does not do is apply those Old Testament texts to that reality in the way Wright does.

As stated above, *it should not be the default that we simply assume the whole larger context of this or that Old Testament passage or whole book when Paul draws on language from the Old Testament.*[89] Paul, like John Wesley, spoke "Biblese," and so when Wesley called himself "a brand plucked from the burning" after being rescued from the parsonage fire in Epworth, we should not simply assume that Wesley thought a text from the apocalyptic prophets was being fulfilled in his life and that it was then necessary to probe the whole context of that phrase and see how it was also fulfilled in Wesley's experience. No, he was simply using apropos scriptural language to describe his own experiences. That's all. Paul from time to time does the same thing. The idea of the Spirit as the

[89]I have now dealt with this problem in the intertextuality studies of Hays, Wright, and others in Ben Witherington III, *Isaiah Old and New: Exegesis, Intertextuality, and Hermeneutics* (Minneapolis: Fortress, 2017); *Psalms Old and New: Exegesis, Intertextuality, and Hermeneutics* (Minneapolis: Fortress, 2017); *Torah Old and New: Exegesis, Intertextuality, and Hermeneutics* (Minneapolis: Fortress, 2018).

coming of the Shekinah glory, the living presence of God, into the lives of believers can of course be found clearly enough in Paul, and it is a bit of a surprise that Wright doesn't refer to 2 Corinthians 3, where we are told that by the indwelling Spirit we are being changed from one degree of glory to another. True enough, the Spirit is Immanuel, God with us, just as "Christ in us" is God with us. This, however, does not entail downloading the whole package of events mentioned in the Old Testament when it refers to the return of Yahweh to Zion. Some of those things are still outstanding and are not currently happening in the context of the church; otherwise Paul would never have spoken about the regrafting of temporarily broken-off Israelite branches from the people of God back into the people of God when Jesus returns.[90] Discerning which bits are being fulfilled and which bits are yet to be fulfilled requires careful exegesis and discernment.

Toward the end of his monotheism discussion, Wright is mainly engaged in an interpretation of the pneumatic monotheism as expressed in 2 Corinthians 3–4 in particular. There are some good things about this exegesis. In particular, he is right that Paul is contrasting the Old Testament people of God with the New Testament people of God in regard to the issue of hardheartedness. But there is more to it than that. There is also a contrast between the ministry of Moses and the glory involved in it, which faded, and the ministry of Paul. It is quite impossible to talk about covenant *renewal* from 2 Corinthians 3, when what Paul says is there is the thing which is to be abolished. What is that *thing*? What used to be glorious, says Paul, has come to have no glory at all. He is surely here talking about the old covenant. It would make no sense to talk about the abolition of (1) Moses (obviously he is dead) or (2) God's glory. It fades but is not abolished. No, it is the ministry of Moses and its product, the Mosaic covenant, that is abolished. One should not lump together the fulfillment of Old Testament texts and prophecies with the renewal of the Mosaic covenant, but that is what happens in these pages.

[90]*PFG*, 717.

There is one more problem with all this. It is simply not true that there was no problem with the Mosaic law. There was: it was impotent to change fallen human beings, hence the contrast with the Holy Spirit. Even if Israel did not involve fallen persons, it is doubtful Paul would ever say the law without the Spirit in one's life would be adequate. But, for sure, the effect of the Mosaic law on fallen persons is death-dealing, not life-giving, and Paul says so in 2 Corinthians 3. The letter kills, he says, but the Spirit gives life.[91] Wright deals with monotheism and the single united family of God. Here his basic thesis is, "It is, after all, the *unity* of the Messiah's followers that will demonstrate that they are indeed the new humanity, the true people of the one God of Israel." For Wright this segment, and the focus on the community, is crucial, not least because mere new ideas are not sufficient to create a new worldview. He puts it this way on that same page: "The symbolic praxis of Paul's worldview—the place where the worldview became visible and tangible—was the concrete reality of the united community, for which Paul works in letter after letter, against one danger and another, from one angle after another."[92] The new temple is the new humanity, and within that is the living presence of the living God, now understood to involve Christ and Spirit as well as the Father, reformulated around Christ and Spirit.

CONCLUSION

We have concentrated in this chapter on the way Wright articulates his understanding of God, and of Christ, and the Spirit as part of the divine identity, and also early in the chapter focused on assessing Wright's view of whether Paul is reacting to the imperial cult. We have concentrated on these important aspects of Wright's larger argument because other aspects have been dealt with at great length by others in recent publications, such as those listed in the notes of this chapter.

---

[91]*PFG*, 718-27.
[92]*PFG*, 728.

Because Wright sees Christ and then his people as the fulfillment of Israel and Israel's mission, he quite rightly rejects the two-track proposal most recently advocated by Jewish scholars, such as Mark Nanos or Paula Fredriksen, sometimes called the "radical new perspective on Paul."[93] That perspective at points even wants to argue that Paul was writing his letters *exclusively* to Gentiles and that his critique of the Mosaic covenant, including circumcision, was simply that it did not apply to Gentiles. They had another way of salvation through Christ. Alas, for this view does not do justice to Paul's more radical critique of the Mosaic covenant itself and its deficiencies, especially in the light of the coming of Christ and the inauguration of his eschatological kingdom. Furthermore, Wright is also on target in affirming with other proponents of the new perspective on Paul that by *pistis Christou* Paul is using shorthand for the faithfulness of Christ even unto death on the cross. That is the objective means of salvation Paul is talking about in Galatians and Romans, while faith and trust in Christ is the subjective means of salvation, which Paul also speaks about.

As we said at the outset of this chapter, Wright is a global thinker with few equals among New Testament scholars, and we are indebted to him for shedding fresh light on so many Pauline topics in his magnum opus and elsewhere. The critiques of his work in this chapter should not be taken to neglect or diminish the positive aspects of his work. Perhaps more than anyone else in the broadly conservative Protestant camp, he has advanced our understanding of Paul in numerous ways, showing us why "the Paul quest" is still alive and must go on.

---

[93]See most recently Paula Fredriksen, *Paul: The Pagan's Apostle* (New Haven, CT: Yale University Press, 2017), and see my detailed critique of the book on my Patheos blog, The Bible and Culture, in February and March 2018.

four

DUNN, WITH PAUL AND THE BOUNDARY MARKERS

When thou hast done, thou hast not done, for I have more.

JOHN DONNE, "A HYMN TO GOD THE FATHER"

James D. G. Dunn is the emeritus Lightfoot Professor of Divinity chair at Durham University, a post he held for thirteen years (1990–2013). Over the course of his career, he has contributed to the study of early Christianity through numerous articles, monographs, and his three-volume work, *Christianity in the Making*. As stated in the introduction, Dunn is credited with coining the phrase "the new perspective on Paul" in his 1983 T. W. Manson lecture, which was a response to and interaction with the work of E. P. Sanders. Dunn's influence in Pauline studies can be felt not just through several important articles and books on Paul, or even his landmark Romans commentary, but most acutely in his most thorough work on Paul, laconically titled *The Theology of Paul the Apostle*.[1] At some eight hundred pages, this is the most detailed treatment of Paul's thought by Dunn and has only been supplemented and slightly updated by the second volume of his *Christianity in the Making*, titled *Beginning from Jerusalem*.

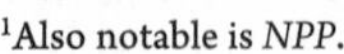

[1]Also notable is *NPP*.

PROLEGOMENA

In his *Theology of the Paul the Apostle,* Dunn begins his work with the historical and philosophical considerations relevant to pursuing the task of constructing Pauline theology. Is it a dead-end endeavor? Such questions are not trivial. One of the primary questions Dunn raises is, "When we talk of 'Paul's theology' are we talking about the theology of any particular letter or the theology of all the individual letters aggregated into a whole?" Dunn rightly notes the distinction between the person who stands behind the letters and the letter writer himself, noting that we do not have all of Paul's letters preserved for us. The hermeneutical concern takes center stage for Dunn when identifying Paul's letters as a "sequence of occasional conversations" whereby Paul's theology transcends the mere letters. Letters do not have theologies; persons do. In an apt statement, Dunn notes that if all we studied were the letters, at best we would have a "theology of Paul's controversies."[2] According to Dunn, the way forward in this thicket of interpretive weeds is a theology that is more than the sum of its parts, but certainly not less. One might characterize Dunn's process of theologizing Paul as a dialogue with Paul himself and not merely a description of what he believed. In turn, this forces a recognition that Paul's theology contains both doctrine and praxis, and they are in constant interaction with each other.

Such concerns remind interpreters of Paul of the one-sided nature of the Pauline correspondences. Stated more directly, the information we have in the letters is not all that Paul could have said on given topics but are indeed contextualized messages to specific churches. Even the very topics addressed are shaped by the controversies he engages in with local communities. For example, Paul's discussion of the Lord's Supper appears in 1 Corinthians and not in Galatians. Likewise, references to Abraham are primarily confined to Galatians and Romans. To put a finer point on it, let us ask a theoretical question: If the Corinthians had

---

[2] *TPA,* 12, 14, 17.

not had problems with the Lord's Supper, would we have any of Paul's thoughts on the matter? Most likely not. Such a question reveals the provisional nature of the letters themselves.

It has often been said that Paul is no systematic theologian. This of course should not be taken to mean that Paul is not theological. He certainly is theological. Rather, the issues Paul confronts are first and foremost issues that face his churches and are not driven by a desire to systematically treat abstracted concepts such as pneumatology or ecclesiology. These theological concepts are refracted through the lens of conflict and confrontation, either within churches themselves (as 1 Corinthians) or between Paul and his communities (as in Galatians).

Several issues further complicate this endeavor of discovering a theology of Paul. First, Dunn points us to the multilayered texture of Paul's letters, which includes several important features. He begins with the referential nature of Greek language, which must guide the interpretation of Paul from the outset. Although a basic concern, it bears repeating that Paul did not write in English with the conceptual patterns of the modern West. Paul was an ancient thinker and writer who used Koine Greek and ancient rhetoric to communicate with his mainly Greek-speaking audience in patterns, images, and metaphors that resonated with their first-century historical context. In the absence of such knowledge, one will merely read one's own insights into Paul and miss the theological depth and impact of Paul in his first-century context.

A second layer to the resonances of Paul's discourse is of course his use of the Jewish Scriptures, especially in their LXX form, which Dunn identifies as the "substructure" of Paul's theology. These move beyond mere examples of direct quotations from the Pentateuch, the Psalms, or Paul's favorite prophet, Isaiah.[3] Paul's use of the Old Testament also includes the larger themes of Old Testament theology, through various images, metaphors, and nuances latent in the biblical

[3]See Ben Witherington III, *Isaiah Old and New: Exegesis, Intertextuality, and Hermeneutics* (Minneapolis: Fortress, 2017).

stories themselves.[4] Not all of what we identify as Paul's theology is *unique* to him; much of it is rooted in the witness of the Old Testament, and particularly in the Pentateuch and Isaiah. Such points press home the concern that whatever we call "Paul's theology" has already been deeply imprinted before the letters by his own reading of the Old Testament. The topic that plagues interpreters of Paul is, How much of what Paul believed about the Old Testament is taken over whole cloth? What is adapted or modified? Or, even more controversially, is anything rejected? And what new content has been injected into the mix?

Third, Dunn also rightly places before us the oft-neglected issue that the faith already common to Paul's communities included the kerygmatic tradition, which was a range of substantial, basic Christian teaching. We ought to remember that, though a founder of many communities, Paul had predecessors who went before him. Indeed, in terms of the community at Rome, which he did not found, Paul can admonish his audience to be "obedient from the heart to the form of teaching to which you were entrusted" (Rom 6:17 NRSV; see also 1 Cor 15). Much of the teaching Paul did with his converts would have been in person, before he moved on from local communities to his next stops on his missionary journeys. We have very little reference to this type of teaching and little insight into the foundational theology that Paul discussed with his new converts. Restating a point made above, the letters at some level are aimed at correcting problems or furthering positive beliefs and behaviors, not at converting the audience. Of course, there are some exceptions to this general rule, such as Ephesians.

A fourth issue influencing the theology of Paul's discourses is references to the Jesus tradition that appear in Pauline paraenesis. Although this is often debated, there is substantial overlap between Jesus' teaching and Paul's ethical admonitions to his communities (see Mt 5–7; Rom 12–15). Dunn rightly reminds readers that the initial teaching and

[4]Richard B. Hays, *Echoes of Scripture in the Letters of Paul* (New Haven, CT: Yale University Press, 1993).

theology of the earliest Jesus communities would have been the teachings of Jesus himself, which contain, like Paul's teachings, their own multilayered texture (through the use of the Old Testament). Certainly the theological formation of these Christian communities must take adequate stock of both the Jesus tradition(s) and Paul's theologizing within these horizons.

Such concerns and issues lead Dunn to offer the following solution to the dilemmas proposed. The four issues above must confront the reader in their full force and reaffirm that the letters alone do not suffice to construct or reconstruct Paul's theology. The situation-specific nature of these discourses resists such extrapolating *from the surface* some sort of theology. The questions Dunn (and others) have focused on are *the source(s)* of such profound theologizing.[5] The theological solutions Paul provides for his communities swell up from deep theological reservoirs, and as a result interpreters of Paul aim to uncover and discover the "substructure" of Paul's thought as a means by which to investigate Paul's theology. The "what" of Paul's theology is as important as the "how" of Paul's theologizing.

Dunn's analysis of the substructure of Paul's thought leads him to identify three main levels. The first and deepest level contains the stories of God and Israel, Paul's inherited traditions, which often operate underneath the radar or below the surface. The second level contains "transformative moments," which includes Paul's own conversion/call and his interaction with the other apostles. Dunn maintains that these were probably some of the most formative aspects of his theology. The third level is also the most obvious and contains the "story/stories" of the immediate issues and Paul's current reflections, resulting in what is on the surface in his letters. This level provides the questions and issues Paul pursues in his writings. Dunn

[5]Fundamental in this regard are the works of Ben Witherington III, *Paul's Narrative Thought World: The Tapestry of Tragedy and Triumph* (Louisville, KY: Westminster John Knox, 1994); and Richard B. Hays, *The Faith of Jesus Christ: The Narrative Substructure of Galatians 3:1–4:11*, 2nd ed. (Grand Rapids: Eerdmans, 2002). See also Bruce W. Longenecker, ed., *Narrative Dynamics in Paul: A Critical Assessment* (Louisville, KY: Westminster John Knox, 2002).

concludes that Paul's theology is the reality of these three levels interacting, as evidenced in his letters.[6]

While I agree in the main with Dunn's construction of Paul's substructure, it needs to be further developed. Rather than simply seeing the story of God and Israel, other chapters must be added to this ongoing unfolding of the divine drama of redemption. Certainly, Paul begins where the story ultimately begins—with God. Paul is a strong creational monotheist (see Rom 1:18-32; 8:26-38). To this story, however, we must have not only God, but God, creation, and the story of the world gone wrong (Rom 5). The story of Israel emerges out of the story of the world gone wrong. Tragically, the story of Israel gets trapped within the story of the world gone wrong, so the story of Christ seeks to address both the story of the world gone wrong and the story of Israel, now caught up in the same mix.

The story of Christ issues forth a new reality, of which Paul is a herald and in which his communities take part. The story of Christ-followers appears to be the penultimate story, before the story of consummation. Paul's communities of course arise out of the four previous stories and are at the crucial turning point of history, called to live in between the twin stories of Christ and consummation. This is not intended to critique Dunn overly but just to add to and to deepen the stories that shaped Paul's thought as he writes to his communities, on whom, in his words, "the end of the ages has come" (1 Cor 10:11 ESV; Rom 13:11-12).

Although the issue of how to construct or investigate Paul's theology seems easy enough to answer, behind such questions and issues is a debate within Pauline studies about the *coherence* of Paul's thought. Not every interpreter answers in the affirmative that there is even coherence and consistency in Paul's thought. In fact, E. P. Sanders himself judged Paul's statements on the law to be contradictory, and some have gone further. The late Heikki Räisänen held that at a core level Paul was an inconsistent thinker: "Paul's gospel itself also implies a grave *problem.*

---

[6]*TPA*, 18-19.

At the very core of his thought, Paul has 'conflicting convictions.'" Räisänen goes on to state in a footnote, "I render him [Paul] completely incoherent."[7] Although Räisänen certainly represents an extreme position, Dunn's work and that of others takes place within such a context, and his work certainly counters such radical and flawed proposals.

PAUL: BEFORE THE LETTERS

What was Paul's view of himself and his identity? In *Beginning from Jerusalem,* Dunn argues that Paul's description of himself in Philippians 3:4-7 helps us establish Paul's own convictions about his identity. From the phrases that appear in his self-description, a strong consensus emerges that Paul saw his upbringing as one of a faithful Jewish family. Of keen interest is that Paul knows his genealogical heritage ("of the tribe of Benjamin") and that his was the only tribe that remained faithful after the civil war that struck the house of Solomon and divided the kingdom. Paul's pedigree was firmly intact.

But what are we to do with the fact that Paul was born and raised not in Jerusalem but in Tarsus? This raises the question of how Hellenized Paul would have been from his Diaspora upbringing. The now-defunct history-of-religion school took his Hellenistic upbringing as primary evidence that Paul was influenced not as much by the Jesus tradition but by Greek philosophical thought. From that school's vantage point, the Hellenistic world that Paul grew up in then affected how he understood issues such as Christ's resurrection, baptism, and the Lord's Supper as modeled on the myths of dying and rising and Greek mystery cults. Dunn roundly rejects such an approach and argues that Paul would have been "entirely antagonistic to any ascription to him of the epithet 'Hellenist' beyond that of simply 'Greek speaker.'"[8] In terms of Greek influence on Paul, Dunn does note that Paul's letters indicate a good understanding of Greek rhetoric, which shaped his correspondences.

---

[7]Heikki Räisänen, *Paul and the Law*, 2nd ed. (Eugene, OR: Wipf & Stock, 2010), xxiii, emphasis original.

[8]*BJ*, 329.

Acts 22 indicates that Paul grew up in Jerusalem, perhaps from the time he was a young man, a preteen. In any case, he seems to have been educated in Jerusalem in his most formative years.[9]

Paul's background raises an issue that every Pauline interpreter must deal with: To what degree did Paul's experience with the risen Jesus on the road to Damascus come to shape his convictions? One may notice that I have not used the terms *conversion* or *call*; the latter term, of course, has become popular in Pauline studies ever since Krister Stendahl. Dunn weighs in on this particular conversation and thinks that, properly speaking, such a dichotomy is "rather pointless."[10] He rightly notes that we must avoid anachronism and should not think of Paul "converting" from one religion to another. Such an idea of conversion is fraught with modern baggage that ought to be avoided. The issue is not whether he was converted *from* Judaism, but rather what he was converted *to* when he became a Christ follower.[11]

For example, in the modern conversation, *conversion* is usually used to talk about moving from one religion to another. The case for Paul and the early Christians is a bit more complex. Paul of course did not go from being a polytheist to being a monotheist—that remained the same. Likewise, Paul continued to believe that the Old Testament was God's revelation. Statements such as "the law is holy, righteous and good" could certainly have been made by Paul both before and after the Damascus road event. Such continuity for Paul, on this and certainly more topics, can render the term *conversion* problematic.

In the ongoing debate over whether Paul was called or converted, Dunn seems to land on the side of the latter. Dunn takes Paul's statement in Philippians 3:7, "But whatever were gains to me I now consider loss for the sake of Christ," as a clear indicator of a stark change of position and is "as clear of a 'conversion" as one could imagine." The devil

[9]For a more in-depth discussion of this point see Ben Witherington III, *The Paul Quest: The Renewed Search for the Jew of Tarsus* (Downers Grove, IL: InterVarsity Press, 1998), 90-98.

[10]*BJ*, 353.

[11]See the discussion of Sanders above.

is in the details of how we define such terms such as *conversion*. Dunn notes, however, that if we think of conversion from one form of Second Temple Judaism to another, "that is, from Pharisaism to Jesus messianism," then we are on much firmer ground both theologically and historically.[12] Dunn concludes that although *conversion* is the language of the historian of religion, *commissioning* is closer to Paul's own self-description, but these two should not be set in sharp antithesis.

How did Paul see his commissioning? Dunn draws attention to several key Pauline texts on the matter. For Paul, it is clear that the prophetic callings of both Isaiah and Jeremiah form the profile that he sees himself stepping into. In Galatians 1:15-16, Paul echoes both Jeremiah 1:5 and Isaiah 49:1-6 in stating that he was "set apart from my mother's womb" and saw his role as fulfilling Israel's commission to be a light unto the nations. Dunn rightly notes,

> What happened on the Damascus road *was* a conversion, a conversion from Saul's previous understanding of how God's will and purpose for Israel was to be carried forward. But Paul saw it as a conversion *to* a better, indeed to the correct, understanding of that will and purpose for Israel. Apostle to the Gentiles, yes, but not thereby an *apostate from* Israel; rather an *apostle of* Israel, commissioned to carry forward Israel's destiny as "a light to the nations."[13]

Another question that emerges out of this key conversation on Paul and Damascus is, To what degree did the experience with the risen Jesus shape Paul's thought? Perhaps even more important, were such issues *immediately* apparent, or did they *develop over time*? If over time, then when did these changes or modifications take place, and how might we discern them? One perennial example of such thought in action is the tenor and tone of Paul's discussion of the law in Galatians and Romans. Does Paul show a maturation of his view of the law in a

---

[12]*BJ*, 353.

[13]*BJ*, 355, emphasis original. Dunn is reacting here to Alan Segal's contention that Paul was indeed an apostate Jew, from a normal first-century Jewish perspective. See Segal's *Paul the Convert: The Apostolate and Apostasy of Saul the Pharisee* (New Haven, CT: Yale University Press, 1992).

later letter such as Romans, where he has toned down some of his more inflammatory statements in Galatians? Perhaps more controversial is the relation of Paul's changing thought when it comes to the topic of eschatology and Christ's return. Did Paul's belief in the *imminent* return of Christ, which many see as readily apparent in a letter such as 1 Thessalonians, eventually dissipate with the reality that Christ had not come back as soon as he had expected? These issues and more are all directly related to the topic of Paul's thought and whether his thought changed over time. Underlying such debates is a running argument, spanning several decades now, between Dunn and Seyoon Kim. Dunn credits Kim with "bringing Paul's conversion back into fame as a, if not the, major creative influence on Paul's gospel."[14] Dunn identifies two key areas for possible change in Paul's thought after Paul's conversion (as defined above): Christology and atonement.

On the first matter, the identity of Jesus in Paul's thought certainly underwent change from before to after the Damascus road encounter. The change involved a recognition that Jesus had been raised from the dead, that he was the Messiah of Israel, that he was God's Son, that he had been made Lord, and that this was good news for Jews and Gentiles.[15] In terms of the second area of immediate change, the atonement and the conviction that Christ "died for our sins," Dunn regards this feature of Paul's thought as coming to him very early. Paul's conception of the death of Jesus as a sacrifice for sins is rooted in the sacrifices associated with the Day of Atonement (Lev 16). Such dual themes are summed up in one of Paul's main kerygmatic themes: Christ crucified.

Less certainty and more controversy surrounds other central elements of Paul's theology in relation to his conversion, specifically the issue of justification by faith and the role of the law. In my estimation, one must be careful with the assumption that justification by faith was somehow unique to Paul. If one takes such an approach, one will certainly create problems when addressed with a simple question: If the

---

[14]*BJ*, 357.
[15]*BJ*, 357-58.

doctrine of justification by faith was unique to Paul and a result of his Damascus road experience, then what was Peter preaching this whole time? Or, for that matter, Jesus himself?

Dunn highlights that justification by faith was certainly the starting point for Paul's experience, not only on the Damascus Road but, one may even suggest, in terms of the way he viewed Judaism itself. The important issue that Dunn raises is precisely "whether Paul *developed* that basic insight through his own missionary experience and/or in light of the confrontation with other missionaries."[16] Put another way, that Paul believed in justification by faith is certain; what is less certain is whether the unique Pauline emphasis on such a concept was a result of his interaction with Gentile audiences or, more negatively, a result of confrontation with other missionaries. Was justification by faith for Paul a pragmatic reality or a product of the crucible of confrontation? Dunn affirms the latter.

One of the issues that makes the justification issue more complex is its connection to another thorny dilemma in Paul's thought: his view of the Mosaic law. Did Paul's Damascus road experience relate to his view of the law? According to Dunn, Paul's view of the law and its relationship to the Christ event and his Gentile audiences developed over time and was not a direct result of his Damascus experience. Rather, Dunn posits, the critical component for understanding the law in Paul's thought is in its "Israel-defining role," and this Dunn ties to Paul's revolutionary zeal before the Damascus road event. It was Paul's zeal that led him to persecute the early Jesus movement where he saw it breaching the law in terms of its boundary-marking roles. It is evident that when Paul began preaching to the Gentiles, circumcision was no longer a requirement, at least for Gentiles. This perhaps marks one of the most salient differences between Saul the former Pharisee and Paul the apostle. Dunn's treatment of the boundary markers of Israel is perhaps one of his most enduring contributions to Pauline studies, but also one that has gone

[16] *BJ*, 360.

through its own development and is the perhaps the most misunderstood element in Dunn's thought.

DUNN AND "THE WORKS OF THE LAW"

Perhaps the feature of Dunn's treatment of Paul that has undergone the most transformation over his career is his understanding of the "works of the law" in Paul's thought. This phrase has also been a touchstone of debate within Pauline studies, with his proposals proving to be watershed moments within the history of interpretation of Paul in the modern period.

We must situate Dunn's work within the broader movements afoot in the 1980s in Pauline studies. By way of reminder, E. P. Sanders published his now widely influential *Paul and Palestinian Judaism* in 1977. Although certainly important in terms of the understanding of the Second Temple period of Paul, Sanders's portrait of Paul left many dissatisfied, particularly Dunn. Within this context of dissatisfaction with Sanders's understanding of Paul, Dunn gave his now-famous T. W. Manson lecture in 1983. In his own words, this lecture was his attempt to "give a better answer," and essential to this answer for Dunn was Galatians 2:16 and correctly interpreting the phrase "the works of the law."[17]

In the 1983 lecture Dunn picked up several strands of Pauline interpretation before pressing forward in a new direction. Both citing the influence of Krister Stendahl's emphasis on the particular context of Paul's ministry and combining these insights with that of Sanders on a new portrait of Second Temple Judaism, Dunn pressed forward to take both of their conclusions and apply them to Paul's Jew-and-Gentile context in Galatians. The definition of "the works of the law" in Galatians 2:16 becomes central for Dunn's contribution. Dunn contrasts traditional readings of the phrase, which take the phrase to refer to any work prescribed by the covenant, with his offering that "by 'the works

[17]*NPP*, 8.

of the Law' Paul intended his readers to think of *particular observances of the law like circumcision and food laws*."[18]

Dunn more narrowly defines the phrase "the works of the law" frequently in his lecture to refer to the specific issues of circumcision, food laws, and Sabbath keeping.[19] It is this set of particular practices that Paul denies in his Galatian context. In the letter to the Galatians, Dunn argues that the phrase carries quite a specific meaning, "epitomized in this letter by circumcision."[20] In light of the role of Jewish identity within the Greco-Roman world, it was this set of practices that began to define the communal or national identity. The practices of circumcision (acutely so), food laws, and Sabbath keeping defined ethnic Jewish identity within the first century (and a bit prior), and according to Dunn it was this concept, so radically defined, that Paul rejected.

To put it rather straightforwardly, in Dunn's 1983 lecture, "the works of the law" would *not* refer to, for example, the commandments about tithing or clothing, but specifically to these "badges" of national identity that marked out the Jewish people in their Greco-Roman world. Dunn stresses the unique specificity of this phrase in the letter to the Galatians. The "works of the law" is not functioning as a synonym for *law* in general.[21] Dunn states it thusly:

> Lest the point still be confused, I repeat, Paul here is not disparaging works in general or pressing a dichotomy between outward ritual done in the flesh and inward grace operative in the spirit. Once again, we must observe the limited target he has in his sight. It is works which betoken racial prerogative to which he objects, acts done in the flesh because faith in Christ is reckoned insufficient as the badge of covenant membership which he denounces. Over against Peter and the other Jewish Christians Paul insists that God's verdict in favour of believers comes to realisation through faith, from start to finish, and in no way depends on observing the works of law

[18]James D. G. Dunn, "The New Perspective on Paul," in *NPP*, 108, emphasis original.

[19]Dunn, "New Perspective on Paul," 108-11, 113. That this narrower definition is in view is clear from statements where Dunn emphasizes the demand for a "*particular* work" that Paul denies (115).

[20]Dunn, "New Perspective on Paul," 116.

[21]Indeed, Dunn cites this as a critique of Sanders in 1983 of both *Paul and Palestinian Judaism* and Sanders's *Paul and the Jewish Law* ("New Perspective on Paul," 117).

which hitherto had characterized and distinguished the Jews as God's people.[22]

In 1984 Dunn expanded on this lecture, taking his working definition of "the works of the law" as circumcision, food laws, and Sabbath and emphasizing the *social function* of these practices to mark off or separate Israel from the nations. The observance of the law functioned socially as a boundary marker.[23] Such insights were followed up on and built on in Dunn's magisterial Romans commentary, published in 1988.

It was Dunn's Romans commentary that came to be the most influential in terms of transmitting Dunn's view of the "the works of the law" to a broader audience. Dunn reiterates:

> A sociological perspective also helps us to see how the conviction of privileged election and the practice of covenantal nomism almost inevitably comes to expression in focal points of distinctiveness, particular laws and especially ritual practices which reinforced the sense of distinctive identity and marked Israel off most clearly from the other nations. In this case three of Israel's laws gained particular prominence as being especially distinctive—circumcision, food laws, and Sabbath. . . . This, then, is the context within which and against which we must set Paul's treatment of the law in Romans. . . . They would, I believe, recognize that what Paul was concerned about was the fact that covenant promise and law had become too inextricably identified with ethnic Israel as such, with the Jewish people marked out in their national distinctiveness by the practices of circumcision, food laws, and Sabbath in particular.[24]

The statement above then became the operating understanding of how Dunn viewed the phrase "the works of the law." Such an interpretation, if now commonplace, was not so at first and provoked strong reactions from a wide range of scholarship.[25]

---

[22]Dunn, "New Perspective on Paul," 117.

[23]*NPP*, 7-8.

[24]James D. G. Dunn, *Romans* (Dallas: Word, 1988), 1:lxxi.

[25]One of the first and more critical reactions to Dunn's thesis was C. E. B. Cranfield, "'The Works of the Law' in the Epistle to the Romans," *Journal for the Study of the New Testament* 43 (1991): 89-101. Cranfield concludes, "The explanation of ἔργα νόμου in Romans rejected by Professor Dunn is the true explanation, namely, that it denotes (the doing of) the works which the law requires, obedience to the law; and that, when Paul says that no human being will be justified in God's sight by

In 2005 Dunn offered a retrospective on his work on Paul and in particular his role in the development of the new perspective on Paul. Such a moment allowed Dunn to reflect on the benefits and shortcomings of over two decades of work on Paul. In his chapter "The New Perspective: Whence, What, and Whither?" Dunn offers some clarifying remarks and addresses misunderstandings of his work. His interpretation of "the works of the law" forms one of four main areas he seeks to clarify.

Dunn expresses regret that his first proposal for a definition of "the works of the law" permitted a larger degree of scrutiny and pushback than he had initially intended. He argues clearly that the phrase "the works of the law" refers to

- "what the law requires"
- "the conduct prescribed by the Torah"
- "whatever the law requires to be done can be described as 'doing' the law."[26]

However, Dunn is keen to stress that the context of the announcement of Galatians 2:16, "no one is justified by the works of the law, but through faith in Jesus Christ," is a reminder that "the general principle can be put to the test by particular works of the law."[27] Put another way, although the phrase "works of the law" can refer to more than just the badge markers, the badge markers are sufficient enough to raise the primary concerns Paul has in Galatia. The term can mean more, but certainly not less, than circumcision, food laws, and Sabbath. Dunn acknowledges that if the strict focus on the primary issues of circumcision and food laws appears to be too restrictive, then the notoriously difficult phrase "living like a Jew" in Galatians 2:14 is probably the broader concept that many seek to equate with the phrase "the works of the law."

---

works of the law, he means that no one will earn a status of righteousness before God by obedience to the law" (100).

[26]*NPP*, 23-24.

[27]*NPP*, 25.

One must also consider the issue of the works of the law from the sociological viewpoint of Gentile converts and the broader Greco-Roman world at large. Certainly, those unaccustomed to the Mosaic law would not associate the phrase "the works of the law" with the more peculiar laws of the Mosaic code, such as not planting two different kinds of seed in the same field (Lev 19:19), or for that matter any of the Levitical laws concerning the priesthood and the temple. Non-Jewish people certainly did not care enough, nor did they scrutinize the legal codes of Moses to find out how various Jews worshiped.

What would, however, stand out to much of the non-Jewish world would certainly be the bigger-ticket items that could easily be observed, such as the dietary restrictions, as this shaped whom various Jewish groups could eat and associate with from the home to the marketplace. Indeed, in Rome, Jews had their own markets to do their kosher grocery shopping. Likewise, the keeping of Sabbath would have been easily observed by non-Jews, not just in terms of the workforce but even with more specific instances. For example, Philo indicates that Augustus made concessions for the Jewish groups in Rome in terms of the picking up of free grain (*Laws* 158). If the doling out of free grain fell on the Sabbath, Augustus would allow Jews to pick up their grain on weekdays. Such a benefit would surely have been noticed by those who were not Jewish.

Finally, there is the issue of Jewish circumcision. One may wonder how non-Jews would know whether a Jewish male was circumcised. To state a rather obvious fact, stereotypes of Jewish males probably sufficed for most non-Jews so that they simply *assumed* that if someone was Jewish and male, then he was circumcised. Further, if Jews participated in any of the gymnasiums in the major cities of the ancient world or frequented the baths, the nudity at various points and places would have provided glimpses of such a reality. Although the phrase "the works of the law" is certainly broader in meaning, it is simply not less than these large issues, especially when the issue is considered from a Greco-Roman viewpoint on Jewish practices.

Paul could certainly have meant more by the phrase, and his communities could have assumed more, but the broader Roman world would have assumed nothing *less* than the boundary-marking badges of Jewish identity.

In a move that may appear surprising to those opponents of Dunn who continue to criticize his understanding of works of the law, Dunn readily admitted in 2005 that "I do not want to narrow 'the works of the law' to boundary issues." Rather, Dunn insists that even if one wants to take the broadest definition of "the works of the law" to indicate *any* work of the law, one must certainly grant the "fact," as Dunn calls it, of the issue of Jews and Gentiles eating together.[28] The response in 2005, although brief, certainly showcased a turning point in Dunn's understanding of the phrase "the works of the law."

Eight years later, Dunn returned once again to the state of the discussion on the new perspective on Paul in his article "A New Perspective on the New Perspective on Paul." Dunn acknowledges the issues of justification by faith and the works of the law are central to understanding the arguments of the new perspective on Paul. He once again returns to the all-important Galatians 2:1-16, where these phrases first appear. In returning once again to Galatians 2:16 and the parallel phrases "the works of the law" and "faith in Christ," Dunn now notes, "By 'works of the law,' of course he [Paul] means what the law requires." In a footnote on the same page, he says he emphasizes this because his T. W. Manson lecture "caused some misunderstanding or confusion on the point."[29] Dunn shows that although "the works of the law" can refer to whatever the law requires, within the context it seems to surround the issues key to the Antioch incident: trying to circumcise Titus (Gal 2:3-6), laws of clean and unclean (Gal 2:14), separation (Gal 2:12), and living like a Jew (Gal 2:14). Although there is some repetition of his argument from previous books and articles, it leads to a rather new conclusion:

---

[28]*NPP*, 28.

[29]James D. G. Dunn, "A New Perspective on the New Perspective on Paul," *Early Christianity* 4 (2013): 174 and n67.

> To repeat, "works of the law" is a more general phrase, which refers to the principle of keeping the law in all its requirements. But when the phrase comes in the context of Paul's mission to Gentiles, and particularly of Jewish believers trying to compel Gentile believers to live like Jews, then its most obvious reference is particularly to the law in its role as a wall dividing Jew from Gentile, the boundary markers which define who is "inside" and who is "outside," that is, inside the law/covenant and outside the law/covenant people.[30]

Such a statement shows the movement within Dunn's own thought from his initial 1983 lecture on the topic. From 1983 to 2013, Dunn moved from a rather restrictive definition of "the works of the law" as only circumcision, food laws, and Sabbath to understanding the phrase in a more general sense, all the while maintaining that the situation on the ground in Antioch as represented by the Galatian correspondence should not be underestimated in showing how this phrase functioned within the early Christian movement. In sum, it appears that Dunn has moved to a both/and approach.

A few conclusions are in order for the student of Paul. First and foremost, Dunn shows critical scholarship at its best, whereby one offers a reading of the evidence; that evidence is critiqued by one's colleagues; one interacts with interlocutors, listening to both their affirmations and conclusions; and then one modifies and adapts one's view. Although this process is all too infrequent within scholarship, it is refreshing to see when it does occur. Dunn's view of "the works of the law" provides one example of this process.

Another important conclusion is to realize that the field is ever changing. Not only so, but scholars' own views grow and mature over time. In a more negative light, some contemporary scholars of Paul have not kept up to speed with a given author's work, growth, or development and wrongly attribute old views to other scholars. Sometimes they are even painfully unaware, whether intentionally or unintentionally, of the changes that have taken place. Dunn shows the need to

[30]Dunn, "New Perspective on the New Perspective," 174-75.

stay engaged and up to date on the state of research, even more so with some of the most pressing issues within the field.

THE LAW

As we widen our scope from the specific phrase "the works of the law" to the law in general, Dunn offers several arguments about how to understand the law in Paul's thought. It ought to be stated that Paul's view of the law is multifaceted and largely dependent on the context within which the discussion takes place (Jew/Gentile). One of the inherent dangers of discussing the law in Paul's thought is the tendency toward reductionism and simplistic categories.

Dunn's first point on the law begins traditionally. The law played a role in defining sin. The law identifies sin as a transgression and issues a guilty verdict on that transgression. The law, for Paul, does this for Jews and to some degree Gentiles (Rom 2:14-15). Interestingly, Dunn notes that this point is not mentioned in Galatians, which might reflect the contingent aspect of Paul's thought.[31] However, even this is not novel to Paul but is reflected within the law code as a whole in the Old Testament. Indeed, the entire sacrificial system operates on the assumption that law violation would occur. This would not have been a point of controversy for Paul and his fellow Jews. Although this is the traditional starting point for discussing the law, it is only one spoke of the proverbial wheel in terms of how Paul discusses the law.

Second, Dunn raises the issue of the law and its connection with Israel, especially its protective and disciplinary aspects. This was indeed the "temporary" aspect of the law, which Paul makes explicit, especially in Galatians. Dunn tackles a number of the thorny passages that indicate that the law was given "for" the sake of transgressions. Dunn suggests that these texts should not be read pejoratively but rather as a gracious act of God, who gave the law to "deal with transgressions" and to provide a solution through the sacrificial system. It is also in this

---

[31]*TPA*, 134.

sense that Israel's being "under the law" should be understood—it was under the protective and instructive aspect of the law.[32] As stated above, the entire atonement system not only assumes that law violation will occur but also provides at the time the requisite means for dealing with transgressions through the various sacrifices. Both problem *and* solution are addressed from the onset in terms of how the law functioned in the Old Testament and for Paul as well.

Third, Dunn argues that Paul's primary critique against his fellow Jewish contemporaries is their failure to note the *temporary* aspect of the role of the law. He notes that in this aspect a "fundamental feature" of Paul's perspective comes to the fore. For Dunn and certainly others, this may be Paul's unique contribution to the early Christian movement. Paul's insight is that the coming of Christ "marked a climax and completion in God's overarching purpose."[33] This fulfillment meant that Israel no longer needed the protective custody of the law. Paul's critique of the law is then *primarily eschatological*. Such a criticism of the law would certainly put him at odds with those who assumed the "historic status of privilege" under the law even after the coming of Messiah, hence his debate with the Judaizers in Galatians.

On this point, Dunn needs to go further. Such statements concerning the temporary nature of the law are clear in Paul; however, what has not been addressed is what the common assumption was about the role of the law in the messianic age. This is a question that Albert Schweitzer initially raised and was subsequently raised by E. P. Sanders. Dunn provides no clear answer on the role of the law in the coming age to substantiate his or Paul's conclusions on the law. An engagement with the various views of the law among other Jewish groups of the first century is needed. Certainly, some regarded the law as eternal in nature, and it is on this point that Paul would have distanced himself and appeared most novel to contemporary Jewish thinkers, such as Philo and others. The temporary nature of the Torah is one of the more controversial aspects of Paul's thought.

---

[32]*TPA*, 139, 141-42.
[33]*TPA*, 143.

Though Paul courted controversy over his view of the Mosaic law, this did not in turn mean he became an antinomian. Rather, it is interesting that the more precise question Paul is asking is *which* law should be operative for his Gentile converts. The Mosaic law is part of a different covenant, of which the Gentiles are not a part (Gal 3–4). In the place of the Mosaic law, Paul does not just substitute the Spirit. Instead, we see Paul discussing the enigmatic "law of Christ" (Gal 6:2; 1 Cor 9:21). Further, although not formally a reference to the law, Paul praises his Roman congregation for their obedience to a "pattern of teaching" (Rom 6:17) that they had been given. Broadly speaking, Paul is not antithetical to notions of instruction and obedience. To the contrary, Paul nearly everywhere is giving his communities teaching to which he expects their obedience, going as far as explicitly stating this with the important obedience of faith (Rom 1:5). The key point for Paul seems to be, as it is in Galatians 4:1-6, that the time has changed and the eschatological age has dawned. However, even in the eschatological age, a law still remains operative—the law of Christ, empowered and aided by the Spirit. To understand Paul's view of the law, one must have a firm grasp of the eschatological landscape, something Dunn himself undertakes to describe.

It is important for understanding the sometimes-critical stance Paul takes toward the law to remember that the most critical statements about the law come when he is contrasting epochs. As Dunn notes, "When the Moses to Christ phase of God's purpose is set within the Adam to Christ epoch, the more positive function of the law in relation to Israel falls out of sight" and the negative role of the law comes to the forefront.[34] The focus of the argument centers on Galatians 4; Romans 5; and 2 Corinthians 3. It is the imagery of Sinai and slavery, law and death, and divergent covenants that brings Paul's negative statements about the law into sharp relief. Each of those arguments is, however, inherently eschatological as Paul looks from his vantage point of living in the

---

[34]*TPA*, 146.

eschatological age of the Spirit. But this raises a further complicating issue for Paul and the law. What is the nature of the law? Is it life giving or death dealing? From the argument so far, it would appear that the law is an instrument of death. Further, wouldn't this view of the law contradict the witness of Deuteronomy, which views the law as the way that leads to life?

Dunn raises and responds to these questions, arguing that the law is *used* by sin to entrap human weakness. Dunn's primary focus is on Romans 7 for this feature of Paul's thought. He rightly notes that even the critical statements about the law in Romans 7 that seem to align the law with sin actually arise in a "defense of the law" and as an answer to the rhetorical question "Is the law sinful?" Paul's own rebuttal, of course, is "Certainly not!" (Rom 7:7) and that the law is "holy, righteous and good" (Rom 7:12). It is sin that takes over the law and misuses and abuses it. The negative impact of the law is, as Dunn argues, that "the weakness of the law is simply the obverse and unavoidable corollary of its role as the measure of God's will and yardstick of judgment. . . . If there are laws to guide human endeavor and rules to ensure the most fruitful cooperation, it seems to be an inescapable feature of human society that there will be lawbreakers and rule-ignorers."[35]

Dunn concludes that the problem was not the law but sin entangling the law within its cosmic web, sin using the law for its own ends. Using the language of Paul's argument in 2 Corinthians 3, Dunn argues that sin turns law into *gramma* and desire into lust. This leads to Dunn's final point, that the law is now allied with sin and death. However, Dunn maintains that the law should not be viewed as a cosmic power, thus standing in stark contrast to Schweitzer, Bultmann, Käsemann, and even perhaps Beker and Wright.

Dunn holds that one positive feature of the law, even though it is misused and abused by sin and death, is that it "transforms death from a final judgment on the sinner to the final destruction of sin itself." Thus

[35]*TPA*, 157, 159.

the law can function in dual roles. The law can be used as a means given by God to identify transgression and provide for transgression, as well as in the cosmic sense, where sin and death co-opt the law. The law can be used both ways, which explains how Paul can refer to it in both positive and negative terms.[36]

SALVATION

In chapter five of his *Theology of the Paul the Apostle,* Dunn turns to the topic of salvation in Paul. He begins by noting several important issues that have dominated Pauline scholarship. First, interpreters must take account of the "epochal" shift of Paul and the earliest Christians' message. Eschatology, as always, is a game changer. The death and resurrection of Jesus had shifted the times, and now the world was in a new age, a time of new possibilities. For Dunn, the old epoch of sin and death had been done away with and replaced by an epoch of grace and faith. Although Dunn does not use apocalyptic language to categorize this shifting of times, one wonders whether this is where his language is headed. One small caution is in order in his discussion of epochs characterized by sin and death and by grace and faith. Such generalizations could mislead one to think that grace and faith were not part of the previous age; this would of course be a wrong conclusion. Although Dunn does not necessarily intend his language in this way, it opens up a pathway whereby one could wrongly conclude this is what he means.

In terms of the salvation event, Dunn also emphasizes the radical shift from "first Adam to last Adam," which "must be echoed in human lives."[37] Indeed, the salvation experience was to be embodied in the very lives of those who proclaimed this message. Each person and community was to reflect the transition of the times in their individual and communal livelihoods, a feature we will return to shortly.

A primary focus for Dunn in studying the theology of Paul is the metaphors Paul uses to describe salvation. He notes, importantly, that

---

[36]*TPA*, 159, 161.
[37]*TPA*, 318.

Paul draws on metaphors of his time to communicate effectively. Terms such as *justification, redemption, reconciliation, liberation, citizenship,* and *inheritance,* as well as the most common understanding of *salvation* as "bodily health or preservation," all draw on concepts that would have been familiar from the social world of his audiences. Dunn draws two conclusions from the multiplicity of metaphors. First, these metaphors bring out an experiential reality, something that Dunn states that each community member would have readily identified with. Dunn notes that the frequent Pauline references to salvation as death, life, and marriage are momentous terms used for life-changing events.[38] Something of substance had happened to these early Christians that was not just a minor tweak to a previously good life; rather, a life-altering reality had changed the very nature of their identity and livelihood.

Although Dunn does not draw out this corollary specifically, these profound experiences of a new reality aided the growth of Christianity in the first few centuries. Something dramatic had happened in the Mediterranean world, and people took notice of that change. One only needs to think of the members of the Christian community embodied in a Pauline slogan such as Galatians 3:28, whereby the very makeup of the community provided its own built-in apologetic/evangelistic impulse within the very fabric of the community. Christians through their very own lived-out experience offered unforeseen vistas to a watching world.

A second feature of the multiplicity of metaphors is that each metaphor was an attempt to express an idea that transcended a single description. Or, to put it another way, no one metaphor could adequately express the complete reality of what God had accomplished in Christ. Let the reader take notice. In seeing not just *what* Paul wrote, but *how* he wrote, Dunn draws out a subsequent point that takes aim at contemporary Pauline scholarship. *Dunn regards it as mistaken to take one metaphor and make it the central or primary way of understanding Paul's*

---

[38]*TPA*, 328-29, 331.

thought, along the way noting the tendency of popular evangelicalism to stress new birth and the metaphor of justification in Protestant theology.[39] Dunn's pedagogical aim for interpreters of Paul is that we speak of salvation in the way Paul did, with a rich variety of provocative metaphors uniquely aimed at the unique situations his communities faced.

Dunn continues his discussion of salvation by focusing on the doctrine of justification by faith. He sets the issue of justification within the context of twentieth-century scholarship and notes that it has been part of one of two trends in the history of scholarship. Typically, justification is seen as the center of Paul's theology and considered to be the ultimate doctrine of the church.[40] This is the approach taken by both Rudolf Bultmann and his student Ernst Käsemann. One negative consequence of this approach is that it can often take an anti-Jewish stance and can often be pitted as a reaction of Paul *against* Judaism. Here Christianity itself is placed in antithesis to Judaism.

The second trend within twentieth-century scholarship on Paul sees justification as a dispute not between Paul and his ancestral religion but between various groups within Christianity. This ultimately goes back to F. C. Baur's analysis of early Christianity as a conflict between Jewish and Gentile Christianity. In such a view, Paul's insistence on justification by faith put him at odds with other Jewish-Christian missionaries. A particular example of such a reading would be the argument between Paul and Peter in Galatians 2. Two years prior to the publication of *The Theology of Paul the Apostle,* Dunn organized the third Durham-Tübingen research symposium to address the issue of Paul and the Mosaic law. In the proceedings from the symposium, with an article titled "In Search of Common Ground," Dunn takes it as a point of agreement that

> Paul's principal treatment of the law in his letters was formulated in dialogue and dispute not with non-Christian Jews, but with fellow Jewish Christians. . . . Protests against Paul's gospel in reference to the law arose because so many of Paul's fellow Jewish believers felt their own identity as children of

---

[39]*TPA*, 332.
[40]*TPA*, 336.

> Abraham and their heritage as the people of Israel to be under question or even threat from the success of Paul's mission.[41]

The primary issue of Paul's continuity and discontinuity with his heritage emerges from both trends of twentieth-century scholarship on Paul. Scholars range on a spectrum concerning the degree of continuity versus discontinuity. However, the precise arguments about justification take on different nuances when placed within the two trends of readings of Paul. One particular element that stands out with the second trend takes us all the way back to the beginning of the new perspective. If Paul is not engaged in a debate with or against first century Judaism but in an in-house argument with Jewish-Christian missionaries, then, in the words of Dunn, "the doctrine of justification by faith was formulated within and as a result of the early mission to Gentiles. It was a polemical doctrine, hammered out in the face of Jewish Christian objections to that mission as law-free and not requiring circumcision."[42] We might recall from our initial chapter that this was one of the primary points of Krister Stendahl, who proved quite prescient about future Pauline discussions. The debate over Paul's understanding of justification enters us into one of the most vigorous and contentious debates within Pauline studies.

Dunn begins his own analysis of justification with a survey of the key issues and aspects: the righteousness of God, the works of the law, and the *pistis Christou* debate. Regarding the righteousness of God, Dunn stresses its Hebraic character and emphasizes the relational aspect and the obligation laid on each individual. God's righteousness is understood as his faithfulness to uphold his obligations to humanity, his covenants. Indeed, Dunn sees the faithfulness/righteousness of God as one of the principal concerns of Paul in Romans. Paul's doctrine of justification is rooted in this Old Testament theme, including the initial grace in God's calling his people Israel, and thus justification

[41]James D. G. Dunn, "In Search of Common Ground," in *Paul and the Mosaic Law*, ed. James D. G. Dunn (Grand Rapids, Eerdmans 2001), 310.
[42]*TPA*, 340.

was not a reaction against his heritage but an affirmation of its fundamental principle.[43]

Concerning the issue of "the faith/faithfulness of Christ," Dunn offers his own stimulating contribution.[44] He begins by noting that the phrase by itself, *pistis Christou,* is grammatically indeterminate. It is context that must decide the meaning of each instance. Before moving on to contextual issues, Dunn notes that one would expect a definite article if it were to be understood as the subjective, as "the faith of Christ." Interestingly, we never find the phrase with the article, which is a strong point in Dunn's argument. By way of summary, Dunn takes all the Galatian references of *pistis Christou* as objective, as "faith in Christ." As he moves to Romans, he notes that the occurrence in Romans 3:21-26 provides a stronger case for the alternative than most, but even here problems remain. Dunn's primary objection is that the phrase being understood as a subjective genitive assumes that it was a familiar theme for his audience. Dunn concludes that to understand the phrase as "the faith of Christ" in Romans depends too much on "atomistic study" or on an "assumption" of an underlying narrative. The texts "in their flow" naturally refer to "faith in Christ."[45]

Several issues ought to be noted as related to the issue of translating *pistis Christou.* Although Dunn does note that the phrase lacks a definite article, and, as he notes, it would have been easy to add one, such an argument cuts both ways, as there is also a Greek preposition *en* (in) that would be just as easy to add and likewise does not appear here in Galatians, while Paul does use it in Colossians 2:5. Arguments from absence should be avoided. Second, if one looks at Romans 4:16, there is a similar construction in regard to Abraham's faith. It's the same type of grammatical phrase that appears in Galatians. However, no one doubts that in Romans 4:16 Paul means the faith "of" Abraham, not

---

[43]*TPA,* 341, 345.

[44]On the importance of this phrase within Pauline scholarship see the helpful volume edited by Michael F. Bird and Preston M. Sprinkle, *The Faith of Jesus Christ* (Peabody, MA: Hendrickson, 2009).

[45]*TPA,* 381, 384-85.

faith "in" Abraham. Third and last, in Galatians 1:1, notice that Paul juxtaposes human activity and divine activity in Christ. Paul seems to be juxtaposing both issues in Galatians 2:16 too. If the issue were works of the law versus a believer's faith in someone, Paul would be comparing two human activities. Rather, it seems Paul is contrasting a form of human activity (works of the law) with the faithfulness of Jesus to God.

What, then, does the phrase "faithfulness of Christ" refer to, and why does Paul juxtapose it with works of the law? At a general level, Paul is referring to Jesus' obedience to God's will. To use the language of Romans 5–6, as the "new Adam" Christ perfectly obeys God. More precisely, though, Paul is most likely referring to the act of Jesus' death. Such is the point made in Galatians 1:4, where, right after Paul mentions Christ, he immediately mentions "who gave himself for our sins," referring to the death of Christ. We might also mention Philippians 2:5-11, which makes precisely the same point.

Moving on, as Dunn concludes his section on justification he lists several features that flow out of this doctrine for Paul. These include acceptance, peace with God, access to God, boasting in the glory of God, unity of Jew and Gentile, and liberation from the law. The item at the end, regarding which Dunn maintains that Paul experienced his coming to faith as liberation, bears closer scrutiny.[46] Dunn says that Paul experienced liberation from the law as liberation from slavery. He regards Paul as coming to this conclusion in hindsight: that he now views his previous life as one characterized by slavery. But where do we find this in Paul's letters as a description of his own personal experience? Undoubtedly Paul refers to the law as slavery, but only in relation to his Gentile converts accepting this and as a misunderstanding of the climactic act of God in Christ. There in Galatians, Paul is using the rhetoric of avoidance to ward off his Gentile converts from making the wrong move.

This, however, does not seem to be Paul's view of his own experience. We get no sense that Paul had any undue guilt or anxiety that burdened

---

[46]*TPA*, 385-88.

him. From Paul's letters, we gain very little insight into his own personal conversion experience and what he underwent. Even when we look at the book of Acts, we do not learn anything largely different. While it is true that Paul does regard his previous accomplishments as "loss" in relation knowing or gaining Christ (Phil 3), is loss equivalent to slavery? One would be hard-pressed to make the case or to mix the metaphors. It would be a mistake to assume that Paul's discussions with his Gentile converts regarding the law were the same as his own reflections on his personal relationship to the law. Again, Paul's apostleship as directed to the Gentiles ought not to be neglected. Since the Spirit has been given, there is no way for Gentile converts to turn back now to the former things. On this point, Dunn is rather unclear, and such statements about Paul's experience seem to run counter to his previous arguments.

Dunn's section on participation in Christ, although substantially smaller than the justification section, belies the importance of the motif for Dunn's understanding of Paul's theology.[47] Dunn offers a brief history of scholarship noting the important players who championed this view as central to Paul's thought in the previous century—Adolf Deissmann, Bousset, and Schweitzer—and more recently Sanders, among others. This view had initial difficulties in gaining ground in Pauline studies in a post–world war context, but Dunn signals a renewed call to investigate this theme as central to Paul's theology, as so many other features are covered by it, including Christology, pneumatology, the Christian life, baptism, and the body of Christ. "In Christ" language is important not only because of its ubiquity in Paul's letters (some eighty-three times) but also because it is almost entirely found in Paul alone.[48] In terms of the imagery Paul uses to discuss salvation, this little phrase bears much of the load.[49]

Dunn places Paul's "in Christ" language into three main categories:

---

[47]*TPA*, 390-412.

[48]*TPA*, 396.

[49]Subsequent scholarship has taken up this emphasis with renewed vigor, as is seen in the work of Constantine R. Campbell, *Paul and Union with Christ: An Exegetical and Theological Study* (Grand Rapids: Zondervan), 2012.

1. an objective sense, which focuses on the redemptive act that happened in Christ (e.g., Rom 3:24; 6:23; 8:2; 1 Cor 1:4; 2 Cor 5:19)
2. the subjective sense, wherein believers are spoken of as *being* in Christ; this sense emphasizes the experience of the believer (Gal 2:4, 3:28; Rom 6:11, 8:1; 1 Cor 1:2)
3. the sense wherein Paul's own activity or his own commands are central (1 Cor 4:15; Phil 1:13)

Paul is called "in Christ," and believers are to "hope in the Lord." Dunn reiterates that a wide range of Paul's theology, and most notably the objective saving work of Christ, is summed up in the "in Christ" language, and this makes it a very significant theme for Paul.[50] One would be misguided to think that this is a throwaway line for Paul and that it merely represents an inadvertent addition to Paul's thought.

Dunn rightly goes on to caution that this language should not be reduced to a label but that "at the heart of the motif is not merely a belief about Christ, but an experience" of Christ himself.[51] The language of "in Christ" not only transcends the metaphor but also does not leave behind the actual person of Jesus. Given the massive debates about the center of Paul's thought within the academy, it is an unfortunate reality that this phrase has not received its due attention until recently.

As with the topic of justification, Dunn draws several corollary conclusions from the "in Christ" language. These include the two soteriological moments of Christ's death and resurrection (the objective category from above), such that participation with Christ is always participation in his death and pointed toward resurrection. Second, the corporate nature of the language is evident and provides a good antidote to the rampant individualistic readings of Paul that dominate much of the landscape of Pauline interpretation, both within the academy and the church. Third, Paul ties the ethical component of his teaching to the language and imagery of being "in Christ." The "in

[50] *TPA*, 399.
[51] *TPA*, 400.

Christ" language is thus the starting point for the "new creation" or new life. Dunn explicitly states that the "in Christ" language is the "resource and inspiration" for the ethical life.[52] It is only by being in Christ that a community can begin to live out the reality or realities of new life that Paul describes. The Christian virtues require both Christ and community, and one must be in both to live out the Christian life.

Fourth, the "in Christ" language is both eschatological and cosmic. The language congregates most strongly in Romans 8:16-29, which describes the salvation process of not only the individual but the entire cosmos. Paul ties together the threads of Christ, Spirit, creation, and rescue into a tapestry of redemption. Those who are "in Christ" have no condemnation (Rom 8:1) but, having been set free by the Spirit to life, are also set free from slavery and death—a slavery experienced not only by humanity but by creation too (Rom 8:21). The setting free and resurrecting of those "in Christ" is part of a larger liberation of community and creation itself. In this way, Paul says, those who are set free are firstfruits of the redemption and liberation God has planned for the cosmos itself. Or, to put it another way, we're all in this together.

PAULINE ETHICS

Near the end of the monumental *Theology of the Apostle Paul,* Dunn's discussion turns to how believers should live in light of unification and participation with Christ as creatures of the new eschatological creation. Dunn begins by noting that one major feature of Paul's theology is its "vigorous ethical concern."[53] Contrary to popular opinion, Paul *is* concerned with how Christians live in light of the gospel. Complicating this scenario and leading to the confusion that perhaps Paul does not have much to say about behavior is the oft-posed dichotomy between "theology" and "ethics" in Paul's letters. Such an approach is misguided, as the two are woven together in Paul's discourses (see Rom 1:5). By dividing Paul's letters up into the two sections of

---

[52] *TPA,* 411.
[53] *TPA,* 626.

"theology first, ethics second," one is given the false impression that ethics are secondary to Paul's supposed "true theological concerns." The ethical concerns of Paul are far from ancillary, as ethical concerns consist of the raison d'être for some of the letters themselves (e.g., 1 Corinthians!). Such concerns are not relegated to the end of Paul's letters but, as one notices in Romans 5–6, are directly in the middle of the letters themselves.

Following both Bultmann and Victor Furnish, Dunn agrees with the traditional framing of Paul's ethic under the rubric of the indicative and the imperative. The indicative for Paul consists of two events: the death and resurrection (and, to some degree, the life) of Jesus, and the "beginning of salvation" or justification language.

The imperative also consists of two emphases: the "sustaining grace of God," also called sanctification, and human responsibility. Dunn rightly emphasizes that the indicative-and-imperative structure is caught up in the eschatological tension of the already/not-yet aspect of Paul's thought, and this is the crucial issue in interpreting Paul's ethics.[54] As such, all action is to some degree flawed in the current age and, according to Dunn, "principled compromise" is a characteristic of living between the ages and making ethical decisions. Dunn therefore sets out to categorize Paul's ethics along three lines: faith, Christ, and Spirit.

Dunn summarizes his conclusions on Paul's ethic by affirming that it is one of balance between internal motivation and external norm. By external norm he means traditional wisdom, law (a.k.a. Torah), virtue/vice lists, and notions of right and wrong and good ordering for society. By internal motivation he means the renewed mind that can discern the will of God, "living in Christ," and Christian liberty.[55] An overemphasis on the former leads to *gramma* or legalism, and an overemphasis on the latter leads to antinomianism and libertine lives. Paul expects his communities to act according to the conduct and *charism* befitting of a life lived "in Christ" as a new creation.

---

[54] *TPA*, 629.
[55] *TPA*, 668-69.

CONCLUSION

For the past several decades, James Dunn has highlighted some of the most pertinent issues of Pauline studies: Paul's conversion, the Mosaic law and works of the law, justification by faith, Pauline ethics, and a theological analysis and summary of Paul's thought. Dunn's influence on the guild has been enormous, to say the least. Perhaps Dunn's particular gift is his attention to the details of Paul's thought in his attempts to synthesize as much of the Pauline corpus as possible. One may note that this stands in contrast with his colaborer N. T. Wright, who, though offering a wide-angle lens on Paul, has been frequently criticized for his lack of attention to the details of Pauline thought. Few have offered such a nuanced and wide-ranging reading of not only Paul's world but his thought, exegesis, and theology as James Dunn. His close reading of the letters and effort to allow Paul's thought to stand in all of its own nuance is laudable. Not without criticism, Dunn has responded to the critics over the course of his career and shown how biblical studies ought to work. That some have not taken notice of these changes speaks more about the critics than it does Dunn himself.

Dunn's contribution to the study of Paul and his work within the new perspective has continued to influence generations of scholars, who, though they may not agree with him, must nonetheless engage with his influential contributions. As we will see going forward, Dunn's work stands at the fount of the next series of conversations, and he remains one of the main voices within the study of Paul, within both the church and the academy.

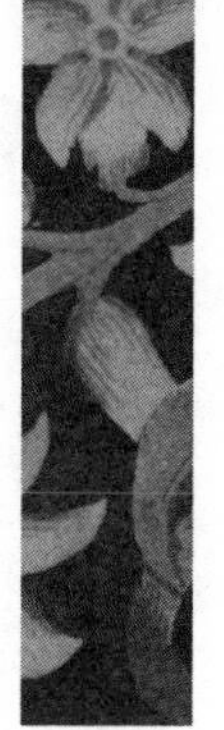

five

THE NEW APOCALYPTIC PAUL

Apocalyptic is the mother of all Christian theology.

ERNST KÄSEMANN, "THE BEGINNINGS OF CHRISTIAN THEOLOGY"

It is clear that the apocalyptic study of Paul is in a renaissance period that is now in full swing.[1] But before a survey of the older and current apocalyptic interpreters of Paul, we must confront the perennial problem of defining our terms. Over the course of the past few centuries the term *apocalyptic* and its related cognates (*apocalypticism, apocalypse,* etc.) have been hard to define, let alone finding a consensus about definitions among scholars from a variety of fields. The lack of coherence in terminology has contributed to the disarray among the responses in the field as to just what is being argued, debated, agreed, or disagreed about.

WHAT IS APOCALYPTIC/APOCALYPTICISM?

The word *apocalypse* was introduced into the academic discourse in 1832 by Gottfried Christian Lücke in his introduction to the book of Revelation. The term is a modern label that is used to analyze a set of texts and

[1]Just some of the recent titles are Ben Blackwell, John K. Goodrich, and Jason Matson, eds., *Paul and the Apocalyptic Imagination* (Minneapolis: Fortress, 2016); Beverly Roberts Gaventa, ed., *Apocalyptic Paul: Cosmos and Anthropos in Romans 5–8* (Waco, TX: Baylor University Press, 2013), J. P. Davies, *Paul Among the Apocalypses?: An Evaluation of the "Apocalyptic Paul" in the Context of Jewish and Christian Apocalyptic Literature* (New York: T&T Clark, 2016).

ideas. Early research into apocalyptic focused primarily on Daniel and Revelation. It was the discovery of numerous apocalyptic texts in the early nineteenth century, such as 1 Enoch, that reinvigorated the field. Early interpretations of such books, with their expectation of the end, hope for another world, and use of complex images, led to the conclusion that apocalyptic came from a distinct form of Judaism in the first century that was in contrast to those based on careful interpretation of the law of Moses. Christopher Rowland has highlighted this in an illuminating quote from Philip Vielhauer, who helped define the field: "We may designate apocalyptic as a special expression of Jewish eschatology which existed alongside the national eschatology represented by the rabbis. It is linked with the latter by many ideas, but is differentiated from it by a quite different understanding of God, the world, and humanity."[2] Several issues in the statement above, such as the appeal to "national eschatology" and the role of rabbinics in the first century, have been challenged by subsequent scholarship. However, Vielhauer's assessment of the features *typical* of apocalypticism influenced the subsequent discussion. He included the following elements as characteristic of apocalypticism:

- The present age is temporary and perishable in contrast with the age to come, which is eternal and imperishable.
- The new age is of a transcendent nature breaking in from outside through divine intervention and without the aid of human activity.
- It involves what we might call a more global, as in cosmological, viewpoint rather than just focusing on Israel herself.
- It involves an interest in world history.
- Everything that happens has been predestined by God.
- World history is divided into epochs.
- It includes the expectation that the present world and its negative aspects will end quickly.

---

[2]Christopher Rowland, "Apocalypticism," in *Eerdmans Dictionary of Early Judaism*, ed. John J. Collins and Daniel C. Harlow (Grand Rapids: Eerdmans, 2010), 345.

The late twentieth century saw an attempt to bring order and definition to the categories of apocalyptic.[3] There arose the differentiation between an apocalypse as a literary genre and apocalyptic as a movement or way of viewing the world. From here the rise of a semantic domain of terms also arose, such as *apocalypticism* as a feature of social ideology and the ever-confusing term *apocalyptic eschatology* to refer to thematic issues that were unhelpfully defined too broadly.

John Collins helped define the literary genre of apocalypse in 1979 in the journal *Semeia*. The definition of apocalyptic offered by Collins was based on a survey of Jewish and Christian writings from 250 BCE to 250 CE as well as other texts from Gnostic, Greco-Roman, Persian, and related Jewish writings. Collins and others proposed that an apocalypse was "a narrative in which a revelation is mediated by an otherworldly being to a human recipient, disclosing a transcendent reality that is both temporal, insofar as it envisages eschatological salvation, and spatial, insofar as it involves another, supernatural world."[4]

Although the definition has found wide acceptance, confusion arose as to how various interpreters used similar terms in different, contradicting, and indeed confusing ways. Even in the foreword to a work on the importance of apocalyptic in the New Testament, the editors note, "At times the word describes a genre of literature (apocalypse), at times it describes a type of eschatology, at times it describes a social movement (apocalypticism), and at times it describes a way of looking at the world."[5] Confusion besets the entire edifice, as John Collins has noted that "from the beginning it was not clear whether *Apokalyptic* designated a literary genre or kind of theology."[6]

---

[3]John J. Collins, "The Apocalyptic Genre," in *The Apocalyptic Imagination: An Introduction to Jewish Apocalyptic Literature*, 3rd ed. (Grand Rapids: Eerdmans, 2016) 1-52; Collins, "What Is Apocalyptic Literature?," in *The Oxford Handbook of Apocalyptic Literature*, ed. John J. Collins (New York: Oxford University Press, 2014), 1-18.

[4]John J. Collins, "Introduction: Toward the Morphology of a Genre," *Semeia* 14 (1979): 1-20.

[5]Joel Marcus and Marion L. Soards, foreword to *Apocalyptic and the New Testament: Essays in Honor of J. Louis Martyn*, ed. Joel Marcus and Marion L. Soards (Sheffield: JSOT Press, 1989), 7.

[6]Collins, "What Is Apocalyptic Literature?," 1. For a pathway through the often-confusing maze, see the helpful work of R. Barry Matlock, *Unveiling the Apocalyptic Paul: Paul's Interpreters and the Rhetoric of Criticism* (Sheffield: Sheffield Academic Press, 1996).

Such matters are important, as we will see, for the latter issue of apocalyptic as a "kind of theology" came to dominate the discussion surrounding the apocalyptic Paul and which issues are and are not apocalyptic touchstones. By way of example, there is the scene in 2 Corinthians 12:1-4, where Paul speaks of having visions of the apocalyptic variety that we might expect. Likewise, Paul speaks of the "present evil age" in Galatians 1:4 and then even uses the term *apokalypsis* in Galatians 1:12. Such evidence supports the use of the term *apocalyptic*. But what about other features of Paul's thought? Is the sending of Christ an apocalyptic event? Is his death on a cross viewed apocalyptically? What are we to make of the resurrection of Christ, not to mention his return? These issues and more are the precise battleground on which the apocalyptic debate comes to the fore.

Our understanding of the nature of the apocalyptic material is vastly aided by the insights from the Dead Sea Scrolls. The discovery revolutionized New Testament studies in general and the apocalyptic conversation in particular. By *revolutionized* I mean complicated our simple definitions. As mentioned above, the scholarly assessment was at one point dominated by the apocalyptic features of Daniel and Revelation. However, in light of the evidence from the Dead Sea Scrolls, this vista became enlarged, deepened, and to some extent problematized. In addition to the canonical books of Daniel and Revelation, one must now take account of 1–2 Enoch, 2–3 Baruch, the Assumption of Moses, and the Apocalypse of Abraham, as well as numerous other texts. As Jörg Frey has argued, and it should not be underestimated, "any further discussion of apocalyptic must be deemed insufficient if it does not take into consideration this vast amount of evidence."[7] As we will see, the study of apocalyptic in Paul has often failed to do this. Of course, we cannot anachronistically judge scholars who did not have such sources available to them. However, we must gauge the more recent and current apocalyptic

[7]Jörg Frey, "Demythologizing Apocalyptic?," in *God and the Faithfulness of Paul*, ed. Christoph Heilig, J. Thomas Hewitt, and Michael F. Bird (Minneapolis: Fortress, 2017), 513.

interpretation of Paul alongside such findings, or we are destined to repeat the errors and confusion of the past.

In a helpful analysis, Jörg Frey has gathered together the "new insights" from this vast amount of literature. I draw out the relevant ones for our discussion, and these include the variety of genres and subgenres and the spatial-versus-temporal orientation of the apocalyptic material. The discovery of numerous apocalyptic texts has shown that "the variety of genres and sub-genres includes a variety of motifs and themes, and there is no motif or theme that is represented in all apocalypses."[8]

Frey's conclusion means that we cannot define apocalyptic on the basis of any particular feature, such as symbolic features, various dualisms, or even the idea of dividing time into two stages (this age versus the age to come). These features alone do not make an apocalypse or make a person of the first century more (or less) apocalyptic than anyone else. To posit distinctions such as *apocalyptic versus salvation historical* fails to take adequate stock of how apocalyptic features are incorporated into various programs of the Second Temple period. Placing this matter within the discussion of Paul, a conclusion is perhaps more apparent. Paul can include apocalyptic elements within various frameworks. If apocalyptic thought, images, and motifs can be incorporated into various genres and programs of Second Temple writers, then Paul is capable of this as well. As will be seen below, it is just this attempt to separate out the Pauline material to which criticism must be directed.

In discussing the spatial-versus-temporal orientation of apocalyptic works, Frey draws on the Book of Watchers and the Apocalypse of Weeks and criticizes approaches that focus on the temporal aspects of apocalypses, noting:

> Apocalyptic as such . . . from its very beginnings [was] not focused on that dimension, nor is it generally characterized by temporal aspects in later

[8]Frey, "Demythologizing Apocalyptic?," 516.

> periods. Jewish (and Christian) apocalypses always imply the spatial dimension in their worldview, and it is, and always has been, erroneous and misleading to "define" apocalyptic from certain kinds of future-oriented eschatology or even "imminent expectation" of the kingdom or a near end.[9]

Frey's conclusion is perhaps most relevant to our discussion below, as it bears on the fraught conversation on the relationship of apocalyptic to history. This conclusion also draws out another corollary of subsequent apocalyptic debate in Paul that came to describe the idea of apocalyptic as an invasion. In light of that ensuing conversation below, we ought to remind ourselves of the following: "Although the expectation of a final defeat of the evil powers is not always related to the earlier (biblical) promises but expected from a new and, in that sense, unexpected divine intervention, *it is actually an expression of faith in God the king and ruler of the universe even though his kingship is often invisible and hidden to humans*."[10] Likewise, Christopher Rowland, among others, has shown how further study has upended some of Vielhauer's distinctions. One important correction is, "Subsequent study has shown that this neat distinction of *Apokalyptik* from other strands of Judaism is fallacious. Not only is eschatological expectation a key aspect of most varieties of ancient Judaism, but a work like *4 Ezra* indicates that the law of Moses could play a key part in apocalyptic literature."[11]

The conclusions can be drawn out even more clearly. We should avoid sharp distinctions when discussing the nature of apocalyptic; as Rowland cautions regarding the apocalyptic content and apocalypticism, "We need to be careful not to assume that there was this radical, and widespread, shift from 'this-worldly' to 'otherworldly in the eschatology of the apocalypses.' The apocalypses reflect the biblical hope for fulfillment in this world."[12] Concerning Pauline texts, some things should now be more evident. Several of the features of the previous list

---

[9]Frey, "Demythologizing Apocalyptic?," 515.

[10]Frey, "Demythologizing Apocalyptic?," 517, emphasis added.

[11]Rowland, "Apocalypticism," 346.

[12]Rowland, "Apocalypticism," 346.

have come to dominate various apocalyptic interpreters of Paul. The critiques of Frey, Rowland, and indeed others have not been heeded.

As will be seen subsequently, one prominent feature emphasized by the emerging apocalyptic school is this "radical" break. However, undercutting such a radicalness is the actual study of the commonness of such elements and inclusion of such features within apocalyptic texts. One might conclude that the matter is, at most, a hermeneutical one. It is an insight, using revelation, that causes one to reread biblical texts and come to somewhat different, perhaps not-before-seen conclusions. An apocalyptic approach is not in spite of scriptural witness, not always in contradiction to the scriptural witness, but sometimes involves its dramatic and paradoxical interpretation.

A SHORT HISTORY OF READING PAUL APOCALYPTICALLY: WHENCE AND WHITHER

A good starting point for the rise of apocalyptic in New Testament studies is Johannes Weiss. He turned the focus of New Testament scholarship to apocalyptic eschatology, by emphasizing apocalyptic as a theological concept rather than a literary one (see the discussion above on apocalyptic as form versus content). Weiss focused on the image of the kingdom of God as a *messianic* kingdom and thus an eschatological/apocalyptic concept. Therefore, nearly all of Jesus' teaching about the kingdom was now deemed apocalyptic.

If it was Weiss who focused on the apocalyptic elements of Jesus, it was Wilhelm Bousset who linked Jesus and Paul on this matter as a consistent aspect of their thinking. The ground work of an apocalyptic reading of Paul had been laid. However, it was Albert Schweitzer who fundamentally altered the course of Pauline research in his *The Mysticism of Paul the Apostle.*[13] He maintained that Paul's thought is "always uniformly dominated" by the return of Jesus, his judgment, and eschatological glory, or, in Schweitzerian terms, Paul is eschatological

---

[13]Albert Schweitzer, *The Mysticism of Paul the Apostle* (New York: Seabury, 1968).

through and through.[14] According to Schweitzer, once the realization of the significance of the death and resurrection of Jesus as a cosmic event was understood in terms of eschatological expectation, then Jesus' own resurrection was seen as the beginning of the resurrection of the dead.

Thus, a traditional eschatology could not be maintained but had to be modified. For Paul, then, the eschatological reality awaiting all believers had to be in line with the very facts of the Messiah appearing in the flesh, dying, and rising again.[15] Schweitzer strongly emphasized the messianic component of apocalyptic thought. There was a tendency during the early apocalyptic readings of the New Testament to focus on the imminent expectation of the end of the world, or the parousia/ return of Christ, or both. However, since this didn't happen, what is one to do with all of the apocalyptic elements within the New Testament? The stakes were high as apocalyptic thought dominated two of the most prominent figures of the New Testament: Jesus and Paul.

If Schweitzer's Paul was a thoroughgoing apocalyptic thinker, half a century later, it was up to another towering figure in New Testament studies to dismantle such a project. By way of summary, if the general atmosphere of the mid-twentieth century was that the authors of the New Testament had wrongly believed the end of the world was nigh, a salvage attempt needed to be made. One might note the very specific definition of apocalyptic at work in such a climate.

Enter Rudolf Bultmann.[16] It was precisely the apocalyptic elements of both Jesus and Paul that Bultmann sought to render in a modern vernacular in order to understand their message. Such an attempt was necessitated by the context of New Testament studies both prior to and

---

[14]Schweitzer, *Mysticism of Paul the Apostle*, 52.

[15]Schweitzer, *Mysticism of Paul the Apostle*, 100.

[16]In recent years, a renaissance of sorts is underway in the study of Bultmann and his works. See Bruce W. Longenecker and Mikeal C. Parsons, eds., *Beyond Bultmann: Reckoning a New Testament Theology* (Waco, TX: Baylor University Press, 2014); David W. Congdon, *Rudolf Bultmann: A Companion to His Theology* (Eugene, OR: Cascade Books, 2015); Congdon, *The Mission of Demythologizing: Rudolf Bultmann's Dialectical Theology* (Eugene, OR: Cascade Books, 2015).

during Bultmann's day.[17] Bultmann translated the apocalyptic elements of the Gospels and Paul's letters into an existential plea rather than an apocalyptic one. As Richard Hays has wisely noted, Bultmann's *Theology of the New Testament* "is neither an explanation nor a defense of the program of demythologizing; rather, it presupposes the necessity of such a program. The book therefore functions as a *performance*" of that program and its assumptions.[18] It was decades until Bultmann's formidable reconstruction of Paul was challenged. However, the challenge eventually arose and came from none other than one of Bultmann's own students: Ernst Käsemann.

The rediscovery of apocalyptic features of Paul's thought was at the heart of Käsemann's work and a direct challenge to the ideas of Bultmann, his teacher. If Bultmann saw apocalyptic as a trapping to be explained away or translated into a modern *lingua*, Käsemann saw it as the generative center of Paul's thought. Such an insight led Käsemann to argue, famously, that apocalyptic is the "mother of all Christian theology."[19] Käsemann places the apocalyptic character of Paul's thought back into the conversation. For him, the apocalyptic view dominates not only Paul's outline of history (defined in epochs such as Adam, Moses, Christ, etc.) but also the fate of people, the world, and even his mission to the Gentiles.[20] Apocalyptic is all-encompassing. Essentially, for Käsemann, apocalyptic is ultimately the history of the cosmos; its creation; its ruler, Jesus the Lord; God's righteousness; and justification. Apocalyptic thought is tied to the sovereignty of God over his creation and the attempt to get creation and its creatures back under their rightful ruler. Although sidelined for decades, the apocalyptic Paul was now back in play, thus setting the stage for subsequent studies. Such

[17]See Angela Standhartinger's excellent essay "Bultmann's *Theology of the New Testament* in Context," in Longenecker and Parsons, *Beyond Bultmann*, 233-55.

[18]Richard B. Hays, "Humanity Prior to the Revelation of Faith," in Longenecker and Parsons, *Beyond Bultmann*, 72.

[19]Ernst Käsemann, "The Beginnings of Christian Theology," in *New Testament Questions of Today*, trans. W. J. Montague (Philadelphia: Fortress, 1969), 102.

[20]Ernst Käsemann, *Perspectives on Paul* (Philadelphia: Fortress, 1971), 24.

an emphasis on apocalyptic positioned Käsemann as the intellectual grandfather to the new apocalyptic school.[21]

How might we assess Käsemann's view of apocalyptic? Since the term is used ambiguously in New Testament studies, it is always helpful to know how a particular author is using the term, and even more so in this case given the influence Käsemann had on subsequent studies. His view of apocalyptic is indebted to Philipp Vielhauer, focused on the aspects of a dualistic worldview involving two stages (eons) and a deterministic view of history, rendered a negative view of the present, and finally involved the imminent expectation of the parousia.[22] Within this approach, then, two features came to dominate Käsemann's proposal on Paul: that Christ is taking over a rebellious cosmos—he is the rightful *Lord* of the world—and that God's righteousness is the avenue that Paul chooses to pursue. According to Käsemann, this inbreaking of God creates a new world, which causes one to wonder, What is the relationship between the old world and the new one?

One of the perennial questions surrounding an apocalyptic reading is whether apocalyptic thought is opposed to history. As criticisms of apocalyptic interpretations of Paul go, one sees this question raised often in current debates. The issue of the relationship of apocalyptic to history can be traced back to the work of Gerhard von Rad. As Richard Sturm notes in an immensely helpful article, there is an inherent assumption that "apocalyptic has an inadequate appreciation for history."[23] Von Rad states that salvation in apocalyptic thought "has moved out to the fringes of history . . . to the dawning of salvation at the end . . . or, to be more precise, soteriological depletion of history."[24]

[21]A title given to Käsemann by Jörg Frey in "Demythologizing Apocalyptic?," 503.

[22]Philipp Vielhauer, "Apocalypses and Related Subjects," in *New Testament Apocrypha* (Louisville, KY: Westminster John Knox, 2003), 2:542-68.

[23]Richard E. Sturm, "Defining the Word 'Apocalyptic': A Problem in Biblical Criticism," in *Apocalyptic and the New Testament: Essays in Honor of J. Louis Martyn*, ed. Joel Marcus and Marion L. Soards (Sheffield: JSOT Press, 1989), 29. Sturm provides a wonderful outline of the history of research and was immensely helpful in providing contours to frame the historical debate in this chapter.

[24]Sturm, "Defining the Word 'Apocalyptic,'" 29, quoting Gerhard von Rad, *Old Testament Theology* (New York: Harper & Row, 1965), 2:273.

Käsemann reinvigorated this discussion of the relationship of apocalyptic to history by including cosmology within his apocalyptic frame and thus sees the Christian faith as bearing on the issues of history and time itself. According to Frey, Käsemann's view of apocalyptic was shaped by the cross event. Frey notes the "apocalyptic event in which all worldly wisdom was turned upside down (cf. 1 Cor 1:18-25) [so] then the essence of the Christian faith could also be characterized as radically other worldly, fundamentally questioning other human religious views."[25]

What are we to make of such claims and arguments? One of the primary challenges is that this radical break with "the world" has implications for Paul's relationship to Judaism. One key assumption made by Käsemann and others is that Paul has added his Jewish contemporaries to this category of "worldly wisdom." Is this so? It would be obviously problematic to assume such a relationship between Paul and his Jewish contemporaries were it not for a certain reading of the issue in 1 Corinthians 1:18-25, where Paul is *not* mainly talking to Jewish contemporaries but to Corinthian Gentiles, shaped as they were by the Hellenistic sophist tradition.

Yet, one ought to note that in 1 Corinthians 1:18-25, every time Paul talks about wisdom, he associated it with the Greeks, not Jews. There it is Jews who demand "signs" and Greeks who desire "wisdom" (1 Cor 1:22). Christ is a "stumbling block" to Jews, but "foolishness" to Greeks—notice the contrast between foolishness and wisdom (1 Cor 1:23). While Paul says both Jews and Greeks are called, and while Paul notes that Christ is the power of God and the wisdom of God, both these nicely line up with the previous comparisons whereby wisdom aligns again with the Greeks. It is pressing too hard to take an argument Paul aims at Greek thinkers and reverse it and apply it to other first-century Jewish questions. To put it more precisely, according to Paul, the issue of the cross in 1 Corinthians 1:18-25 for his Jewish

---

[25]Frey, "Demythologizing Apocalyptic?," 508.

contemporaries is one of a stumbling block and weakness, not necessarily "worldly wisdom" on how one views the cross. Difficult to comprehend, yes, but it's not foolishness.

To return once more to Käsemann, given the context in which he operated, that is, against the backdrop of the towering figure of Bultmann and a history-of-religions school aiming to Hellenize Paul, one ought to note his success in recovering a critical piece of Schweitzer's thought that it was *Jewish* apocalyptic that shaped Paul rather than Hellenistic categories. The pendulum had swung back to Jewish soil. Likewise, in contrast to Bultmann, Käsemann did not go the route of demythologizing and negating the future-oriented aspects of Paul's thought but instead came to view them as essential and at the center of Paul's thought. Käsemann put forth a radical vision of Paul that captured and enraptured his students as well as subsequent interpreters of Paul. His work reinvigorated, if not established, an apocalyptic stream of Pauline interpretation. Apocalyptic interpretation of Paul was back on center stage.

APOCALYPTIC READINGS OF PAUL TODAY

The stage having been set, a new generation of scholars took up the mantle of Käsemann and continued down the path laid out by him, with some modifications, as will be seen shortly. The renewal of apocalyptic trends in the study of Paul is a unique feature of what may be called the Union school due to the influence of Martyn and Beker on a generation of students who passed through the halls and classrooms of Union Theological Seminary in New York. The following section traces the work of J. Christiaan Beker, Louis Martyn, Martinus de Boer, and Beverly Gaventa and their impact, which has set the current trajectory for the apocalyptic renaissance.

Beker and the coherence of apocalyptic. J. Christaan Beker was the Richard J. Dearborn Professor of New Testament Theology at Princeton Theological Seminary for thirty years. He was the author of the influential *Paul's Apocalyptic Gospel: The Coming Triumph of God* (1982) and

The Triumph of God: The Essence of Paul's Thought (1990).[26] He is perhaps best known for his terminology of coherence and contingency to describe Paul's thought, combined with an emphasis on the apocalyptic character of Paul's thought. Beker maintains that Paul's unique contribution as a New Testament writer is not necessarily any new theological or doctrinal observation but instead *his hermeneutic*. It is Paul's interpretive ability to translate the consistent elements of the gospel (coherence) into specific situations and communities (contingency) that is his lasting legacy. Furthermore, as Beker wades into the raging waters of Pauline interpretation, he champions the view that the center of Paul's thought is "the triumph of God in Christ." Beker's "double thesis" is concerned not only with Paul's hermeneutic of coherence and contingency but also the apocalyptic theme that shapes the entire project.

Beker argues that Paul's hermeneutic has been divorced from Paul's thought and that Paul's thought has been stripped of its apocalyptic character, especially by figures such as Bultmann. Beker sets forth that Paul's "coherent center" must be understood as a "symbolic structure" seeking to express the Christ event (the death and resurrection) in the language of apocalyptic Judaism. However, Beker argues that the Christ event "modifies Paul's traditional apocalyptic language" so that it becomes a "Christian apocalyptic structure of thought." As such, the Christ event is unintelligible without attention to its apocalyptic character. He further claims that, both implicitly and explicitly, all of Paul's apocalyptically infused contingent hermeneutical strategy points to the coherent core of Paul's thought, the "imminent cosmic triumph of God."[27]

According to Beker, the coherent center of Paul's theology is thoroughly apocalyptic, and this predilection for apocalyptic *preceded* Paul's

---

[26]J. Christiaan Beker, *Paul's Apocalyptic Gospel: The Coming Triumph of God* (Philadelphia: Fortress, 1982); Beker, *The Triumph of God: The Essence of Paul's Thought* (Philadelphia: Fortress, 1990).

[27]J. Christaan Beker, *Paul the Apostle: The Triumph of God in Life and Thought* (Philadelphia: Fortress, 1980), 15-16, 19.

conversion/call and was part of his Pharisaic background but was modified by the Christ event. Beker, following the impetus of Käsemann, seeks to offer a fresh understanding of Paul based on a "consistent apocalyptic interpretation of Paul's thought." Beker identifies three main features of apocalyptic that characterize Paul's thought: (1) historical dualism, (2) universal cosmic expectation, and (3) the imminent end of the world. He notes that Paul is not the only figure who is misunderstood outside an apocalyptic frame of thought, and he mentions the Qumran community, the Sicarii, and the Zealots as other groups similar to Paul.

The brief description above is as close to a definition of apocalyptic as we receive from Beker. What is interesting about Beker's treatment is that by his time of writing, well after Käsemann, he is still reliant on the same sources of Philipp Vielhauer (1963) and Klaus Kloch (1972), which results in an inadequate notion of apocalyptic. A dualism alone does not an apocalypse make, nor do the other two features he points out. Beker responds to criticisms of his limited approach to apocalyptic in his 1990 work, *The Triumph of God,* where he notes that his definition of apocalyptic was lacking, and that he had "neglected perhaps the most important aspect of biblical apocalyptic: the faithfulness and trustworthiness of God."[28]

Beker, more than others that followed him, argues for a via media in the debates between salvation history and apocalyptic categories for interpreting Paul. Although working with an inadequate definition, he comes to some rather startling conclusions on the role of the faithfulness of God vis-à-vis apocalyptic. We might characterize his approach as a both/and rather than an either-or. Beker's persistent refusal to allow apocalyptic dualism to slip into a Gnostic dualism perhaps gave room for new proposals. Certainly, the addition that the faithfulness of God was at stake in an apocalyptic conversation provided new insights, even if subsequent interpreters did not follow the path he laid down.

[28]Beker, *Triumph of God*, 64, 136, 143.

Such conclusions led Beker to an astute comment on the nature of the relationship between God's action before and after Christ. Beker wisely notes, "The history of Israel is for Paul not simply the old age of darkness," but rather, as Beker sees, "the past is not just the age of sin and death but also the era of God's salvation-historical imprint. . . . The past contains the footprints of the promises of God, and these promises are taken up into the new rather than cast aside."[29] Beker argues that even in spite of the ensuing events of the apocalyptic moment for Paul, this does not render everything that has come before as incomplete or unnecessary. Beker stands within these two traditions of reading Paul (apocalyptic versus salvation historical) but attempts to maintain the best of both. It seems, however, in the current state of things that Beker has not been as influential on the apocalyptic school as his contemporary and colleague to whom we now turn.

J. Louis Martyn: (Re)enter apocalypse now. J. Louis Martyn was the Edward Robinson Professor of Biblical Theology at Union Theological Seminary in New York from 1959–1987. Martyn had a prolific career that spanned Jesus studies early on and Pauline studies in the second stage of his career. His work issued forth in a landmark volume on the Gospel of John and later the Anchor Bible commentary on Galatians. Much of Martyn's work on an apocalyptic reading of Paul appeared in numerous journals, which were helpfully collected in the volume *Theological Issues in the Letters of Paul* (1997) and culminated in his landmark commentary on Galatians (1997). Several of his articles bear on our task here and not only form the contours of Martyn's apocalyptic Paul but exerted quite an impact on subsequent scholarship.

We begin with Martyn's foundational article, published in 1967 and titled "Epistemology at the Turn of the Ages: 2 Corinthians 5:16," which lays out some of the philosophical underpinnings of his apocalyptic reading of Paul. According to Martyn, to make sense of these verses we must understand that Paul establishes "an inextricable connection

[29]Beker, *Paul the Apostle*, 150.

between eschatology and epistemology."[30] Martyn's understanding of Paul's way of *knowing* is shaped by his understanding of 2 Corinthians 2:14–6:10. From this, he draws several implications. According to his reading, Paul's prior knowledge of Christ was *kata sarka*, or according to the flesh. Taking the domain of *sarx*/flesh as negative in Paul (although one may note this is not always so), Martyn offers a comparison to an unlikely contemporary, Philo, perhaps one of the most nonapocalyptic writers of the first century. It is not clear that Philo's distinction between dual understandings of flesh and how it is perceived is altogether parallel to that of Paul's. Paul's way of knowing is fundamentally shaped by the cross. We quote Martyn at length here:

> It is clear that the implied opposite of knowing by the norm of the flesh is not knowing by the norm of the Spirit, but rather knowing *kata stauron* ("by the cross"). Those who recognize their life to be God's gift at the juncture of the ages recognize also that until they are completely and exclusively in the new age, their knowing by the Spirit can occur only in the form of knowing by the power of the cross. For until the parousia, the cross is and remains the epistemological crisis, and thus the norm by which one knows that the Spirit is none other than the Spirit of the crucified Christ.[31]

A significant shift in the apocalyptic conversation takes place here with Marytn's work. In contrast to Käsemann, who sees the parousia as the apocalyptic event, Martyn reframes the apocalyptic focus on the cross as the sine qua non of Paul's apocalyptic thought. In this article, the apocalyptic foundations are laid for the future direction of Martyn's contributions. We see the buzzwords of apocalyptic resonating through his thinking, such as "the juncture of the ages," the concentration on knowing, the language of epistemology, and the centrality of the cross as the apocalyptic event par excellence. Such intertwining threads will soon be woven together to form the apocalyptic backdrop of Martyn's reading of Paul.

---

[30]J. Louis Martyn, "Epistemology at the Turn of the Ages: 2 Corinthians 5:16," in *Theological Issues in the Letters of Paul* (Edinburgh: T&T Clark, 1997), 92.

[31]Martyn, "Epistemology at the Turn of the Ages," 108.

One of Martyn's lasting contributions was the shift in focus of the apocalyptic conversation by bringing Galatians into the apocalyptic orbit. A corollary of Käsemann's concentration on the parousia as the main apocalyptic event is that Galatians was thought to have little to do with apocalyptic thought, since the parousia does not appear in the letter. The irony is deep in light of Martyn's subsequent work. Not only does Martyn attempt to show that Galatians was apocalyptic through and through, but the letter to the Galatians also has the word *apokalypsis* in it (Gal 1:12)!

One of the earliest attempts of Martyn to reread Galatians apocalyptically was his 1985 article "Apocalyptic Antinomies." Several problems plague Martyn's apocalyptic reading of Galatians. The key that opened the apocalyptic lock on Galatians for Martyn is in the final paragraph of the Galatian letter, and he highlights Galatians 6:13-15. Martyn notes: "Paul refers . . . to two different worlds. He speaks of an old world, from which he has painfully been separated, by Christ's death, by the death of that world, and by his own death. And he speaks of a new world, which he grasps under the arresting expression, new creation."[32] It is the language of the death of a cosmos and new creation that Martyn takes as pivotal to understanding Galatians in apocalyptic categories and thus forces a rereading of the letter as a whole. The death of the old world and the rebirth of a new creation in a new cosmos expresses, for Martyn, a central opposition, or what he identifies as an *antinomy*.

As Martyn states in a footnote and implies in the title of his 1985 article, he is concerned with *antinomies*. By this term he means, "Paul embraces as a major factor in his theology the pattern of mutually exclusive opposition" and notes that the concern of the essay is to "approach the question of 'Paul and apocalyptic' by taking one's bearings from pairs of opposites."[33] He does stress that he is not speaking of an

---

[32]Martyn, "Apocalyptic Antinomies," in *Theological Issues in the Letters of Paul*, 114. In a note to this sentence in the article, Martyn himself admits that the expression itself "scarcely decides the issue" but that new creation language is "at home in apocalyptic."

[33]Martyn, "Apocalyptic Antinomies," 114n12.

antithesis but rather *antinomy* in the full Greek sense of the word, where it relates to the philosophical view of the cosmos as being composed of opposites (right and left, male and female, etc.). However, it is hard to see how antinomy does not slip into outright antithesis as he proceeds in his argument.

Martyn takes Paul to be denying a fundamental aspect of the ancient world, that it thought in terms of opposites as a foundational part of the cosmos, with his statement in Galatians 6:14 that neither circumcision nor uncircumcision is anything. By denying this ontological reality, Martyn argues Paul is showing, and the Galatians would have known, that in "denying real existence to an antinomy" Paul shows the "old cosmos has suffered its death."[34] By this analogy Martyn derives an insight that is central and illuminating to his project and deserves full quotation. Martyn states:

> Perhaps in this final paragraph Paul is telling the Galatians that the whole of his epistle is not about the better of two mystagogues, or even about the better of two ways, and certainly not about the failure of Judaism. He is saying rather, that the letter is about the death of one world, and the advent of another. With regard to the former, the death of the cosmos, perhaps Paul is telling the Galatians that one knows the old world to have died, because one knows that its fundamental structures are gone, that those fundamental structures of the cosmos were certain identifiable pairs of opposites, and that, given the situation among their congregations in Galatia, the pair of opposites whose departure calls for emphasis is that of circumcision and uncircumcision.[35]

The whole edifice of Martyn's proposal is based on the centrality of the idea of antinomy. One should not underestimate the weight that this proposal places on one philosophical concept that is assumed to be common knowledge on the part not only of Paul but of those in Galatia as well. It is the death of the old cosmos, including the law, that bears on Paul's apocalyptic message. The proposal is no less tantalizing

[34]Martyn, "Apocalyptic Antinomies," 117.
[35]Martyn, "Apocalyptic Antinomies," 118.

than it is all-encompassing. For Martyn, the dismantling of antinomies is an apocalyptic event. Such a thesis on the death of the old cosmos has implications, and this leads Martyn to place the law in the old cosmos.

In speaking of law, Martyn employs nothing less than a process of demythologization, which is all the more paradoxical in light of the work of Käsemann and does not seem to comport with the argument of apocalyptic post-Käsemann. Martyn states, "Paul repeatedly reinforces this matter of loss of cosmos. Using Jewish terms, because of the nature of the Teachers' message, Paul nevertheless presents a universal picture."[36] It is hard to see any other way of reading this than a kernel-and-husk approach to Paul and apocalyptic. To put it rather bluntly, Paul really had a universal message but couched it in Jewish terms for his audience. Our task is to dehusk the Jewish aspects, and that leaves us with the universal, timeless principle.

Such a universalizing of Paul's message, especially after Stendahl's emphasis on the uniqueness of Paul's message, runs radically counter to other major interpretations of Paul. Such an attempt leads Martyn into another problematic issue. Given the universalizing aspect of Paul's message, this turns Paul's opposition to "religion" itself, or one might say in light of the argument by Martyn, to "mere religion." As Martyn states, "For crucifixion with Christ means the death of the cosmos of religion."[37] Such a statement is profound because it occurs after Sanders's *Paul and Palestinian Judaism*. We will return to this problematic issue of Martyn below, but for now we must address the conclusion of Martyn's proposal. The death of the cosmos and its antinomies is not the death of antinomies itself but of *specific* antimonies, as Martyn argues that new antinomies emerge.

These new antinomies are essential, as they came to introduce the language from which subsequent apocalyptic interpretations of Paul drew. The new antinomies that emerge are apocalyptic, since they are

---

[36]Martyn, "Apocalyptic Antinomies," 118.

[37]Martyn, "Apocalyptic Antinomies," 119.

"cosmic in scope" and "they are being born in the apocalypse of Christ." The Spirit and flesh are two of the new antinomies of the new apocalyptic eon. The sending of Christ and the Spirit is fundamental, as it was "*the* cosmic apocalyptic event. There was a 'before,' and there is now an 'after.' . . . It is at this point at which the 'after' *invades* the 'before.'" As Martyn states: "The Spirit and the Flesh constitute an apocalyptic antinomy, in the sense that they are two opposed orbs of power, actively at war with one another since the advent of the Spirit. The territory in which human beings now live is a newly invaded space, and that means that its structures cannot remain unchanged."[38]

The language and imagery of invasion, warfare, and orbs/spheres of power came to characterize apocalyptic interpretation of Paul, and it began here with Martyn. In this paradigm, the law, circumcision, and all pairs of opposites have been replaced or at least rearranged under a new antinomy. Now the law and circumcision have been realigned under the power "Flesh," which stands in opposition to Spirit. One wonders whether Paul was attuned to these categories.

A few issues stand out for comment. There is no doubt about the changing of the eons for Paul, namely, that this age is "evil" and the Galatians have been delivered from it by the death of Christ (Gal 1:4). Likewise, it is undoubtedly clear that baptism is identified with death in Christ and ultimately death to the world and its way of knowing. It is not entirely clear, however, that the categories are so binary and opposite.

It is convenient if one can pick and choose one's antinomies, to talk about the death of antinomies, only to reintroduce "correct" antinomies later on. While Martyn wants to discuss the end of antinomies as the death of the cosmos and the law, one is struck by the reintroduction, seemingly without argument, of the new antinomies he proposes. Further complicating this picture, even if one takes the antinomies offered by Martyn, is law itself always opposed to Spirit? Particularly problematic is Paul's ambiguous phrase "the law of Christ" in Galatians

[38]Martyn, "Apocalyptic Antinomies," 120-21, first emphasis original, second emphasis added.

6:2. Although we do not have space here to investigate a phrase that has perplexed many, we can at least note that in the antinomies that Martyn has set up, we are at least intrigued if not confused to see the reemergence of law. That Paul can refer to the law of Christ within this new apocalyptic age at least challenges the strong binary that Martyn proposes and blurs the lines Martyn seeks to establish. This is especially the case when one probes a little deeper and discovers that by the phrase "the law of Christ" Paul means Jesus' interpretation of some things in the OT law that he reaffirms, for instance no adultery.[39]

A further critique has to do with the use of "invasion" language to describe apocalyptic thought. The critical evaluation of Jörg Frey is immensely helpful on this precise point. Apocalyptic writers and texts could and do speak of the radical corruptibility of the world (see the Apocalypse of Weeks). However, they are also able to discuss how God might interact or intervene with this problematic situation, whether through a messianic agent (or not), through some form of judgment, or even through destruction. There is an extensive range of options available. As Frey perceptively and judiciously states, seemingly with Martyn and the apocalyptic interpreters of Paul in mind:

> If some exegetes use the military imagery of a divine "invasion" into the cosmos, this is rather anachronistic. In antiquity, the world was not considered a closed space of "immanence," strictly separated from the realm of "transcendence," since God the creator and ruler of the universe was always thought to be able to intervene in his creation. Even if evil powers were thought to rule the world or a portion of it (cf. the Treatise on the Two Spirits from Qumran; 1QS III, 13-IV, 26), such an authority was always thought to be given only for a certain time or space and subject to God's permission. In the final visitation or in various acts of judgment God was considered to make an end to the evil powers. But an eschatological purification (1QS IV, 23-26) or even battle (1QM) was not considered an "invasion" of God into a realm that was not originally and legitimately his own. On the other hand, the strict presupposition of a "space-time

[39]On which see Ben Witherington III, *Grace in Galatia* (Grand Rapids: Eerdmans, 1998), on Gal 6.

> continuum" is likewise a modern concept that should not be used to limit the creative and judicial power of God.[40]

Martyn's proposal of an invasion is shown to be deeply flawed and to be a seeming modern attempt to make sense of an ancient world. Frey concludes that the approach sketched out above is "inappropriate in view of the variety of Jewish apocalyptic texts." Despite the inadequacy of the invasion language, it came to shape the apocalyptic discussion of Paul dramatically, as will be seen in subsequent interpreters.

In 1993 Martyn penned "God's Way of Making Right What Is Wrong" and introduced the concept and influential wording of "anti-God powers," which came to characterize his students (most notably Gaventa) and the subsequent apocalyptic interpretation of Paul. In this article, Martyn takes as his central focus Galatians 2:16 and the testimony of Paul to a Jewish-Christian legacy he inherited, referred to as "rectification" (this is Martyn's preferred term for justification). Martyn employs what he labels "a Jewish-Christian tradition about rectification," a tradition that Martyn argues Paul uses in Galatians 2:16, Romans (Rom 3:25; 4:25), and 1 Corinthians (1 Cor 6:11). He argues that this tradition was agreed on by Paul, other Jewish-Christians, and most notably by the "teachers" in Galatia. Paul's contribution, according to Martyn, which differentiates Paul from the Jewish-Christian leadership as well as the teachers, is his inclusion of what Martyn calls the "anti-God powers." It is Paul who conceives of the law as an anti-God power as it pronounces a curse on all humanity, and so God is now on a collision course with the law itself, which has subsumed humanity in slavery. In stunning prose, Martyn describes that "with the appearance of these anti-God powers, the landscape is fundamentally changed. . . . The cosmic landscape now proves to be a *battlefield*, and in that setting the need of human beings is not so much forgiveness of their sins as deliverance from the malignant powers that hold them in bondage."[41]

---

[40]Frey, "Demythologizing Apocalyptic?," 519.

[41]Martyn, "God's Way of Making Right What Is Wrong," in *Theological Issues in the Letters of Paul*, 141, 152-53, emphasis original.

Several issues are worthy of note in Martyn's presentation of the law. One of the striking problems is that Martyn's reading of Galatians 3:6–4:7 is entirely devoid, and one might indeed say stripped, of its references to the Hebrew Scriptures. Such a move is quite necessary to make such profound statements about the law. One example of note relates to the law and the curse terminology. Paul writes in Galatians 3:13, "Christ redeemed us from the curse of the law." Two questions emerge: Who is "us," and what is the "curse of the law"? We will take the latter question first, as it provides insight to the former.

Those not attuned to the language and resonances of the Hebrew Scriptures might mistakenly read Paul's phrase to mean "the law *is* the curse," in that it burdens us and points out our wrongdoings. Such a generalized reading, of course, is not indebted to Paul as much as to the theological inheritors of Paul. Likewise, if one wants to talk about an *actual* curse that the law produces, one might take notice of the language of blessing and curse at the end of Deuteronomy. It is here that a national curse is placed on Israel for failing (ultimately) to obey the covenant, and the *actual curse* of the law of Moses is national exile or scattering, enacted in 722 and 586 BCE in two stages. Deuteronomy ends not on the note of curse but blessing. If Israel repents and turns back, God will bring it back from the foreign lands and restore its fortunes. Likewise, Deuteronomy discusses the exile as a return to slavery (Deut 28:68) and explains why Paul, if he is evoking the national curse of Deuteronomy, might use the verb *exagorazō*. This also explains why Martyn sees Paul talking about not the forgiveness of sins in relation to the law but "deliverance from genuine slavery."[42]

To return to the first question, the identity of the "us" who are redeemed from the law, it is not humanity in general (contra Martyn) but specifically Israel. Paul and his fellow Jewish Christians are in view. Christ redeems Israel from the curse of the law *so that* the Gentiles can receive God's blessing (Gal 3:14; see Gen 15). It is not, as Martyn would

[42]Martyn, "God's Way of Making Right What Is Wrong," 153.

have it, that the law has brought "all humanity" under its curse, for the Gentiles are not under the Mosaic law. Indeed, Paul's point is exactly the opposite. It is precisely because the Gentiles are not under a curse that they are not at the present state under the law. Hence Paul's adamant statements to not turn back.

Although there are issues with Martyn's reading of Galatians 3–4, what is clear is that his language to *describe* his interpretation of Paul has come to influence the discussion in its present form. One will notice below just how much the current conversation on Paul and apocalyptic is indebted to Martyn's language and imagery. Such should not be surprising, as the discussion has been guided by two of his former students: Martinus de Boer and Beverly Gaventa.

Martinus de Boer: Extending and expanding Martyn. Martinus de Boer is Emeritus Professor of New Testament at the VU University Amsterdam, a post he held until 2012. De Boer received his PhD in 1983 from Union Theological Seminary under the supervision of Martyn. De Boer's dissertation, "The Defeat of Death: Apocalyptic Eschatology in Romans 5 and 1 Corinthians 15," came to be influential in Martyn's thinking about Paul and apocalyptic.[43] De Boer's discussion of apocalyptic and Martyn's have informed and reinforced each other's work. The thrust of de Boer's work has been through a series of articles, culminating, like Martyn, in a commentary on Galatians.[44]

A primary emphasis of de Boer's work on Paul is the term *apocalyptic eschatology,* as he states: "In publications devoted to the 'apocalyptic Paul,' I have consistently used the term 'apocalyptic' as an adjective modifying the noun 'eschatology.'" By this he uses the argument of Paul D. Hanson to argue that Jewish apocalyptic eschatology involved "a religious perspective, a way of viewing divine plans in relation to mundane realities" and concerns God's "final saving acts." Further, these final

[43]Martinus C. de Boer, *The Defeat of Death: Apocalyptic Eschatology in Romans 5 and 1 Corinthians 15* (Sheffield: Sheffield Academic Press, 1988).

[44]Martinus C. de Boer, "Paul and Apocalyptic Eschatology," in *The Origins of Apocalypticism in Judaism and Christianity*, vol. 1 of *The Encyclopedia of Apocalypticism*, ed. John J. Collins (New York: Continuum, 2000), 345-83; de Boer, *Galatians* (Louisville, KY: Westminster John Knox, 2011).

divine saving acts involve "deliverance out of the present order into a new transformed order" of reality."[45] Building on a reality seen in Revelation, de Boer appeals to Revelation 21:1-2 and the passing away of the first heaven and earth along with the arrival of a new heaven and earth to argue, controversially,

> The expected new order of reality will not be a rehabilitation or a reconfiguration of the present (social and political) order of reality ("this age"), as is generally the case in OT prophetic eschatology, but its termination and replacement by something completely new ("the age to come"). The new Jerusalem will replace the old Jerusalem. The new order of reality will replace the old order of reality, and it will do so definitively, finally, and irrevocably, i.e., eschatologically. This act of replacement will be initiated and brought about by God and God alone, which is to say that it cannot be initiated by human beings or effected by them.[46]

As we have discussed in several places in this chapter, it is precisely this radical break that is most controversial in the apocalyptic interpretation of Paul. The dividing matter among scholars is the precise nature of this break in reality and to what degree continuity and discontinuity ought to influence our interpretation of Paul and key Pauline texts. Even in the quotation above, one notices the continuity embedded in the reality de Boer describes. It is certainly true that the new Jerusalem will replace the old Jerusalem, but we should not miss that it is still *Jerusalem*.

De Boer, like Marytn, emphasizes that the apocalypse Paul describes is none other than the event of Jesus Christ. The unique Pauline twist on the apocalyptic eschatology of his Jewish contemporaries is that "the coming of Jesus Christ God has inaugurated 'the final saving acts' . . . that mark the definitive end of the old order of reality ('this age') and its irrevocable replacement by the new order of reality." Especially regarding Paul, "The Apocalypse of God in Jesus Christ covers

---

[45]Martinus C. de Boer, "Apocalyptic as God's Eschatological Activity," in *Paul and the Apocalyptic Imagination*, ed. Ben C. Blackwell, John K. Goodrich, and Jason Maston (Minneapolis: Fortress, 2016), 45, 49. See also Paul D. Hanson, *The Dawn of Apocalyptic: The Historical and Sociological Roots of Jewish Apocalyptic Eschatology* (Philadelphia: Fortress, 1979).

[46]De Boer, "Apocalyptic as God's Eschatological Activity," 49-50.

events from the initial sending of the Son and his Spirit into the world to the transfer of Christ's messianic sovereignty to God at the End (1 Cor 15:23-28)."[47] This event, however, is a "revealed" event for Paul and thus inherently apocalyptic.

Key to this understanding of apocalyptic eschatology is that the eschatological situation is *revealed.* As de Boer argues, the term *apokalypsis* itself carries the meaning of "unveiling," and, drawing primarily on the book of Revelation, de Boer concludes, "This eschatology is a matter of divine revelation: apocalyptic eschatology is *revealed* eschatology."[48] Paul's use of the language of revelation (Gal 1:12, 16) places him in the apocalyptic world of Second Temple Judaism. The question taken up by de Boer is, Just what type of apocalyptic thinker was Paul?

To answer this question, de Boer importantly introduced a heuristic model for understanding two distinct tracks or patterns within Second Temple Jewish apocalyptic thought.[49] De Boer identified the two tracks as the cosmological and the forensic. Drawing on the works of David S. Russell and Paul D. Hanson, de Boer understands the cosmological strand of Jewish apocalyptic thought as concerned with the narrative that the created world is held hostage by evil powers in a primeval period (usually Noahic) where evil angels overtook the world God had created.

The scenario described above, de Boer says, has led the whole world astray into worshiping idols, including God's people. However, there remain those who are obedient to God and show that the evil powers will pass away. It is precisely this "righteous remnant" who are awaiting God's deliverance, when "God will invade the world under the dominion of the evil powers and defeat them in a cosmic war." The result of the victorious battle of God will result in (1) delivering the righteous and (2) ushering in a new eon where God reigns without opposition.

---

[47]De Boer, "Apocalyptic as God's Eschatological Activity," 52-53.

[48]De Boer, "Apocalyptic as God's Eschatological Activity," 351.

[49]Much of this section derives from de Boer's "Paul and Apocalyptic Eschatology," 345-83. For further discussion see Martinus C. de Boer, "Paul and Jewish Apocalyptic Eschatology," in Marcus and Soards, *Apocalyptic and the New Testament*, 174-84.

As primary evidence of the cosmological view, de Boer points to 1 Enoch 1–36 and the Testament of Moses. Following the argument of Russell, de Boer argues that such a view of apocalyptic suggests that "the two ages are not only the moral epochs but also two spheres or zones in which certain powers hold sway or in which certain kinds of activity take place. The final judgment entails God's defeat and destruction of cosmic evil forces."[50]

The forensic view is the second distinct track that de Boer identifies within Jewish apocalyptic. This track is a modified version of the cosmological, whereby those cosmological evil forces do not play as central (if at all?) a role in the apocalyptic dilemma. Instead, de Boer argues, the forensic approach focuses on "free will and individual human decision," whereby persons sin by rejecting God, thus receiving the punishment of death.[51] It is the human decision to reject God that breaks the world. Within this schema, God provides the law as a means by which to fix the relationship, and as such one's relationship to the law determines one's eschatological outcome. Within this paradigm, the last things do not focus on a cosmic battle but on a courtroom with God as the judge (hence the forensic or judicial label). Further added to this track is an emphasis on Adam and his transgression and the need for humans to decide whether to acknowledge God as creator and the law. As examples of this track of apocalyptic, de Boer points to 4 Ezra and 2 Baruch.

What is somewhat perplexing about de Boer's analysis is the blurred approach he takes in describing these two tracks of apocalyptic eschatology. At the beginning of his argument in "Paul and Apocalyptic Eschatology," de Boer states that these two patterns are "distinct" from each other. According to de Boer, "angelic forces play *no part*" in the forensic track, in contrast to the cosmological track. Two paragraphs later, however, he states that the forensic pattern is a "modified" form of the first cosmological track. Modified is not the same as distinct.

---

[50]De Boer, "Paul and Apocalyptic Eschatology," 359.

[51]De Boer, "Paul and Apocalyptic Eschatology," 359.

Confusion abounds even more in the next sentence, where now de Boer states that evil cosmic forces "recede into the background" or are "explicitly rejected."[52] It is an overassertion to say categorically that cosmic evil forces play *no part* in forensic models of apocalyptic thought. The two tracks de Boer proposes already show cracks in their foundation.

Finally, even more bewildering, at the end of his discussion of "two distinct tracts" he does acknowledge that "some works exhibit a blend of the two patterns," and he notes both the Dead Sea Scrolls and Paul.[53] In fact, de Boer bases his heuristic model on only two works, 1 Enoch 1–36 and 2 Baruch, works he proposes represent the nearly "pure form" of each track.[54] However, de Boer himself points to at least four other works (Jubilees, Testaments of the Twelve Patriarchs, Dead Sea Scrolls, and Paul) that combine or overlap the categories of cosmological and forensic. It should not be underestimated that de Boer himself notes that more works combine the tracks than purely represent them. Logically, if more works don't conform to the heuristic model proposed, the problem may be with the model itself, that it is too reductionistic. Likewise, Frey has also criticized the approach of de Boer, noting that his approach "basically draws on a taxonomy inspired from elsewhere and on an outdated view of Jewish apocalyptic and its basic features."[55] To say that the schema of de Boer is unclear would be an understatement. At various points, de Boer says the tracks are distinct, with certain themes absent, except when they appear, and then the tracks ultimately overlap. Apparently, they more often do.

Weaknesses aside, we return to the discussion of Paul within the proposed categories of Jewish apocalyptic, where de Boer contends that within the letters of Paul there are concerns and ideas of both tracks of

[52]De Boer, "Paul and Apocalyptic Eschatology," 359, emphasis added.

[53]De Boer, "Paul and Apocalyptic Eschatology," 360.

[54]De Boer "Paul and Jewish Apocalyptic Eschatology," 176.

[55]Frey, "Demythologizing Apocalyptic?," 509. In the same section, Frey also notes, "It is remarkable, however, that in the basic characterization of apocalyptic, de Boer still draws on the handbook knowledge Käsemann had presupposed, in particular Philipp Vielhauer's introduction to apocalyptic" (509).

Jewish apocalyptic eschatology. As is evident to any interpreter of Paul, the character of Adam is important in several places to Paul's argument, such as in 1 Corinthians 15:21-22 and most notably in Romans 5:12-21. De Boer points to this as a feature of Paul's concern with the forensic track. He also draws attention to the cosmological by noting Paul's references to Satan as a hostile power in Romans 16:20; 1 Corinthians 5:5; and so on as Paul's "indebtedness to the worldview of 'cosmological' Jewish apocalyptic eschatology."[56] Further, Paul's identification of sin and death in Romans 5 also represents the concerns and ideas of the cosmological apocalyptic track.

Drawing on the influence of Martyn, de Boer is an advocate of invasion language to describe the apocalyptic character of Paul. Given the cosmological apocalyptic bent of Paul's thought, de Boer argues that at the end of all things "the Last Judgment has the character of an invasion, a military metaphor." To this end de Boer has coined the phrase "the apocalypse of God" to describe this divine warfare. Within this world of evil and cosmic forces, God has waged war against hostile powers that, in the language of de Boer, "have oppressed and victimized human beings." The oppressive factors of sin and death not only victimize human beings but actually pull the Torah into the sphere of oppression. De Boer notes, "the Law is not only too weak and ineffectual for expurgating Sin, and thus also Death from the cosmos, it has also (ironically and lamentably) become a major tool in the hands of Sin for solidifying its Death-dealing hegemony over human beings."[57]

When reading de Boer, or Martyn for that matter, it is easy to see difficulties with the arguments as presented. Yet, we can certainly agree that humans are under the power of sin, which takes on a suprahuman quality. Additionally, the sending of Christ is surely a cosmic event. Indeed, it is interesting that in speaking of the death and resurrection of Christ de Boer notes, "The death and resurrection of Christ has inaugurated a unified apocalyptic drama that reaches its conclusion at the

---

[56]De Boer, "Paul and Apocalyptic Eschatology," 360-61.

[57]De Boer, "Apocalyptic as God's Eschatological Activity," 57-58.

Parousia / the End."[58] It is this idea of a "unified drama" that is most intriguing. It is precisely this matter of unity to a story that those outside the new apocalyptic school have been arguing for, a unified drama that extends not only to the New Testament but right from the Hebrew Scriptures, through the New Testament, and on to the apocalypse proper.

The role of unity and diversity within apocalyptic thought requires more scrutiny and attention to a few issues that remain blurry if not obscured by de Boer's proposal. If there is a unified drama in apocalyptic thought, how then does it relate to what has come before? Putting the matter a bit more directly, in many of the articles where de Boer sets out to explain apocalypse in Paul at a heuristic level, there is a notable absence of a primary character for Paul: Abraham. If Paul's gospel is apocalyptic throughout in the manner as described by de Boer, his proposal certainly works better for Romans, where Paul spends a good deal of space talking about Adam, sin (with a capital *S*), and death (with a capital *D*). Even in Romans, though, the proposal runs into problems in Romans 4 and the character of Abraham, to say nothing of the difficulties presented in Galatians, where the crux of Paul's main argument revolves not around Adam but Abraham. Let us turn to address the matter of the law in Galatians and the matter of Abraham in Galatians and Romans.

In speaking of the law, de Boer wants to argue that in Jewish apocalyptic, "the Law functions as a bridge for crossing the otherwise unbridgeable chasm—death—that separates human beings from God and thus from life in the world to come."[59] But this says nothing of the argument that Paul makes in Galatians 3–4, that the law was given for a *temporary* purpose. Paul in Galatians 3–4 seems to be operating with a unified drama from the Old Testament, a story that begins with Abraham (not Adam) and finds the discussion of the law within that narrative of the First Testament. Abraham looms significantly not only in Galatians but also in Romans, precisely in the books

---

[58]De Boer, "Apocalyptic as God's Eschatological Activity," 52-53.

[59]De Boer, "Apocalyptic as God's Eschatological Activity," 56.

where Paul discusses the law, sin, and death—cosmic, capitalized, and otherwise.

Yet the character of Abraham is notably absent from de Boer's discussion of apocalyptic in Paul. In both the cases of Galatians and Romans, Abraham is key to the argument. Even within Romans, where Paul does move in Romans 5–7 to talk about Adam, sin, and death, the Abraham story is not left behind. Rather, the conversation of heirs, weak bodies, and hope of Abraham in Romans 4:16-25 mirrors the conclusion of Paul in Romans 8:12-25. Thus, the apocalyptic categories and the covenantal categories are indispensably linked with each other. In "Paul and Jewish Apocalyptic Eschatology" (1989), "Paul and Apocalyptic Eschatology" (2000), and "Apocalyptic as God's Eschatological Activity" (2016), Abraham plays no central role in de Boer's argument.[60] The most detailed discussion of Abraham occurs in de Boer's 2011 Galatians commentary.

There, in a convoluted explanation of Galatians 3:6, de Boer takes up the role of Abraham in Paul's argument to the Galatians. In terms of shaping the discussion, de Boer sees Paul taking on the Galatian teachers' argument, which is a christological modification of forensic apocalyptic eschatology of the Jewish apocalyptic patterns mentioned above.[61] Paul then reframes the forensic apocalyptic approach of the teachers with a cosmic (track one) focused argument. Hence, one could concede, in alignment with de Boer's argument, that Paul discusses Abraham only because it was crucial to the teachers but perhaps was not crucial to him. Such an explanation, though, which involves all sorts of questionable mirror reading of Galatians, does not solve the issue of Paul's use of Abraham in Romans.[62] Returning to Abraham, de Boer sees the argument of Abraham as "*only* an analogy," one he states is a "rough one."

[60]References to Abraham only appear in "Apocalyptic as God's Eschatological Activity" in two footnotes (8n38, 13n56).

[61]De Boer, "Paul and Jewish Apocalyptic Eschatology," 185.

[62]On the problems with mirror reading of Paul's letters, by which is meant thinking that Paul is quoting his opponents and not agreeing with them, see Jerry L. Sumney, *Identifying Paul's Opponents: The Question of Method in 2 Corinthians* (London: Bloomsbury, 2015).

In a rather tortured distinction, de Boer views the object of Abraham's faith and the Galatians' as different. He states, "The 'believing' of Christians is thus not only different in kind from that of Abraham; it is also directed to Christ, not God."[63] In de Boer's estimation, Abraham believed God, and the Galatians believe Christ. But is this a distinction with merit? Later on, de Boer notes that the God of Jesus is the same God of Abraham, so his distinction ultimately collapses on itself. To put it simply, Abraham believed God would provide a seed, and the Galatians believed that seed to be Christ. The distinction seems trivial, if not arbitrary.

Problematic as well is that de Boer argues that Paul does not use Abraham as a model for his Galatian converts. He further posits that the justification of Abraham and the Gentiles is different. Although de Boer provides no definition or explanation of the justification of Abraham, he argues that the justification of the Galatians is unlike Abraham's, as their justification is "already contained in God's prior act in Christ: his faithful death on the cross." So what, then, is the purpose of Abraham, one might ask? De Boer concludes that Paul's appeal to Abraham "serves a specific and limited purpose, to show the Galatians . . . that the exclusive relationship between 'believing' (*pisteuein*) and justification . . . posited in 2:16, 21 has its precedent, and thus its anticipation, in (the story of) the first patriarch himself."[64] But what precedent appears in the parameters set out above by de Boer? One might hope that Paul could construct a better argument than the "rough analogy" conceded to him by de Boer.

Two further issues remain. If it is such a poor analogy, why would Paul return to the same analogy in Romans? Second, if Paul assumes a cosmic Jewish apocalyptic category, why not shift the argument from Abraham to Adam, as Paul does in Romans 5–8? Questions such as these plague the portrayal of Abraham that de Boer offers.

By contrast, Paul affirms some degree of continuity between the promise made to Abraham and the promise of the Spirit that the

[63]De Boer, *Galatians*, 190.

[64]De Boer, *Galatians*, 190.

Galatians now experience (Gal 3:29), although the discussion of promise in Galatians 3:29 gets little attention from de Boer. But it is precisely this issue of *promise* that appears to be the Achilles' heel of the argument at hand. De Boer even states, "What was promised was the Spirit (3:14) and the Spirit has been given (3:1-5). . . . The promises to Abraham have been fulfilled."[65] What this raises, at least at a cursory level, is that if the Spirit is the cosmic apocalyptic gift that results from the apocalyptic action of God in Christ (both his sending and in the cross event), then at what level is the term *invasion* appropriate? Was this never before seen or anticipated? The sending of the Spirit as a sign of the new age to come derives not from an apocalyptic revelation of previous unknown avenues but from Joel 2 and the prophets. We have the fulfillment of prior promises rooted in the story of the Hebrew Scriptures. The giving of the Spirit is not an outward invasion to an alien context but rather the divine fulfillment in a long and winding story, and thus Abraham for Paul is the chief cornerstone that the apocalyptic builders have rejected.

Beverly Gaventa: Taking Martyn to the masses. Beverly Gaventa is Distinguished Professor of New Testament at Baylor University, a post she has held since 2013. Previously she held the Helen H. P. Manson Professor of New Testament Literature and Exegesis at Princeton Theological Seminary, where she taught from 1992–2013 and was colleagues with Beker. Gaventa received her PhD from Duke University but, most importantly for our discussion here, received her master of divinity from Union Theological Seminary, where she was a student of Martyn. The influence of Martyn and Beker runs throughout Gaventa's work on Paul, and in many significant ways she carries on their legacy.

As part of the reinvigoration of this stream of Pauline interpretation, she hosted the conference Creation, Conflict, and Cosmos at Princeton Theological Seminary in 2012, subsequently published as *Apocalyptic Paul: Cosmos and Anthropos in Romans 5–8*. Gaventa has made numerous

[65]De Boer, *Galatians*, 247-49.

contributions to the apocalyptic reading of Paul and is situated within the so-called Union school, associated with the work of Martyn and de Boer. Her work *Our Mother Saint Paul* represents a collection of her essays and the most comprehensive summary of her approach to the apocalyptic Paul.

Drawing on the influences of Martyn, Gaventa not only supplements but extends the apocalyptic conversation in new directions. Like Martyn, she identifies apocalyptic as a revolution of epistemology and as an unveiling of invisible powers that hold humanity under their sway. She also raises the importance of the cosmological aspects of salvation, wherein the twin destinies of humanity and the cosmos are intertwined, in a nod to Käsemann. But first Gaventa articulates the power of an apocalyptic gospel for the person of Paul himself.

Central to Gaventa's portrayal of Paul and a unique contribution to the apocalyptic stream is her emphasis on Paul's own apocalyptic experience via Galatians 1–2, where the "new creation" language of Galatians 6:15, noted by many as an apocalyptic touchstone, is applied by Paul to himself. In the words of an apocalyptic reading of Paul: the old Paul is gone; all that is left is new apocalyptic Paul. Bucking the trend of the exegetical tradition, Gaventa argues that Galatians 1–2 is not consumed by an apologetic bent but rather, "Paul presents himself as an example of the working of the gospel." Or to put the matter more precisely, later on, Gaventa comments, "Paul's calling as an apostle and his gospel are inextricably linked."[66]

Through the first two chapters of Galatians, Paul uses his experience as the paradigmatic example of the revolutionary nature of the gospel he proclaims and expects his Galatian audience to maintain. According to Gaventa, this apocalyptic gospel consumed Paul himself, and he uses this "paradigm of reversal" as a pedagogical tool for his audience to imitate. Indeed, Paul's presentation of his own life in Galatians 1–2 is an entryway for Gaventa into the apocalyptic nature of his gospel, whereby

---

[66]*OMSP*, 88, 91.

"the repetition of the theme of the gospel's singularity, the inbreaking of the apocalypse, and the insistence on the gospel's reversal of prior value systems . . . [are] presented in the form of autobiographical material."[67]

In the presentation of Galatians 1–2 one might note that missing from Gaventa's first argument about Paul's conversion is that it is couched in the language of Jeremiah and Isaiah (Gal 1:15-16). There is no mention in her chapter of the echoes of the Old Testament prophetic call narratives that Paul himself uses to describe his apocalyptic calling. She argues for the dramatic reversal Paul experienced. But would the same statements apply to both Jeremiah and Isaiah as well? To use her categories from above, what value systems were reversed for Jeremiah or Isaiah? Such a conversation causes us to return to the argument made by Stendahl decades ago about Paul's call/conversion and is undoubtedly crucial at this juncture. The prophets receive revelations about God and his message to and for his world, and they are certainly frequent at times, as reading through the prophetic corpus will indicate. Radical, then, need not mean discontinuous. Our analysis of Paul's language in Galatians 1–2 must be attuned to the argumentative texture and scriptural residue that saturates the reversal in his autobiography.

In "The Singularity of the Gospel," Gaventa lays out her most thorough case for an apocalyptic reading of Paul and his gospel. Building on her previous argument about Galatians 1–2, she turns to analyze Galatians 3–4 within the proper context of Paul's discussion in the letter as a whole, which does not stand alone but follows from the premises of Galatians 1–2. The argument is summarized as follows: "The singular gospel results in a singular transformation." Gaventa uses the language of Martyn to argue that in Galatians 3–4 the "governing theological antithesis in Galatians is between Christ or the new creation and the cosmos; the antitheses between Christ and the law and between the cross and circumcision are not the equivalent of this central premise but follow it."[68]

---

[67]*OMSP*, 99.
[68]*OMSP*, 101-11.

The echoes of Marytn's 1989 antinomies language to describe Paul's activity in Galatians loudly reverberate. Although notice that now antinomies have become antitheses! Many interpreters have seen the primary issue in Galatians as the role of the law and its subsequent stake in the lives of Paul's Galatian community. Gaventa ultimately argues that this is a subset of a much larger antithesis for Paul, one that crucifies the whole cosmos (Gal 6:12-14). Taking her cues from the end of the letter, Gaventa argues, "The primary antithesis is not between Christ and the law or between the cross and circumcision. These are but subsets of the more fundamental antithesis, which is between Christ/ new creation and cosmos."[69]

One wonders whether Paul's two passing references to *kosmos* can bear the weight that this interpretive argument places on it. The term *kosmos* only appears twice in Galatians (Gal 4:3; 6:14), and the term translated "age"—*aiōn*—only appears in Galatians 1:4. No doubt these ideas are much larger than the occurrences of them within the letter, but one might expect more emphasis on these if the other themes of the letter are but mere subsets of the cosmological issue. By contrast, the term *kosmos* appears fourteen times in 1 Corinthians.

Likewise, Gaventa sees, as does Martyn and de Boer, that the crucifixion is the theme that dominates Paul's letter to the Galatians. Gaventa is emphatic on this point, "Although the letter refers to Christ's resurrection, it is *the crucifixion* that dominates Paul's Christology in Galatians."[70] Gaventa adduces the evidence from Paul's cryptic reference to Christ appearing to the Galatians as publicly crucified (Gal 3:11), Paul's boasting in the cross (Gal 6:14), the act of Christ himself (Gal 1:4; 2:20), and the effect of crucifixion as redemption from the law (Gal 3:10-14).

The emphasis on crucifixion in Galatians is immediately recognizable, as no less than four verses into the letter, Paul refers to the crucifixion with Christ "who gave himself for our sins." However, we ought to note

[69]*OMSP*, 108.
[70]*OMSP*, 109, emphasis original.

that although we typically think of the progression from crucifixion to resurrection, we get the inverse in Galatians 1:1-4. Paul mentions first that "God . . . raised him from the dead" (Gal 1:1) and then that Christ "gave himself for our sins" (Gal 1:4), and one might wonder why Paul has inverted this traditional, and one might say logical, ordering. Likewise, if, as we have seen, an apocalyptic reading of Paul emphasizes "new creation" or a new age/order, would not the resurrection of Christ be proof positive of this argument? Paul makes this argument in Galatians 6:15 and later in 2 Corinthians 5:17—anyone "in Christ" is a new creation. The "in Christ" motif and language are referring not to being in Christ's death (though not exclusive of this either) but to being in Christ's resurrected life. Gaventa does not pursue this route but negates it. She ponders and then answers, "Do Paul's references to the cross carry an implicit reference to the resurrection as well, as is sometimes suggested? The answer to that question, at least in Galatians, must surely be no."[71]

Gaventa raises and addresses the critical issues of the relationship of the gospel to Israel and Paul's usage of Scripture, the lack of which in many apocalyptic readings of Paul is a frequent criticism. Both issues have been notably absent in previous interpreters, and regardless of agreement, Gaventa strengthens the position of the new apocalyptic school by addressing them head-on. She notes that Paul is born under the law and also born into the particular story of ancient Israel and its relationship with God. However, she broadens this in two significant ways. First, although identifying the birth of Christ as "God's intervention in a particular history," she says it is now "radicalized to include all humankind."[72] A pause is needed to consider the ramifications. God's intervention *now* includes all humankind? What then of God's promise that through Abraham's family all the nations of the earth (i.e., humanity) will find blessing? Do such promises negate both the terms *intervention* and *radical* in Gaventa's argument?

---

[71]*OMSP*, 109. In a footnote Gaventa cites Martyn affirmingly that Paul is concerned with the advent, sending, and death of Christ as the focus in Galatians.

[72]*OMSP*, 110.

Second, Gaventa states, "It is precisely within history, in the person of a son of a woman, in the person of one crucified, that God reveals the end of history's distinctions between and among peoples."[73] On first glance, there seems to be an affirmation of the historical issues, but on further review one notices an absence that speaks profoundly. It is God's revelation within *Jewish* history that a *Jewish* son is born of a *Jewish* woman, where that same *Jewish* son is crucified as the king of the *Jews*. Indeed, right under the guise of the proposal sketched above, one finds the key to opening the proverbial lock. No fewer than six times in the paragraph quoted above Gaventa uses the term *Christ*. It is Jesus as the Jewish Messiah that is underappreciated. Gaventa ponders the relationship of Christ to the law, but what about Christ to Israel's story? Such matters are omitted or glossed over, even in her attempt to deal with them. These *particular* issues represent the most acute challenge to the *singularity* of the proposal outlined in the new apocalyptic school.

In an afterword to this chapter, Gaventa discusses the developments of her thought on Paul in the intervening period between the article's publication and its publication within the volume *Our Mother Saint Paul*. At first writing, she was ambiguous with her commitment to the term *apocalyptic*, since it is, as has been noted, a slippery term. However, in the subsequent years, she has firmly committed to the term, not least for signaling her appreciation of and relationship to the arguments of Käsemann, Beker, and Martyn. She admits in passing that the term *apocalyptic* "does not do justice to the continuity reflected in the letter (continuity with Israel's history and Israel's scripture)."[74] We have raised objections all along about precisely these issues, although not much in the argument thus far has assuaged these criticisms.

Gaventa also tackles a difficulty presented in previous apocalyptic conversations on the nature of Paul and Scripture. We have noted several times the absence of the Old Testament in the arguments of both Martyn and de Boer. A significant contribution of Gaventa is

---

73 *OMSP*, 110.
74 *OMSP*, 111.

addressing these pertinent criticisms. Although only a brief comment, Gaventa argues that even if Scripture is necessary for Paul, this is not to say that "Paul clings to Scripture as a way of maintaining continuity with tradition itself."[75] One wonders, within the immensity of the silence, what, then, is the purpose of the near-ubiquity of Scripture throughout the letters of Paul? If the radicalness is as radical as proposed, one would think that Israel's Scripture would not be a great resource from which to mount so many arguments. Why return to an empty well?

Gaventa returns to this topic in her chapter "The God Who Will Not Be Taken for Granted."[76] In speaking of Scripture in Romans, she writes, "The God of the promise of Scripture (1:2) is faithful, but faithfulness does not imply predictability. God is also free, not to be confined to human expectations about God's judgments and responses." Gaventa takes this precedent from Romans itself, where she notes that, in the first several verses, though Paul invokes the idea that the gospel is promised beforehand in the Scriptures (Rom 1:2), the fulfillment of that gospel message is unexpected. Paul turns to the obedience of the Gentiles, as evidenced in that "God's actions extends in new directions: God is faithful to the promises but not restricted in fulfilling it."[77]

Such a statement is puzzling and depends on how one defines the gospel. Certainly, God is God and can do whatever God wants. We are but the vessels speaking to the potter (Rom 9:19-26). However, the idea of obedient Gentiles is not foreign to the Hebrew Bible. The role of Gentiles in the eschatological age is debated within Second Temple Judaism, but obedient and faithful Gentiles are one track.[78] One thinks not only of the prophet Isaiah; in Romans 9:19-26, Hosea becomes all the more important. There, precisely when talking about the unpredictability of God, Paul quotes the prophet Hosea in calling those who are "not my people" "my people" and says that those persons become

---

[75]*OMSP*, 111.

[76]*OMSP*, 149-60.

[77]*OMSP*, 151.

[78]Terence L. Donaldson, *Judaism and the Gentiles: Jewish Patterns of Universalism (to 135 CE)* (Waco, TX: Baylor University Press, 2007).

"children of the living God." The question of unpredictability is more precisely, Unpredictable to whom, us or Paul?

Further, to argue that God is faithful to promises but not in how they are fulfilled only makes sense when there is not a covenant involved. It is true that God will not be restricted, except of course when God *does restrict himself*, or what is called making a covenant. To use a somewhat blunt analogy, when God promises Abraham a child, Abraham can't receive anything else. It is precisely the point for Paul that this is the God who makes *particular* promises. Such an issue appears to be precisely what Paul is addressing in Romans 9–11. Nothing less than the faithfulness of God is at stake in Romans, as many subsequent interpreters of Paul have argued. Gaventa takes such issues head-on in a section on Romans 9–11 but merely reverts to the argument that faithfulness does not equal predictability. Again, the ironic nature of this proposal about this section of Romans is that it is widely argued to be the epicenter of Paul's Old Testament quotations. For Gaventa, God's freedom undermines "any notion that God's faithfulness can be predicted in advance, in the sense of being 'taken-for-granted.'"[79] Paradoxically, Paul's aim in the section becomes apparent in Romans 11:17-24, that the "taken for granted–ness" is not about using faithfulness as a means for predictability but is aimed squarely at the Gentiles who think they don't need the Israel story.

Gaventa has returned to this topic of Christ and Israel recently in the edited volume *Paul and the Apocalyptic Imagination* in a chapter titled, "Thinking from Christ to Israel: Romans 9–11 in Apocalyptic Context." Rather than focusing on continuity, an argument is adapted and taken up from E. P. Sanders that the solution precedes the problem for Paul. Namely, the "argumentative logic" at work in Romans 9–11 is not about the faith of Israel but rather "Israel's past, present, and future, as Israel's very identity is revealed in light of Christ." She contrasts her approach with that of Wright, who sees Romans 9–11 as part of the great story

---

[79]*OMSP*, 156.

about Abraham's family. She states in a footnote that her argument is "for Paul, Israel . . . is known though Jesus Christ, not the other way around."[80] What is rather confusing about this reading of Romans 9:6–11:36 is that Abraham and his children are exactly those whom Paul invokes. Likewise, to speak of Israel and not Abraham seems impossible. Of course, the identification of the Israel that Paul speaks of in Romans 11 is a notoriously thorny knot within the study of Romans. Problematic for Gaventa's whole argument is that the term *Israel* clearly in Romans 9–11 refers to non-Christian Jews. It is a term of particularity, not universalism.

Another subsequent discussion of Romans 9–11 occurs in the wonderfully brief, accessible, and brilliantly titled Romans volume *When in Romans*. Gaventa takes up the debate about Romans 9–11 again in a chapter titled "Consider Abraham." One can't help but think that a synonym of consider is *remember*. Gaventa concludes that section by stating, "The only Israel that exists, for Paul, is the one that God called into being with the promise to Abraham, the one that God redeems—along with Gentiles—with Jesus Christ, and the one to whom God's promises are unbreakable."[81] Note the previous arguments by Gaventa above and ponder the question: What is the relationship between irrevocability and predictability?

To sum up, Gaventa has steered the apocalyptic conversation to the most pressing issues and thorniest passages that offer significant challenges to the apocalyptic school. It ought also to be noted that any charge of anti-Jewish readings cannot be laid at the feet of Gaventa, who more than most has argued so stridently against a de-Judaizing account of Paul in his letters. Gaventa straddles the apocalyptic stream by both continuing to affirm the Jewish character of Paul and attempting to maintain the element of newness or "unforseen-ness" of Paul's gospel.

---

[80]Gaventa, "Thinking from Christ to Israel: Romans 9–11 in Apocalyptic Context," in Blackwell, Goodrich, and Maston, *Paul and the Apocalyptic Imagination*, 241, 242n6.

[81]Beverly Roberts Gaventa, *When in Romans: An Invitation to Linger with the Gospel According to Paul* (Grand Rapids: Baker, 2016), 71.

Her concerted effort to value the placement of Romans 9–11 in the context of apocalyptic readings of Paul is appreciated, as it has all too often been neglected. Finally, though, it is perhaps Romans 9–11 that provides the most significant hurdle for an apocalyptic reading, as there is much within Romans 9–11 that depends not only on the singularity and the particularity of Paul's gospel revealed in Jesus Christ but also on what was *promised beforehand* in the Scriptures. It is this tension that is elided, if not lost altogether, in an apocalyptic reading of Paul, but a tension that must remain nonetheless.[82]

CONCLUSION

Throughout this chapter, we covered the ground of the main apocalyptic interpretations of Paul and the resurgence of such readings in the new apocalyptic school. Although there is much to learn from these readings about the Christ event and how challenging it may have been in the first century, we noted several key issues worth further investigation that must be addressed by subsequent apocalyptic interpreters of Paul.

First, we noted the problematic nature of actually defining the terms that are used within the apocalyptic school. Problems arise at the onset with how we define *apocalyptic, apocalypse,* and cognate terms. The slippery nature of *apocalyptic* and its usage has contributed to the confusion across numerous fields. A second linguistic issue is the nature of invasion language to describe the nature of Paul's gospel. Although it is eye- and ear-catching language, it is inaccurate to describe God and

---

[82]There is not time or space here to deal with the vast study of Douglas Campbell titled *The Deliverance of God: An Apocalyptic Rereading of Justification in Paul* (Grand Rapids: Eerdmans, 2009). A couple of points, however, can be made. Campbell's proposals about how to read Rom 1–4 have not been well received. Most controversially, he advocates that Rom 1–4 is actually large quotes of the opponents' message (à la 1 Corinthians style) that Paul is repeating and that Paul's own concerns do not surface until Rom 5–8. It is one thing to see snippets of quotations of Paul's opponents here and there in Paul's letters but quite another to argue that whole blocks of Paul's letters come merely from his opponents. Not many have followed this logic articulated in such a robust manner as Campbell does in *Deliverance of God*. However, we ought not to miss the important implications that flow out of Campbell's reading. Namely, Campbell's reading shifts the central locus of Paul's argument in Romans to Rom 5–8, a section that is clearly more favorable to an apocalyptic reading.

God's action in the world as an invasion. *Intervention* might be a better term.

Such linguistic issues raise a third important problem, which is that our usage of terms must be tied to the data we know from the apocalypses we have. The important work in the last century on the apocalyptic movement(s) that ran through much of first-century Judaism(s) needs to be kept in mind when discussing Paul as an apocalyptic writer. Much of the previous conversations surrounding the apocalyptic Paul have worked either from an inaccurate understanding of apocalyptic or from an underdetermined definition.

Finally, a repeated issue noted at every turn is the nature of the continuity and discontinuity of the apocalyptic interpretation of Paul. At its worst manifestations, overemphasis on discontinuity can rightly lead to charges of de-Judaizing or supersessionism. Not every apocalyptic interpretation of Paul can or even should be burdened with such accusations. It must be said that the more recent apocalyptic interpretations of Paul, by those such as Gaventa, have done the hard work to avoid such charges. Likewise, there is precedent for this within the apocalyptic school from interpreters such as J. Christian Beker who find the means to affirm the radical faithfulness of God alongside the radical nature of Paul's gospel.

A further question remains for the apocalyptic school, and this concerns the notion of human repentance and faithfulness. One catches the whiff that the all-consuming nature of the apocalyptic event of God in Christ may at times verge on overwhelming human response. How do repentance and human volition work within the apocalyptic system thus set up? Do human choices, such as repentance and then obedience to Christ, play a part in the divine economy of God's action in Christ? With all things Pauline, balance is of course the aim, and this might be one area where the apocalyptic school overreaches and needs to rethink parts of the interpretive framework.

One of the significant achievements of the last century in Paul studies is showing that Paul is an apocalyptic thinker and that there really is no other way to understand him, his life, or his work without due attention to the apocalyptic reality. However, just what type of apocalyptic features characterize Paul, and more importantly how these should be interpreted, is where disagreement ensues. The apocalyptic stream in Pauline studies is certainly not slowing down any time soon and is sure to become a rapid in the next years and decades.

six

OTHER VOICES, OTHER VIEWS

BARCLAY AND CHESTER

Grace is everywhere in the OT, early Judaism, and early Christianity, but it is not everywhere the same. Paul is talking about incongruous grace.

John Barclay

BARCLAY ON GRACE, WORKS, AND SALVATION

There are only a few landmark or seminal books in one scholar's lifetime that are written in one's field. One can easily mention E. P. Sanders's *Paul and Palestinian Judaism* (1977), and Wayne Meeks's *The First Urban Christians* (two editions, 2nd edition 2003). It is too early to assess the full impact of John Barclay's *Paul and the Gift* for various reasons, not least that it is the first of a two-volume study, but what can be said is that if one can judge from this first volume, it is must reading for all interested in Paul and in particular in his concept of grace.

Grace and gift. In conversation with Barclay, he described to me what led to his work.

> Ever since grappling with the work of E.P. Sanders and writing my thesis on Galatians (*Obeying the Truth,* 1988) I have felt that there was something about grace in Paul that the "new perspective" had not got right, but I could not put my finger on what that was for a long time. The "new perspective" has a good social explanation of how Paul's theology relates to his Gentile mission, but by lifting up

> values like "openness," "inclusivity" or "equality" (e.g., "equal rights for Gentiles"; Stendahl; Dunn; Wright) I felt that there was something about Paul's theology that was not being grasped. Paul is not just a covenantal theologian with an eschatological or a radical social twist. He has a radical, even dangerous, view of God's grace, but I was struggling to see how to articulate that. I realized that to understand what Paul means by "grace" I had to understand how gifts worked in the ancient world, and the deeper I got into that (which is a fascinating subject in itself) the more I began to see that there are different kinds of "grace" in the ancient world, including the ancient Jewish world.[1]

Barclay lays out the evidence at some length that gift giving in antiquity, more often than not, was not done with no thought of return. Put another way, gift giving, while free in the sense of unprovoked by the "other," was not free in that it was meant to set in motion a reciprocity cycle. So it was not anonymous or disinterested or purely altruistic giving in the modern sense. The epigram from Martial that "gifts are like fishhooks" is apt. As Barclay stresses, gifts were intended to create social ties of various sorts—family ties, patron-client ties, and the like. The receiver was indeed to understand they had a moral and social obligation to respond. Furthermore, this is true in early Jewish as well as Greco-Roman literature. Not even Tobit reflects a notion of pure grace. Even gifts given to the poor, who cannot reciprocate, were thought to "store up treasure in heaven," so there would be a credit or return from God.

According to Barclay, what is characteristic of Paul is that he radicalizes the *incongruity* of grace, *that is,* grace given without regard to worth, and at the very heart of his Gentile mission is the notion that the gift of Christ is incongruous, but God is expecting a return. Romans 6–8 makes evident that believers are under grace and must respond to it. Gifts carry with them obligations—to whom more is given, more is

[1]John Barclay, email to author, October 2015. Some of this material appeared first in another form on my Patheos blog between October 18 and November 25, 2015. See "John Barclay's Paul and the Gift Part One," The Bible and Cutlure, October 18, 2015, www.patheos.com/blogs/bibleandculture/2015/10/18/john-barclays-paul-and-the-gift-part-one/.

expected. The notion of anonymous giving, giving with no thought of return, or disinterested giving reflects the rise of radical individualism in the West, whereas for ancients social or group identity was primary, and thus giving was meant to foster community. Does this mean that Luther and Calvin got Paul's theology of grace and gift wrong, swept up in the early tide of modern individualism?

Barclay thinks that they were both right about the incongruity of divine grace, given without regard to merit or worth, but Luther moved in the direction of seeing the gift as unilateral, a one-way movement that goes well beyond Paul. In the case of both Luther and Calvin, who were deeply indebted to Augustine, their emphasis on grace as the cure for sin, guilt, and anxiety leaves out the social dimensions of Paul's theology of grace, dimensions that allow for the creation of countercultural communities that move against the dominant flow of culture in various respects. What does this mean for Israel, and who exactly is this Israel that Paul speaks of in, for instance, Romans 9–11? Barclay is quite clear in differing from N. T. Wright at this point. Israel means Jews, and Paul believes that at some juncture "Israel's identity will be regrounded and restored in Christ. . . . As the olive tree analogy shows, Israel is not superseded by Gentiles or absorbed into a non-Jewish realm. By believing in Christ, Israel will draw again . . . on grace, thereby becoming not less but more like itself."[2] Paul is concerned to show that Israel itself is constituted by divine mercy alone—and on that basis he has hope for the salvation of all Israel (not just a select remnant) because God's mercy can overcome all disobedience and because his promises of mercy still stand.

Part of the way Barclay sees Paul's view of gift/grace as radical has to do with the notion that God's gifts bear no relationship to human worth; they are not bestowed on worthy recipients. Further, human gifts are always inspired and enabled by divine giving, divine grace. In the light of the Christ event, Paul is struck by the descriptions of the mercy of

---

[2]John M. G. Barclay, *Paul and the Gift* (Grand Rapids: Eerdmans, 2017), 553, 555.

God that go well beyond what is decent or fair, or might even seem fitting, such as God's response to the golden-calf incident (see Ex 33–34 in Rom 9) or God's calling of very flawed patriarchs.

Barclay seeks to create a broad taxonomy of the different ways grace is talked about in Paul and elsewhere. He identifies six perfections of grace: (1) superabundance (the size or character of the gift), (2) singularity (God's character as giver and nothing-but-giver), (3) priority (the timing of the gift before any initiative from the other side), (4) incongruity (the mismatch between the gift and the worth of the recipient, (5) efficacy (the ability of the gift to achieve the giver's intentions), and (6) noncircularity (gifts that escape any system of exchange or reciprocity). In regard to the matter of incongruity, Barclay affirms Luther's old dictum—the love of God does not find but creates what is pleasing to him.

In his important appendix on *charis* and its semantic range, Barclay points out that in fact *charis* can refer to the quality of charm/agreeableness, or to benevolence or the gift/favor given, and also to gratitude. All of these meanings can be found in the New Testament as well as in wider Greek. The word *charis* itself does not have *the specific sense* of an undeserved or incongruous gift. It takes on that nuance in Paul, but only because it there refers to God's gift given in the Christ event. But the word itself relates to the domain of gifts, and gifts are normally given (for good reason) to fitting or worthy recipients. There is no reason to think that *charis* equals undeserved gift. Only the context can indicate whether that is the (unusual) sense required in particular cases. In short, Paul uses the term in an unusual sense when referring to God's gift of Christ. But even Paul can use the term, for instance in regard to the collection for the poor in Jerusalem, in a broader sense, not meaning incongruous grace.

Some of the reasons for the misreading of some of Paul's language of grace have to do with the misreading of the Old Testament language of *ḥesed,* which means "lovingkindness" or "mercy"; in fact, the term is regularly translated *eleos* in the LXX, "mercy." To translate *ḥesed* as "covenant love" and then define that to mean God's exclusive love for the elect to whom he had bound himself does not come to grips with the scope of the meaning or meanings of *ḥesed,* and evidence that the term cannot also refer to God's relating to non-Jews is lacking. Indeed, the term *ḥesed* comes up, for instance, in the book of Ruth, but Ruth was a Moabitess to whom God owed no covenant love, and neither did Naomi or Ruth owe it to each other. Barclay, quite rightly, is concerned to guard against taking one possible meaning of a word and then assuming it means that in all sorts of different contexts. He points to the "recent mistaken opinion that 'God's righteousness' means 'God's covenant faithfulness' wherever that phrase occurs."[3] Barclay says in *some* contexts it may mean that, but the lexeme "God's righteousness" does not mean "God's covenant faithfulness" wherever it occurs, even in Paul, any more than *ḥesed* means "God's covenant love." Reformed readings of these sorts of things tend to narrow the meaning of terms such as *ḥesed* and *charis* far too much, with a resultant skewing of the reading of Paul's meanings.

For example, a certain kind of theology of predestination would say that the "gift" and the relationship between God and believers was predetermined from before the foundation of the universe. Jonathan Edwards, perhaps the greatest of American Calvinistic theologians, when he reflected on Calvin and Luther, said,

> The response to grace is not voluntary (or free) if you mean there was the power of contrary choice involved from the side of the recipient, but if by "free" or voluntary you merely mean that the recipient of grace did not "feel" or "sense" that he was compulsed to do as he did (though in fact he could not have done otherwise), then the term "free" or "willingly" or "voluntarily" could apply.

This is a classic example of the overdetermined used of grace language in some forms of Protestant theology that misses out or gets wrong the semantic range of meanings of this vocabulary in the New Testament.

---

[3]"John Barclay's Paul and the Gift Part Three," The Bible and Culture, October 21, 2015, www.patheos.com/blogs/bibleandculture/2015/10/21/john-barclays-paul-and-the-gift-part-three/.

Barclay mostly agrees with this assessment, saying:

> It would be problematic for Paul, as for us, if our response to grace could not be considered in any sense "voluntary" (i.e., truly willed). Note how much Paul emphasizes in 2 Corinthians 8–9 that the Corinthians' gift (*"charis"*) to Jerusalem should be voluntary and not an extraction (2 Corinthians 9.5); otherwise in his eyes it would not be a gift. Now, "voluntary" in Paul's eyes does not mean "free of any external influence" (see how much effort he puts into persuading them to make this voluntary gift!): he does not labor under our illusion that we can and should act as completely autonomous individuals. But he does expect that God's work in us generates our own willing (Phil. 2.12-13), as freed agents who could do otherwise (it is possible, in Paul's eyes, to fall out of grace).
>
> There is a tendency, in a line of interpretation from Augustine, through Calvin, to Jonathan Edwards, to "perfect" (radicalize or absolutize) the efficacy of grace, to the point where it causes, constrains, or compels our own wills. This is to turn God's agency/will and our agency/will into a zero-sum game: the more of one, the less of the other. But God's will is not on the same level as ours, working in the same causal nexus. To perfect the efficacy of grace in the way you describe is certainly not necessary, even if it is understandably attractive to some.[4]

Barclay adds that the transcendence of God's freedom does not require that our freedom is constrained in the way that is often supposed (i.e., "if God willed this to happen, I can't have had real freedom to choose").

One of the more vexed questions has to do with what to make of Luther and Calvin's theology of grace as it relates to the notion of the imputed righteousness of Christ. Imputed righteousness seems to be something equally important to both Luther and Calvin. But I (Ben) would argue that Paul basically doesn't affirm imputed righteousness, if by that one means something that rules out imparted righteousness through the internal work of the Spirit in the life of the believer. Surely the new birth/new creation and sanctification are precisely about the

---

[4]This is a further quote from email conversation in October 2015. Barclay adds, "The better theological model is what one might call non-contrastive transcendence" (see the introduction to the volume Barclay edited with Simon Gathercole, called *Divine and Human Agency in Paul and His Cultural Environment* [Edinburgh: T&T Clark, 2006]).

replication of the character of Christ in the life of the believer, not a mere suggesting that Jesus' righteousness counts for ours. It is especially striking how Luther and Calvin do such a tap dance when it comes to texts such as Romans 4 and Galatians 3, which say that Abraham's faith/trust was reckoned as righteousness or reckoned for right standing with God, which is a very different matter from saying Christ is righteous for the believer and in the believer's place. Luther gets around the dilemma by suggesting that the believer is in union with Christ, and so he rejects the legal-fiction idea, but he is adamant about there being no *infused* grace or righteousness within the believer, because of his reading of Romans 7 and his *simul iustus et peccator* theology.

When presented with these thoughts, Barclay stresses that the notion of Christ's righteousness "imputed" to us is an attempt to spell out the "imputed" ("reckoned") language of Romans 4:5 and so on as combined with verses such as 1 Corinthians 1:30 (Christ became our righteousness, etc.) and 2 Corinthians 5:20 ("so that in him we might become the righteousness of God"). Theologically, it represents an insistence that whatever is said about our righteousness can be said only on the basis of our union with Christ: it is not (or not just) that grace is infused to aid us in our path of righteousness, but that everything "righteous" about the believer is founded on Christ. Barclay does not find the language of Christ's righteousness being imputed to us the most helpful (or an exegetically necessary) way of spelling that out, but the theological concern is real, and we certainly need to find ways of talking about the believer's righteousness that continually refer back to the gift of the believer's new self and new agency by grace. Luther's *simul iustus et peccator* scheme is one way to do that, but Barclay prefers something like *simul mortuus et vivens* ("simultaneously dying and yet alive") because he does not read Romans 7 as about Christian experience. One thing one can say about the new perspective on Paul is that it is much more wary of or even rejects the notion that Romans 7:7-25 is describing Christian experience of any sort. This is a move in the right direction, and it calls into question the notion that believers are still in bondage to sin.

Concerning final judgment: Barclay affirms that in Paul's thought right standing with God (justification) involves people who are unworthy, even enemies of God, because justification is by grace through faith. Yet Barclay is prepared to say nevertheless that final judgment, which involves an evaluation of human works and can lead to rewards (or the lack thereof), takes into account the fitness of the recipient for such rewards. Salvation itself, however, even final salvation, is not a reward, not earned or merited. This distinction suggests that the Reformed idea that initial justification is nothing more than final justification retrojected to the beginning of the believer's life (so that God's "no condemnation now" guarantees no condemnation later) is probably an overreading of Paul at several crucial points.

Barclay insists that the unfitting gift (to the unrighteous and enemy) re-creates the believer in the life of the resurrected Christ, and it is only out of that new self that any agency on behalf of the believer can arise. But the purpose of that gift is the new, transformed self, who acts in holiness (not continuing unrighteousness or enmity to God), and at the eschaton Paul pictures God scrutinizing, judging, and rewarding that holiness. This is not a second justification, because it recognizes that what is good in the believer's life is the product of the new life created by God in Christ, but it makes sense of the fact that Paul can still talk of the judgment of believers and even their rewards. That there is no condemnation means that as long as I stand in Christ and draw on him (in the terms of 1 Cor 3, as long as I rest on the foundation that is Jesus Christ), God is committed to vindicate the work he has begun in me. But that leaves open the possibility that I might be separated from Christ—the possibility of apostasy, as mentioned several times by Paul.

Barclay reminds us to notice as well that Paul, like quite a lot of the material in the Gospels, has injected into Christian tradition the notion that God does not act in accord with what we consider fair or reasonable: think of the prodigal son and the workers in the vineyard. Barclay stresses that early Christianity was founded in shock: the shock that God raised Jesus from the dead, and the parallel shock that he distributed his Spirit to unworthy Gentiles and slaves and lower-status people, and thus kept tearing up the social rule book. It is this countercultural, counterintuitive dynamic that gives Paul the freedom to conduct his Gentile mission on unorthodox terms, and that freedom created the experimental and unprecedented communities of early believers.

In comparison to the new perspective. Barclay has much to say in relation to various emphases of the new perspective on Paul. He is mostly unconvinced of the arguments that *pistis Christou* means the faithfulness of Christ, and in this he is in agreement with Dunn and in disagreement with Richard Hays and Wright. He thinks Wright in particular favors that view because he sees Christ as fulfilling the role of faithfulness to God that Israel failed to fulfill. Barclay is clear that he does not agree that Christ plays the role of Israel, or that Jew and Gentile united in Christ equals Israel for Paul.

Barclay is in agreement with Sanders that of course grace is to be found everywhere in the Old Testament and that in early Judaism it is not by and large a "works religion," if by that one means a religion where one earns one's way into the good graces of God; rather, covenantal nomism is closer to the mark, which insists that grace precedes response. But unlike Sanders, Barclay does not think that grace in Old Testament and early Jewish texts everywhere has the same sense, nuance, perfection. For example, he thinks Sanders gets right the priority of grace in most Jewish texts, but then confuses this with the incongruity of grace, which texts such as Psalms of Solomon and 4 Ezra call into question. Some early Jews thought God is merciful on the unrighteous and unfitting (incongruity); some thought, for good reason, that God is not (that would undercut the fairness of the universe) but instead exercises mercy on those who are in one sense or another worthy or fitting recipients of grace. Because Sanders confuses the priority of grace with other perfections of grace (such as incongruity), he thus wrongly thought there was no difference between any of the Jewish texts and Paul.

One theme that arises multiple times in new perspective discussions is the notion that not only is Paul addressing specific situations in Galatians and Romans but that in fact his theology of grace and God's righteousness is quite specifically tailored to his dominant audience—namely, Gentiles. This insight can be overplayed, because Paul is not just saying that "justification by grace through faith" is how Gentiles get into the body of Christ. He is saying that that is how *everyone* gets in, including himself, surely. For example, in Romans 1 he stresses that the good news about righteousness and faith in Christ is for "the Jew first" and also for the Gentile.

A two-track model of salvation does not work as an analysis of Paul's thought, especially when Romans 11:25-36 seems to make clear that "all Israel will be saved" in the future, "when the Redeemer comes forth from Zion and turns away the impiety of Jacob." You don't talk about the impiety of Jacob if you think Jacob is already saved by some other means than Christ, and you don't talk about Jewish branches temporarily broken off from the people of God, so they can be reintegrated into that group by grace through faith in Jesus, if you are touting a two-track model of salvation. In short, it seems to me that very few of the new perspective folks, going all the way back to Stendahl, really grasp the nettle when it comes to the radical nature of Paul's thought when it comes to how exactly non-Christian Israel is and will be saved.

So, what does Barclay think about the notion that Paul is only discussing how Gentiles can be saved, by grace through faith in Jesus, but that a two-track model of salvation is actually operating in the Pauline corpus? Barclay says that Stendahl, in consort with John G. Gager and Lloyd Gaston in his day and now followed by the radical new perspective (Magnus Zetterholm, Mark Nanos, and the Society of Biblical Literature's Paul and Judaism study group, etc.), were and are very unwilling to find in Paul anything that suggests Paul expected Jews to change in practice or belief, and one way to argue this is to say that Paul's negative comments about the authority of the law are only as it relates to Gentiles (his only audience). Barclay thinks that Paul does expect Jews such as himself to be challenged and reconstituted by the gospel, even if he finds a deep connection between what God has done in Abraham and so on and what he has done in Christ. In Barclay's reading of Romans 9–11, Paul expects ethnic Israel to be saved by faith in Christ—though this will be not an addition to, and certainly not a denial of, their Jewish scriptural heritage but rather its fulfillment, since God has constituted Israel all along by an incongruous grace (which Barclay takes to be the root of the olive tree in Rom 11).

Yet in fact in Galatians 4; 2 Corinthians 3–4; and Romans 9:1-5; 10:1-5 Paul quite clearly tells us that Christ is the end or fulfillment of the Mosaic law covenant and that the new covenant is connected through Christ with the Abrahamic covenant, not the Mosaic one, which was a *paidagōgos*, a temporary child minder until Christ came. Paul affirms multiple covenants given by God to his people, not one covenant in many administrations. In short, what is at stake is not a Lutheran reading of the Mosaic law but a Calvinistic and Reformed one. Barclay typically takes his own line of approach. He argues that in texts such as Galatians 2:15-16 by "the works of the law" Paul just means the practice of the Mosaic law in general, not singling out or prioritizing any particular boundary rituals such as circumcision.

Barclay adds that in Galatians 3 Paul makes clear that the Mosaic law had authority for a limited time (starting 430 years after Abraham and until Christ): Paul does not think it is wrong as such, but it is no longer the final authority for those in Christ (even if they fulfill its core intention by walking in the Spirit). Romans brings out even more this sense of the core intention of the law ("the requirements of the law," Rom 2:15; or "the righteous requirement of the law," Rom 8:4), which indicates that believers do what the law at heart was looking for. But that its final authority is broken even for Jews is clear in that, even in Romans, Paul can say that he is persuaded in the Lord Jesus that nothing is unclean in itself (Rom 14:14) and that "the kingdom of God is not food and drink but righteousness and peace and joy in the Holy Spirit" (Rom 14:17 NASB). The Torah's rules remain an honorable cultural tradition, which Paul wants the weak to be allowed to continue (Rom 14–15); but they also have to recognize that one can live to the Lord (God/Christ) in ignoring kosher rules as well as in honoring them. Here I fully agree with Barclay's critique of the new perspective. What one discovers is that Barclay is not merely repristinating an older view, for example, the Lutheran view of Paul, but rather is grounding his critiques in a broader and fairer assessment of both early Jewish texts and Paul's appropriation of his Jewish heritage.[5]

Conclusion. Two of the biggest contributions of Barclay's book are (1) demonstrating at some length the various ways *charis* terminology was used in Paul's world, and how differently it was used in a benefaction culture than it is often used in the modern context, when we talk about giving with no thought of return and the like; and (2) the sixfold taxonomy, which is very helpful for sorting out which aspects of grace Paul is indeed perfecting (e.g., its priority) and which he is probably not perfecting. Barclay objects to the regular attempt to always take Paul as an exception to the rule—that other early Jews thought gifts, even from God, required a return, but Paul believed in a unilateral or unconditional gift, requiring no return. For Barclay, the key perfection for Paul is *incongruity* (God gives in Christ without regard to worth), but this

---

[5]Elsewhere Barclay said to me, in an October 2015 email, "In textual terms, Dunn and others appeal to Gal 5.14 ('the whole law is fulfilled in the love-command') to react against the view that Paul is 'anti-Law'; in theological terms, it comes (as Dunn admits) from his Reformed assumptions that there is one covenant (Abraham-Mosaic-in Christ), albeit in different dispensations; in political terms, it is an attempt to avoid, for the sake of contemporary Jewish-Christian relations, any sense that Paul is directly opposed to Judaism. My position is this: if by 'Judaism' we mean the Jewish people and their covenant relationship to God, Paul is not 'opposed to Judaism,' as I think the prayer of Gal 6.16 (for 'the Israel of God') and Romans 9-11 indicate; but if by 'Judaism' we mean (as I think Paul means when he uses the term in Gal 1.13-14: 'my former life in Judaism') a pattern of life for which the Torah is the ultimate authority, then I think Paul propounds something radically different. It is not just that the Torah is not to be imposed on Gentiles; it is also that it is no longer the ultimate norm even for Jewish believers." It seems to me (Ben) that this means that Galatians is not (1) an argument against legalism, (2) an argument against works-righteousness in Luther's sense of the phrase, (3) an argument against obedience or keeping the law (as redefined), or (4) an argument that obedience has nothing to do with final salvation (while Paul is arguing that initial right standing with God is by grace and through faith). Rather, Paul is reminding those already saved about how they came to have that gift, including the gift of the Spirit, and is suggesting that the way they should live going forward is on the basis of the gift, which keeps on giving through the Spirit, and in a fashion that reflects the character and life-rule of Christ.

does not mean that the gift is also given with no thought of return. Barclay believes that the disaggregation of the different perfections of gift is the key methodological work of his book, and the reviews of his work by systematic theologians have suggested that it would have saved an awful lot of controversy in Christian history if these distinctions had been made clear earlier! Barclay also insists that Paul's thinking is teleological: there is no prior fit between God's grace and human worth (that is what makes Paul's theology and practice so radical), but the aim of the gift is to refound human existence and reorient it, so we end up as fitting worshipers created by an unfitting gift. Barclay affirms that God's fitting judgment on human sin does not enable us to repent (a very rare word in Paul) so much as cause us to put our only trust (or boast) in Christ, so that everything that is said about us positively from then on is dependent entirely on the re-creative work of God in Christ ("if anyone is in Christ, the new creation has come," 2 Cor 5:17).

I suspect that, whatever other aspects of grace one emphasizes, its priority and its incongruity are sine qua nons of grace for Paul, from his christological point of view. This why in the end Paul sees grace to either Israel or Gentiles as purely a matter of God having mercy on people. Barclay, however, rightly points out that he is attempting to put Paul's view in perspective, to look at it first from a kind of critical distance, so we can understand what he is doing. It was not self-evident that the notion of God's grace being incongruous was necessarily better or higher: in fact, many in Paul's day had good theological reasons to reject that notion. We can thus see more clearly that Paul's is not the obvious view of grace but was shaped by a particular set of christological convictions and experiences.

CHESTER ON READING WITH THE REFORMERS

Stephen Chester's *Reading with the Reformers: Reconciling Old and New Perspectives* is the most recent book of great significance for evaluating Paul and his thought world.[6] One of Chester's great concerns is to

[6]Stephen Chester, *Reading Paul with the Reformers: Reconciling Old and New Perspectives* (Grand Rapids: Eerdmans, 2017). Some of this material appeared first in another form on my Patheos blog, The

correct false readings of Luther, Calvin, and Philipp Melanchthon and to make clear that later Lutheran thought and later Reformed thought did not always do justice to those great Reformers' ideas. Too often recent Pauline scholarship has reacted to that later Lutheran and Reformed tradition without really engaging with the Reformers themselves. Chester was a student of John Barclay at Glasgow, and in some ways their views of matters overlap. In any case, Chester's indebtedness to Barclay is a good reason to place this discussion here in the second half of this chapter. Recently Chester explained to me what prompted the writing of this book:

> In the late 1990s as a doctoral student at Glasgow University I was working on some texts in Galatians. One day in the university library I happened to look at what Luther had to say about the verses I was working on and found myself thinking, "He's not supposed to say that!" That experience of finding more in Luther, and something different in Luther, than I was expecting planted a seed. I had long been convinced of the value of the New Perspective rejection of stereotypes of Second Temple Judaism as a religion of works-righteousness, but when I read texts like Romans 4:1-5 or Philippians 3:9 I found the exegesis offered by New Perspective scholars unconvincing. There was something that did not tie together correctly and I began to wonder if, in rejecting trajectories of interpretation ultimately derived from the Reformation, contemporary Pauline scholarship had accurately understood what it was opposing. The only way to answer that question was to go back to the sixteenth-century sources. As will become clear to readers of the book I certainly do not believe that the Reformers were correct in all important aspects of their interpretation, but I do think that they have important exegetical resources to offer us as we attempt faithfully to interpret the same texts in and for contemporary contexts.[7]

Bible and Cutlure, starting on November 15, 2017. See "Reading Paul with the Reformers—Part One," The Bible and Culture, November 15, 2017, www.patheos.com/blogs/bibleandculture/2017/11/15/reading-paul-reformers-part-one/.

[7]This was sent to me in an email early in November 2017, which I then put up on my blog with his consent. See "Reading Paul with the Reformers—Part One," Bible and Culture, November 15, 2017, www.patheos.com/blogs/bibleandculture/2017/11/15/reading-paul-reformers-part-one/. Chester starts by helping us understand the dialogues between Erasmus and Luther about the perspicuity of Scripture, about what counts as Scripture, and about the authority of extrabiblical Christian tradition. Erasmus, on the one hand, freely admits Scripture has its obscurities, and therefore

The Reformers and "the works of the law." The phrase "the works of the law" seems to have been a flashpoint during the Reformation and is again today with the new perspective on Paul. Chester helps us to see how ironic it is that, while various members of the new perspective on Paul spend a lot of energy trying to suggest that by "the works of the law" Paul's focus is primarily if not exclusively on "the ceremonies," that is, circumcision, Sabbath keeping, and so on, actually the Reformers themselves say no, the phrase "works of the law" is not a criticism of ethnocentric ceremonies. It is a critique of the whole law, which cannot justify. It seems as though these folks either are ignorant of the Reformation argument by Calvin and others or ignore it.

Chester says we have two connected issues here: (1) what the phrase "the works of the law" means in general, and (2) what Paul's target is

---

one needs allegory at times to make sense of it, whereas Luther insists on the perspicuity of Scripture throughout—but this seems an odd claim when he calls James "a right strawy epistle" and has serious doubts about Revelation being in the canon. It is fair to ask, having read the dialogue or debate, What is really at issue in Luther's beef with Erasmus over Scripture and tradition? Is it just that he wants to reject the role of Catholic tradition so he can have his own say about Scripture?

Chester reminds us that it is important to note the fuller context of Luther's designation of James as an epistle of straw. Luther says, "St. James' epistle is really an epistle of straw . . . for it has nothing of the nature of the gospel about it." The problem for Luther is that an authentically apostolic text should proclaim the gospel, but James barely mentions Christ, concentrating instead on ethical instruction. Luther thinks that James gives us law when it should be preaching gospel, and Luther sees James as standing in tension with Paul concerning justification. Luther therefore regards James as a less important text and wishes to place it at the end of the canon, *but he does not wish to excise it.* He quotes James with approval and preached from James on more than one occasion. Chester stresses that Luther still regarded it as part of God's Word. What Luther does with James is consistent with his hermeneutic of law and gospel and makes sense if one approaches the interpretation of Scripture with that hermeneutic.

While not wanting to accuse Luther of being simply arbitrary in his debate with Erasmus when he asserts the perspicuity of Scripture, Chester admits Luther is less wise than Erasmus in the sense that Erasmus foresees much more clearly the endless divisions over the interpretation of Scripture that have in fact transpired in the subsequent history of Protestantism. But he is perhaps also more courageous and honest in that Erasmus is at key points unwilling to admit the theological consequences of his own immense exegetical scholarship when it brings him into tension with Catholic tradition.

Chester is very clear as well that Luther is very far from opposing tradition just because it is tradition. He insists very sharply in his debate with Erasmus that the church cannot err in its biblical interpretation. Luther is very traditional on this point, and it is his adherence to such a traditional perspective that, ironically, makes him so very radical. Once he has concluded that the Roman church has indeed very seriously erred in its interpretation of Scripture, then the inevitable consequence is that Luther can no longer regard it as the true church. The true church is instead a remnant chosen by grace. Luther insisted throughout his career that he was the true Catholic, not his opponents.

when he says that justification is not by "the works of the law." On point (1) there actually is not too much disagreement among the Reformers. The Reformers insist that the phrase refers to the whole law, that is, to the characteristic Jewish insistence on the swathing of the entirety of life in obedience to divine commandments. However, on point (2), when they exegete the texts where Paul uses the phrase, they always find his target to be works-righteousness.

Chester thinks this exegesis ignores the fact that in Paul's context righteous behavior was synonymous with a nomistic Jewish way of life and sinful behavior with a Gentile way of life. To say that justification does not result from human ethical achievement coheres with and is an inevitable consequence of saying that it does not result from Jewish ethnic identity. Chester argues that Barclay is on target when he states that the underlying issue for Paul in relation to "the works of the law" is the incongruity of grace, which discounts all forms of human worthiness (including both ethnic identity and ethical achievement).

It is fair to say that Chester is mostly in agreement with the main lines of the Reformers' arguments, but in regard to Romans 7 he largely parts company with Luther and Calvin. Interestingly, he thinks there is an autobiographical element to Romans 7:7-25 and that Paul is speaking of himself as typical or representative. He speaks of his former life as a Pharisee, not as it appeared to him then but as it appeared to him now. Chester argues that Paul describes an earlier losing struggle with sin, now seeing the truth of his former condition, particularly in regard to his persecution of the church.[8]

In our opinion, Chester's interpretation of Romans 7 founders on the rocks of Philippians 3:6, where Paul says that before his conversion he was *blameless* in his obedience to the Mosaic law. Indeed, he evaluates his former life as full of positives, except when compared to his life in Christ, whereby it pales into insignificance and indeed can be

---

[8]Chester makes this argument at length both as one of the contributors to *Perspectives on Our Struggle with Sin: 3 Views of Romans 7* (Nashville: Broadman & Holman, 2011) and earlier in *Conversion at Corinth* (Edinburgh: T&T Clark, 2003).

called *skybala.* But this is how Paul reckons it in comparison to something greater, not how he views it in itself. Here Chester seems to agree with the new perspective on Paul on Romans 7 for the most part while disagreeing with the Reformers.

The Reformers, justification, and righteousness. Sometimes in discussion on the new perspective on Paul, misunderstandings crop up in regard to the Reformers taking a forensic view of Paul's language about justification. Chester clarifies things by pointing out that Melanchthon is actually the one who has the more forensic view compared to Luther or Calvin. He demonstrates that while Luther, Melanchthon, and Calvin all freely use the term *imputation* in relation to justification, they do *not* use the term in the way it is typically used today. When we say that righteousness is imputed, the image it evokes for us is righteousness as a substance that is passed across the divine courtroom from Christ to the believer. Wright and others are certainly correct to point out that this idea is absent from the Pauline texts. However, this is not what these three Reformers mean by imputation. For both Luther and Calvin, the believer certainly receives Christ's righteousness, but it is not transferred from one to the other. Rather, faith unites believers with Christ, and within this union of persons those who are in Christ receive his righteousness, inserted into his victorious person. There is exchange, for Christ receives the sins of the world and in return the believer receives his righteousness, but this exchange can only take place within a union of persons. If there is a transfer, it is the believer who is transferred from the realm of sin and death into Christ and the reign of grace. In this way, any danger of a legal fiction is avoided, for Christ is a powerful transforming presence. Calvin in particular is always concerned to place this in trinitarian perspective, seeing the faith that unites the believer with Christ as the work of the Holy Spirit.

Chester goes on to stress that Melanchthon is a little different, since he does not characteristically stress union with Christ in the same way. He speaks of justification as relational, with Christ as the mediator who, through his saving death, intercedes before God and pleads the believer's case before the Father. In Melanchthon's view, the believer is accepted by God on account of Christ. Already in the 1530s Melanchthon's first critics (e.g., Johannes Gropper) saw this as a legal fiction, but Melanchthon at least is always concerned to stress that at the same time as a person is justified, the gift of the Holy Spirit brings about transformation and renewal. This renewing work of the Spirit is not itself part of what Melanchthon understands by justification, but he insists that it always accompanies justification.

Despite this useful explanation by Chester, more of a defense than merely an explanation, there are still major problems with Luther's view, not the least of which is that Luther doesn't seem to be all that consistent in his views of this matter. In our opinion, trying to pin down Luther's view of Christ's "alien righteousness" is more than a little difficult. Sometimes he seems to be talking as if the believer has Christ as a conjoined twin. They are joined together at the hip, but all the righteousness is in the twin and none of it is in the believer, who still is stuck in bondage to sin. When Luther does talk about "Christ in us, the hope of glory" he is still *so* concerned about keeping that righteousness "alien" that it sounds like he's talking about a matryoshka doll. Christ is in us, and he has perfect righteousness, but we don't actually have that righteousness, or it hasn't changed our nature much, hasn't really bled over into us, the outer doll, for we are still stuck with our sins even though Christ indwells us.

On the issue of the wholly alien righteousness of Christ, Luther's interaction with Melanchthon and also Calvin's interactions with Erasmus are worth considering. First of all, the discussion by Luther and Melanchthon on the meaning of *en auto* in 2 Corinthians 5:21 is interesting. *En* (plus the dative) can mean many things other than "in." It can mean, for example, "by." Furthermore, *auto* can mean "it" rather than "him." So, for example, in Romans 1:17 Paul probably means the righteousness of God is revealed "in it" (i.e., in the gospel), not "in him" (i.e., Christ). In 2 Corinthians 5:21 one could certainly read "and the one not knowing sin was made sin for us in order that we might become the righteousness of God by it" or even "in it" (with "it" in this case referring to the atoning death of Christ). Note that "he was made sin" does not mean "he was made a sinner" (and so like us) so that we might become like him through union with him. "He became sin" likely refers to Christ's becoming the sin bearer who takes away the sins of the world (a.k.a. the scapegoat), or possibly it refers to his taking the punishment for our sins in our place. Again, the mere assumption that *dikaiosynē tou theou* refers not to the righteousness of God (as it clearly does in Romans 1) but to the righteousness of Christ is dubious.

In other words, much hangs for these Reformers on a certain kind of reading both of the prepositions involved with dative objects and the phrase itself, which is assumed to refer to Christ, not God's righteousness. But nowhere in the Corinthian correspondence does Paul call Christ *theos* or God's righteousness if not in the above reference, and the only reference to Christ as God in Romans is in the debatable doxology in Romans 9:5. The first-time listeners in Rome to Romans 1 would never have guessed Romans 1:16-17 refers either to Christ's righteousness or to "God's covenant faithfulness." The other supposed reference to Christ as our righteousness in 1 Corinthians 1:30 is not one—it reads as follows: "But from him [the antecedent is *theou,* meaning God] *you are,* in Christ Jesus (who is our Wisdom from God), righteousness and holiness and redemption." Admittedly, this is one of Paul's more convoluted sentences, and clearly Christ is called "our Wisdom" here, but the structure of the sentence shows that *you* is the subject, *are* is the verb, and the object of the main clause is *righteousness* and so on. In other words, this is not about Christ being something for us; it's about what we become when we are in Christ, in his body.

This very sort of argument shows up among the Reformers.[9] Erasmus, focusing on the Greek of Romans 6:11, quite rightly insists that *en* there likely means "by" or "through," whereas Calvin, following the Vulgate, insists it means "in Christ Jesus" because he sees the

---

[9]Chester, *Reading Paul with the Reformers,* 279-85.

discussion as being about ingrafting into Christ. The same problem crops up with their discussion of 2 Corinthians 5:21, where Erasmus says we become the righteousness of God through Christ, and Calvin says "in Christ." Both renderings of the preposition are quite feasible, but Calvin's turns the righteousness of God the Father into the righteousness of Christ. He makes the same mistake with 1 Corinthians 1:30, quite against the flow of the grammar and syntax of the main clause of that sentence. There is no way one can render that sentence to read that Christ is our wisdom and our righteousness and so on and do justice to the grammar. There is no *kai* after the subordinate clause, which ends with the phrase "our wisdom from God."

Chester argues, in regard to 2 Corinthians 5:21, that translating *en auto* as "by it" would be odd given that that the main verb in the sentence—"he made"—is clearly describing a divine action, of which Christ is the object. If Paul intended to say that we become the righteousness of God "by it," then he did not make himself very clear. An instrumental reading, "by him," is certainly possible. There is a symmetry to Paul's argument: since Christ, who knew no sin, was made sin and so shared in the plight of the sinful, sinners are made righteous by sharing in his righteousness.[10] Again, the problem with this is that Jesus did not actually "become sin"; the language likely refers to the scapegoat concept more than that we actually *become* righteousness in his act or through his act (were that the meaning, the word *dikaios* should have been used). Again, Paul says we become the righteousness of *God* because of Christ's death for our sins. Chester simply reiterates that 1 Corinthians 1:30 must imply that Christ is our righteousness, redemption, and so on, but the qualifier *our* is not applied to those words, and furthermore the grammatical structure of the sentence doesn't favor that conclusion. What then would be the object of the subject and predicate "you are"? Does Paul just leave us in the dark about what we are? I don't think so.

[10]Chester agrees with Constantine Campbell in *Paul and Union with Christ: An Exegetical and Theological Study* (Grand Rapids: Zondervan, 2012), 186-87, that the internal logic of the verse supports the idea that believers share in the righteousness of Christ.

Some of Luther's misunderstanding of Paul comes from a misreading of Paul's use of the term *flesh* as if it refers to the whole Christian person (a mistake Bultmann also later made) throughout the entire Christian life, whereas it is far more likely that it is referring to the *yēṣer hara*ʿ Paul's teachers talked about—the sinful inclination that tugs persons in the wrong direction but which in no sense is more powerful that the leading and drawing of the Holy Spirit in the believer's life. Paul in 1 Corinthians 10 tells even the Corinthians that they have a way to overcome temptation, that God provides the means of escape at a minimum. This hardly sounds like the believer being in bondage to sin. The other passage that led Luther down the wrong garden path was of course reading Romans 7:7-25 as referring to the Christian life.

I (Ben) would maintain that the phrase "the righteousness of God," which is a major theme from the outset of Romans 1, has to do with his character.[11] This is made very clear from the next argument in Romans 1:18-32, where one expression of the righteousness of God is

---

[11]Chester points to Max Lee, "Greek Words and Roman Meanings Part 1: (Re)mapping Righteousness Language in Graeco-Roman Discourse," and "Greek Words and Roman Meanings Part 2: A Prolegomenon to Paul's Use of Righteousness Language in his Letters," in *Fire in My Soul: Essays on Pauline Soteriology and the Gospels in Honor of Seyoon Kim* (Eugene, OR: Wipf & Stock, 2014). He admits that undoubtedly one of the principal meanings of the noun *dikaiosynē* in our Greco-Roman sources is "just and righteous character" as a moral disposition. However, it can also mean the administration of a just standard or norm to establish order. The verb *dikaioō* does not in our Greco-Roman sources carry the specific sense of "acquit," but in legal contexts it does mean to declare someone just or to judge someone to be in the right.

So, Chester takes Paul to mean that the righteous person is someone who does what he or she ought to do, that righteousness is doing what ought to be done, and that when a judge justifies a person it is a declaration that this individual has done what is right and not what is wrong. This is why Chester believes that Luther and Calvin in their different ways (ironically, Luther does not often use legal metaphors in relation to justification but prefers marriage metaphors) are on the right track in interpreting Paul when they link justification so closely to union with Christ. For Paul, the declaration that someone is just or in the right is not fictional because it transfers the person who has faith from the dominion of sin to the reign of grace. Within that reign of grace, the believer is united with Christ by the Spirit, and it is in their union with Christ that those who believe receive his righteousness. Christ is the one who has done what is right and not what is wrong. It is therefore when the forensic metaphors get detached from a strong sense of union with Christ (as in Melanchthon's exegesis) that Chester thinks there is the potential danger of uncoupling the forensic from the ethical in the way that I have described. I don't think the danger is merely potential. I think this way of framing things uncouples right standing from righteous behavior, both of which are part of the salvation process, which is not culminated until the believer is fully conformed to the image of Christ at the resurrection. Salvation is not complete at justification.

his *orgē* or wrath against sin now revealed in the world. It does not have to do with "covenant faithfulness," nor does it have a direct connection with "the righteousness of Christ," a noun phrase not found in the New Testament. God in Romans 1 is God the Father, not Christ.

God the Father did not die on the cross for us. God wants his holy character replicated in us ("be ye holy, for I am holy," 1 Pet 1:16 KJV), not merely by imputation but by impartation. Here the Catholics have the better of the argument. So, all this talk about a wholly alien righteousness of Christ being predicated of us, or the idea somehow we get connected to it through union with Christ but that it doesn't result in actual righteousness on our part, seems a far too esoteric and un-Jewish way of reading Paul. Luther is the bigger offender than Calvin, who at least has an adequate doctrine of sanctification. Philippians 3:9 is rather clear—there is a righteousness that comes from God to us (see 2 Cor 5—we become the righteousness of God). Yes, it comes through having faith in Christ, but it is not Christ's righteousness that we are getting in the bargain.

One more thing: if by "alien" all is meant is that it comes from God and in no sense from the one who believes due to her merit, her works, or even her faith, then that is not problematic. But if it doesn't involve the actual change that happens to the believer by means of the new birth but means that instead of guilt by association we only have righteousness by association with or in union with Christ, then we have a truncated understanding of what it means to be a new creature in Christ, with the old having already passed away (not *simul iustus et peccator* and not still in bondage to sin).

If the righteousness we have remains entirely outside us, *extra nos*, this hardly makes us subjectively new creatures, having experienced new birth and working out the salvation that God has worked in us. Christ cannot be righteous for us (if by that one means something more than his once-for-all substitutionary atonement on the cross paid for our sins) any more than he can be saved for us. He can, however, be the source of our salvation and the mediator of God's righteousness to us, of course.[12]

Chester clarifies Luther's hyperliteral reading of Galatians 2 in regard to the "self" by affirming that Luther takes Paul to be saying not that there is no longer a self but that continuity, the sense in which Paul was still Paul, is the continuity of *the sinful self*. It has been crucified with Christ, and it is now Christ who is living, speaking, and acting through Paul. The believer not only receives an alien righteousness but also must live the alien life of Christ. For Paul to continue to live as Paul would be death for him, but to die and to live for Christ is life. The old person and the new creation, the self under sin and the individual in Christ, are opposite possibilities. This means that the believer faces constant strife between two modes of existence occupying the same body. When the believer lives out of union with Christ (living the Christ life, not the life of the self), then she is truly and wholly righteous because Christ is truly and wholly righteous. But when faith falters and the Christian lives from the self (living the life of the self and not the Christ life), the Christian is then truly and wholly a sinner. The Christian daily dwells victoriously in Christ and under his lordship, or falls back defeated into captivity to sin. The Christian lives each day on an apocalyptic battlefield where the Spirit and the flesh are locked in combat.

In other words, Luther doesn't accept Paul's word that the old self has passed away; rather, he affirms that there are two selves in one person

---

[12]Chester clarifies especially Calvin's view by saying that Luther, Melanchthon, and Calvin all freely use the term *imputation* in relation to justification, but they do *not* use the term in the way it is typically used today. "When we say that righteousness is imputed the image it evokes for us is righteousness as a substance that is passed across the divine courtroom from Christ to the believer. Tom Wright and others are certainly correct to point out that this idea is absent from the Pauline texts. However, this is not what these three Reformers mean by imputation. For both Luther and Calvin, the believer certainly receives Christ's righteousness but it is not transferred from one to the other. Rather, faith unites believers with Christ and within this union of persons those who are in Christ receive his righteousness, inserted into his victorious person. There is exchange, for Christ receives the sins of the world and in return the believer receives his righteousness, but this exchange can only take place within a union of persons. If there is a transfer it is the believer who is transferred from the realm of sin and death into Christ and the reign of grace. In this way any danger of a legal fiction is avoided, for Christ is a powerful transforming presence" (email to author, November 6, 2017).

pulling in two directions. But Paul in Galatians 5 is clear enough that the tension in the Christian life is not between old self and new self but between the sinful inclinations (called "flesh") and the leading and pulling of the Holy Spirit. This is a very different matter from suggesting in essence there are two selves at odds in one person. In the end Chester admits that if the Pauline self has died so completely, what are we to say about Paul's continued use of "I," the first-person pronoun? Even if his account of a twofold competing servitude is realistic, what account is to be given on that basis of the growth and development of individuals in discipleship? It seems very strange that Luther, who emphasized so strongly the power of God's grace, did not think it powerful enough to liberate the believer from the bondage to sin such that the believer can say "while sin [i.e., sinful inclinations] remains, it no longer reigns."

Here is where a little training in Paul's rhetoric might have helped Luther. Paul did not cease to be Paul when Christ entered his life. Yes, the old passed away, and he became new creation, a new creature, but Paul was still Paul, and still a "self." He did not suddenly become Jesus! If all Luther means is that one has abandoned one's previous self-centered existence and now has a Christ-oriented and self-sacrificial existence, well and good. But when Paul says we have become new creatures, he is referring to a change, a conversion that affects human nature in various ways, not just in terms of belief but also in terms of affections, willing, and behavior. At the end of the day, Luther's various statements about alien righteousness prevent him from having an adequate theology either of conversion or of sanctification. Yet, elsewhere Luther is prepared to say faith changes us, kills the old Adam, and makes us altogether different persons in spirit, mind, and powers.[13] One is tempted to say: Which is it, Martin? Is the Christian still in the bondage to sin and the old self or not?

Chester agrees that it would be simply bizarre to hold anything other than that God wants his holy character to be replicated in believers. This

[13]Chester, *Reading Paul with the Reformers*, 194.

is a frequent misunderstanding of the whole sixteenth-century debate, in which the Reformers were deeply concerned to reject the medieval view that faith is primarily knowledge (*fides*) of the saving facts of the gospel that must be formed by love in order to justify. Chester points out that they insist instead that faith is inherently active in good works and that faith that does not work is not faith. What they are passionately concerned to deny, however, is that the works of faith are meritorious. Works that are good in the sight of God are impossible for fallen human beings, but not for Christ. Thus, all attempts to claim righteousness as the believer's own can produce only the illusion of transformation. True transformation stems instead from receiving the alien righteousness of Christ, who, through the work of the Spirit, produces genuinely good works in the believer.

For Luther, it is axiomatic that good trees will produce good fruit (Mt 7:17), and Melanchthon and Calvin both frequently express a deep sense of the obligation of believers to be obedient to God. Such works are not a cause of justification, and they are the work of Christ in the believer rather than the believer's own, but justification never exists without them. Chester admits that Luther can be accused of not offering an adequate account of how the believer grows in discipleship, but not of failing to express a proper sense that transformation takes place.[14] I respectfully disagree with Chester at this point. Other than the cognitive side of conversion, Luther isn't usually saying that being a new creature means one's will has been renovated such that by grace one has the power of contrary choice, particularly when it comes to sin. *Simul iustus et peccator*, "always the sinner and yet justified," is a part of Luther's credo he never abandons.

Part of this comes from the legacy of Augustine, which led both Luther and Calvin to think that there could be no such thing as

---

[14]Chester deals with this relationship between faith and works at greater length in "Faith Working Through Love (Gal 5:6): The Role of Human Deeds in Salvation in Luther and Calvin's Exegesis," in *Doing Theology for the Church: Essays in Honor of Klyne Snodgrass* (Eugene, OR: Wipf & Stock, 2014), 41-54.

righteousness, or better said, blamelessness through obedience to God's law, something Paul himself denies. Of course, keeping the law doesn't at the same time have the broader sense of being (1) sinless, or (2) perfect, or (3) free from sinful inclination. It simply means someone is pious and law compliant when it comes to God's law. This is surely what Paul means when he says that in regard to a righteousness that comes from the Mosaic law, he was blameless when he was a Pharisee. No one could call him a lawbreaker.

The Reformers and covenant theology. Another issue that Chester's book raises is of course the issue of covenant theology. It is a great irony that those who most trumpet covenantal theology today don't seem to understand the ancient Near Eastern ways of looking at covenants, much less the early Jewish ways. In that world, when a sovereign made a treaty or a covenant and the people broke it, the sovereign was not obligated any longer to keep that covenant. He could end the relationship, he could invoke the curse sanctions and do so, he could start anew with a new covenant, but there was no talk of renewing a broken covenant.

Where this has a bearing on Paul is of course the interpretation of 2 Corinthians 3 and Galatians 4 especially. In Paul's view, the new covenant is the fulfillment of the Abrahamic one through Christ, "the seed of Abraham" (and in him we are also the seed of Abraham). The Mosaic covenant was an interim arrangement, according to Paul, a child minder until the time had come to send the Messiah to redeem those under the Mosaic law out from under the Mosaic law. Christ is the end of the Mosaic covenant, both in the sense that he fulfilled its just requirements through absorbing the punishment for sin on the cross, absorbing the curse sanctions, and in the sense that the covenant is now *obsolete*, a point that Hebrews makes even more emphatically. So all the arguments about how "the righteousness of God" equals God's covenant faithfulness to the Mosaic covenant simply don't work! It's not Paul's view.

This is not just overreading covenant hither and yon; this is reading a wrong and un-Pauline view of covenant into various texts, especially in Romans. Rather, it is because God is consistent and faithful to his own character of being both just and merciful, both righteous and forgiving, both holy and loving, both compassionate and yet demanding obedience, that we can talk about God's faithfulness. He is faithful to his own character, not to some previous covenant, broken many times. The new covenant is genuinely a new covenant, as Jesus said, and inaugurated in "his blood." It didn't exist before.

Chester points out that Calvin has a strong sense that Scripture contains a single covenant renewed on various occasions, and also a strong sense of the continuing validity of the Mosaic law as a guide to the Christian life. Yet, this is Calvin's canonical view, based on his reading of the whole of Scripture. Paul believed that we receive descriptions of the law in terms only of what was unique to the law (i.e., command and prohibition and the restraining of transgressions). Looked at in this way, abstracted from the promises of the covenant, the time of the law is indeed completely over, and this is what Paul wishes to emphasize.

Chester stresses that this careful distinction by Calvin between the law in Paul's letters alone and the law in Scripture as a whole has some striking exegetical consequences. If one reads Calvin's comments on Romans 1:16-17, he certainly states that the Gentiles have been admitted to participation in the gospel covenant, but he does not expound the righteousness of God primarily in terms of covenant faithfulness. Instead, the righteousness of God is that which is approved at God's tribunal, that is, presumably that which reflects what is right according to God's own character. Chester adds that while Calvin certainly happily reflects on the theme of covenant whenever Paul uses the term, and he certainly regards covenant as significant for Paul, he does not make it the overarching theological category within which the Pauline letters are to be read in the manner of recent "covenantal" interpretations of Paul. Covenant is a category that Calvin develops more strongly in relation to other parts of the canon.

The Reformers and merit theology. It is clear enough that because of the medieval Catholic theology of merit an awful lot of energy was expended by the Reformers to refute the idea that our good works earn merit or that anything we could do could fall into the credit category (although Paul is clear enough in both Gal 3 and Rom 4 that faith did fall into that category for Abraham) insofar as it could contribute to our salvation or justification. The problem with this is that the New Testament says nothing about *merit*, and it says quite a lot about rewards for good works (e.g., 1 Cor 3).

This whole idea of rewards "in heaven" or the eschaton, with salvation not being viewed as a reward itself, comes up a lot in early Judaism, as Chad Thornhill shows, and it also appears in the New Testament.[15] Chester provides us with an example of how hard the Reformers fought against the merit theology of Catholicism. Calvin is so wanting to deny anything meritorious in a good work that he says the work is rewarded just because God loves the worker, not because of the quality of the work. Yet this is just the opposite of what Paul says about the work of ministers in 1 Corinthians 3—those who build with precious stones get the reward, while those who build with hay and so on will be lucky to escape through fire. Calvin seems rather clearly off base here and out of touch with the early Jewish discussions about rewards (see both Sanders and Thornhill). Also, why would Christ's righteousness need to cover for the imperfections of our good works? Can't their shortcomings simply be dealt with by divine forgiveness and compassion? Why drag the imputed righteousness into this discussion when Paul doesn't?[16]

Chester clarifies Calvin's remarks, saying the basic point is the incommensurability of divine holiness and human calculations about merit. Even in theologies that propose that God graciously accords to human deeds a worth far beyond their actual worth, there is still a calculation of relative achievement. Calvin's point in rejecting this is not that God rewards the work just because God loves the worker, but that it is not what we achieve (which will always be pitiable when measured

[15]A. Chadwick Thornhill, *The Chosen People: Election, Paul and Second Temple Judaism* (Downers Grove, IL: InterVarsity Press, 2015).

[16]See Chester, *Reading Paul with the Reformers*, 309.

by divine standards) that counts and is valued by God but rather our affection and willingness to obey. Human reciprocity matters, and God rewards the right use of God's gifts of grace, but this is more like living into an inheritance to which you are already the heir than it is like meriting something that would otherwise not be yours. This is helpful, but it doesn't reckon properly with the difference between "merit" and reward, for example, in 1 Corinthians 3, when Paul talks about the rewards at the eschaton for good ministry. Paul is not saying the rewards have been "earned" or "merited"; he is simply saying that God has chosen to respond to good behavior and good ministry with rewards.

What does Calvin add to the Reformation discussion about salvation that we don't fully find in Luther? Chester believes Calvin's biggest contribution is to distinguish between justification and sanctification as the principal saving benefits of Christ but to position them jointly as benefits simultaneously received in union with Christ. In making a clear distinction between justification and sanctification, and in making extensive use of forensic imagery to describe justification, Calvin is similar to Melanchthon. However, in integrating his understanding of justification by faith with union with Christ, Calvin is much more like Luther.

AND SO?

We have grouped together Barclay and Chester's important recent work on Paul because they both serve as a corrective in various ways to recent readings of Paul that are often based on Reformation misreadings of Paul. The important distinctions Barclay makes, his taxonomy of grace, should be a reliable guide going forward to understanding why Paul affirms both the incongruity of grace and the divine initiative of grace but does not perfect the notion of the efficacy of grace in the way the Reformers do. Barclay is right that Paul believes that apostasy is possible for the saved person.

Chester, in some ways, takes a more traditional Reformed perspective than does Barclay on some of the issues discussed in this chapter, but his most important contribution is clarifying what the Reformers actually did and didn't say on justification, imputed righteousness, covenant theology, and the like. He is also able to deflate the notion that the Reformers should be charged with reading Paul's soteriology in too individualistic a way rather than in a more corporate sense. Often the new perspective on Paul is reacting more to the Lutheran and Reformed descendants of Luther and Calvin than to what the original Reformers actually said. While certainly the Reformers did us all a great service in stressing Paul's theology of grace over against any kind of theology of meriting salvation, or even purchasing indulgences and thereby saving years in purgatory, the Reformers themselves did not adequately know or deal with the proper Jewish context of Paul's theology, as Sanders, Thornhill, and Barclay himself have helped us to see.

The new perspective on Paul has done us a good service in opposing anti-Semitic readings of Paul's view of the Mosaic law, but more could be done in regard to recognizing, as Barclay does, that God is not finished with Israel yet, that the church is not Israel, and that Christ does not simply complete the role God intended for Israel in the world. Furthermore, a better understanding of covenants in light of how ancient Near Eastern and early Jewish covenants worked would have helped both the Reformers and the advocates of the new perspective on Paul. The works of Barclay and Chester are recent, however, and their impacts will continue for some time to come. They may yet help us correct a variety of taken-for-granted misreadings of Paul.

seven

CONCLUSIONS

AN APPALLING AMOUNT OF PAUL?

Bear in mind that our Lord's patience means salvation,
just as our dear brother Paul also wrote you with the wisdom that God gave him.
He writes the same way in all his letters, speaking in them of these matters.
His letters contain some things that are hard to understand, which ignorant and
unstable people distort, as they do the other Scriptures, to their own destruction.

2 Peter 3:15-16

No one understood Paul before Marcion . . . and he misunderstood him.

Attributed to Adolph von Harnack

The year 2017 was the five hundredth anniversary of the Protestant Reformation, which more than anything else was a celebration of a new perspective on Paul and on the salvation he preached that dawned on Luther, and then Calvin, and then Wesley and many others. The Reformation produced not only a printing revolution when it came to putting the Bible into the hands of laypersons but also a lot of furrowed brows, wrestling with "brother Paul" and the thirteen letters attributed to him in the New Testament. We are still wrestling and, like Jacob with the angel, hoping for a blessing, or at least not to leave the encounter with some part of our anatomy out of joint. No wonder John Donne said he heard a thunder that resounds throughout the earth wheresoever he opened St. Paul's letters. We still hear

the thunder, and we wrestle with the letters that make up almost 40 percent of the New Testament. No wonder, too, that some have complained in the last five hundred years that there is an appalling amount of Paul in the New Testament.

What you have encountered in this book is some of the most recent wrestling with brother Paul and his profound thoughts, and you will have noticed that the wrestling was not without considerable sweat being produced, and other sorts of heat as well, as scholars have tried to tug Paul first this way and then that. The question is, Has the recent heat also produced more light on those seminal documents? The answer is yes, in various ways but first in regard to Paul the man.

PAUL THE EARLY JEW

There is no missing the fact that Paul was a gifted communicator, and a variety of recent studies have recognized that Paul was rhetorically gifted and that it shows in his letters. He was good at the ancient art of persuasion and argumentation, and his letters, while not examples of canned systematic theology, reflect a keen and consistent thinker capable of articulating all sorts of theologizing and ethicizing in the form of rhetorical arguments.

So Paul clearly shows evidence not only of learning Greek quite well but also of learning the Greek method of persuasive discourse. But does that make him a Hellenistic or Diaspora Jew? Sanders clearly thinks so, but the other scholars focused on in this study are less sanguine about that conclusion. What all the scholars in this study agree on is that the older attempts by Bousset and others to locate Paul's thought within the parameters of Greco-Roman thought about mystery religions and the like seems clearly to have failed. In these recent large tomes on Paul we find little or no real reflection on Paul's being a Roman citizen, and that despite scholars' interest in his possible critique of the imperial cult in some spots in his letters. In fact, these recent studies generally abstain from reflecting in any way on the relationship of the Paul of Acts to the Paul of the letters, concentrating instead on the content of the letters, and in some cases exclusively concentrating on the capital Paulines, about which there are few if any authorship questions.

Instead of Paul the Diaspora Jew or Roman citizen, there is general agreement in these studies that Paul must be clearly situated somewhere in the midst of the spectrum of worldviews that constituted early Judaism (while recognizing that Judaism itself, including Palestinian Judaism, had been Hellenized to one degree or another prior to the time of Jesus). Equally, none of the scholars focused on in this study think that Paul fits neatly within the parameters of Diaspora synagogue life, as just another argumentative early Jewish person who was not expelled from the synagogue or set up a separate community. Despite the best arguments of Mark Nanos and other Jewish New Testament scholars, neither Sanders, nor Wright, nor Dunn, nor Martyn, nor Gaventa, nor Barclay, nor in general the new perspective folks think that Paul fits in that niche at all well.[1] The Jewish-Christian Judaizers in Galatia make clear that they didn't see Paul that way either.

So the question becomes, Just how radical a Jew was Paul? Would he have been considered apostate by most early Jews, as Alan Segal suggests? It seems clear from Paul's suffering the forty lashes minus one various times that he tried to communicate the gospel in some synagogues, believed the good news was for the Jew first (Rom 1) even though he was the apostle to the Gentiles, and was rebuffed time and again. Furthermore, the evidence of Paul's letters makes clear he did set up communities that were separate from the synagogue and involved both Jews and Gentiles. There would be no need for discussions such as those in Galatians 2 about Jews and Gentiles meeting and eating together, or the discussions in 1 Corinthians 8–10, or the discussions in Romans 14, if there were not Pauline communities where Gentiles were

---

[1]Not all Jewish scholars have tried to resituate Paul and his converts in the synagogue context. There are a variety of views (see Paul Fredriksen, Daniel Boyarin, Shaye Cohen, Mark Nanos, and Magnus Zettterholm, among others). The major thrust of some of those studies is to try to suggest that Paul is only arguing about whether Gentiles should Judaize, but there are too many clues, such as those we find in 1 Cor 9 or Gal 3:28, that Paul sees Christ-followers of whatever ethnic extraction as a third sort of thing—neither Jew nor Gentile any longer, but simply persons "in Christ."

largely setting the agenda and establishing the ethos of the community but in which *there were Jews as well participating in the same house-church meetings.* The parting of the ways between early Christianity and early Judaism had already begun de facto in the Pauline communities, even though Paul continued to visit and try to evangelize in the synagogue.

But was Paul a practicing Jew—did he keep the Sabbath, the food laws, the purity rules? The evidence suggests that while he could be the Jew to the Jew in order by all means to win some for Christ (1 Cor 9), nevertheless, *he did not feel obligated to do so as a follower of Christ.* It was for him an option but not required as a follower of Christ. It was an *adiaphoron.* This certainly made him a radical Jew, one who even irritated many of his fellow Jewish Christians who had not yet worked out the radical implications of the gospel of Jew and Gentile united in Christ (Gal 3:28), as Paul had done. He was ahead of the curve, and his communities were previews of coming trends.

Paul, while indeed a radical Jew, was still very much a Jew who believed in a Jewish Messiah, in a form of Jewish eschatology, who believed in the God of the Old Testament as Jesus' Abba, who affirmed the importance of a harmonious religious community and a covenantal relationship between God and his people. But what sort of covenantal relationship? Wright, and to a lesser degree Dunn, see the new covenant of Paul as a renewal of the Mosaic one rather than being something genuinely new. Wright even wants to read Paul's thought and the new covenant in the light of Deuteronomy 27–30, indeed in the light of both exodus and exile. But as the other studies surveyed in this work have shown, this configuration of Paul's worldview and thought world is problematic in various ways. Many early Jews did not see themselves as being in exile, and many, unlike the Qumranites, did not see the Herodian temple and its religion as hopelessly corrupt.

There is a general agreement among these scholars—except perhaps Sanders, who sees Paul as inconsistent—that Paul ultimately did *not* maintain a two-track model of salvation, one for Jews and one for pagans, and there is also agreement, again excepting Sanders, that Paul was not a universalist. At the eschaton, only one community of Jew and Gentile together are envisioned by Paul as among the saved. The sheer agony Paul expresses in Romans 9:1-5 about the rejection of Christ by many early Jews, and his willingness to even be cut off from God himself if they could be reclaimed, should make clear he views them as lost, cut off from the olive tree of God's people for the time being. But Paul believes that when the Redeemer returns from heavenly Zion, he will successfully remedy this problem so that Israel might indeed be saved. Paul was thoroughly Jewish, but a radical Jew, at least as radical as the Qumranites, if not more radical. No Jew who could say what Paul says in Philippians 3, probably speaking late in his life, about his heritage being regarded as *skybala* in comparison to the benefits of being in Christ, could possibly be viewed by most early Jews as anything other than radical, if not an apostate from the mainstream of early Judaism.

PAUL THE THINKER

All of the scholars surveyed in this study recognize that there is evidence of development in Paul's thought over time, but because there is not general agreement about the order of Paul's letters, there is also not agreement about the nature and scope of this development. Even though Albert Schweitzer was laid to rest over fifty years ago now (in 1965), his ghost still haunts twenty-first-century discussions of Paul, as is clearly in evidence in chapter two. There is still no agreement on the character of Paul's future eschatology, though there is general recognition that Paul acknowledges that Jesus' return, like a thief in the night, was *possibly* but not certainly imminent. What is not the case is that Paul shows signs of disappointment, whether early or late in the corpus of his letters, about a "delay" in the parousia. This is not surprising, however, when one realizes that Paul was not into date setting for that event, and the idea of a delay presupposes that one knows when it was supposed to happen and that it didn't. He offered great expectations about the certainty of Christ's return but no prognostications about the timetable.

But there is another problem as well: working with too truncated a canon of Paul's letters. Some scholars surveyed in this study do not for the most part extend their scrutiny beyond the undisputed Pauline letters—Romans, 1 and 2 Corinthians, Galatians, Philippians, 1 Thessalonians, and Philemon. The criteria by which this list was decided frankly hasn't been closely reevaluated in many years. It's simply taken for granted as a starting point. What's wrong with this picture? Well, for one thing, it ignores the recent gains from rhetorical studies that have shown, for instance, that Ephesians is an example of a specific kind of rhetoric, Asiatic rhetoric, and so the difference in style has to do not with the difference in authorship but the difference in the character and kind of the rhetoric. Or let's take another example, 2 Thessalonians.

The reasons for leaving 2 Thessalonians out of account don't have to do with style or vocabulary but rather with an assumed difference in eschatology. Second Thessalonians 2 indicates that there are preliminary events that have not yet transpired that will precede the parousia of Christ. This is assumed to be at odds with 1 Thessalonians 4–5. Why? If one is prepared to suggested that Paul's thought developed over time in regard to his discussions of eschatology and the afterlife anyway (take, e.g., Sanders's discussions of 1 Cor 15; 2 Cor 5), why not a development between the writing of 1 Thessalonians and 2 Thessalonians?

But the real issue here is a failure to interpret 1 Thessalonians 4 properly. Paul is dealing with two unknowns: (1) the timing of Christ's return and (2) the timing of his own death (and that of other Christians). Paul could not say "we who are dead before the Lord returns" because he knows neither the date of that return nor the date of his own demise. What this text attests to is that Paul believes it is *possible*, but not certain, that Christ could return soon, but he is not prepared to make calculations. Rather, he merely insists that believers should always be ready. But the thief-in-the-night metaphor, which suggests a coming at a surprising and unknown time, along with the focus on reassuring the Thessalonians that their deceased fellow believers will not be left out when Christ returns, should make clear to us that Paul never said anything like, "We know Jesus is definitely coming back very soon."

Or let's take one final example: Colossians. Wright and Dunn are prepared to suggest that at least in substance Colossians is Pauline. Why then do many scholars still place it in the non- or post-Pauline dustbin? Chiefly because of its cosmic Christology, found in Colossians 1. But again, *if one is prepared to allow some development over time in Paul's thought, why not this development?* After all, cosmic Christology is already hinted at in other Pauline letters that suggest that Christ preexisted (see, e.g., 1 Cor 10; Phil 2). There is nothing in Colossians 1 that is *at odds* with what Paul says in his earlier letters. What is especially odd is that one would think that those enamored with an apocalyptic reading of Paul would find the material especially in Colossians 1–2 congenial to their approach.

There is a further consideration. Colossians, like Romans, was written to a congregation Paul himself had apparently not visited but that was having problems Paul needed to address because one of his coworkers had in fact planted this church in the Lycus Valley and Paul felt responsible. As with Romans, Paul is not able to take a completely direct approach to the problem because these are not his personal converts, nor had he visited them yet. These facts should alter the calculus of whether Paul could have written a letter like this. If Colossians is indeed Pauline, then it also becomes more plausible that Ephesians is a Pauline circular letter written to a series of churches that draws on Colossians toward the end of the composition and shares with Colossians the same Asiatic rhetoric so popular in the provinces in that whole region, including the province of Asia.

The overall point in noting these examples is that *if one starts with a truncated Paul, one gets truncated results.* It would be like studying the early speeches of Abraham Lincoln when he campaigned for the presidency and then ignoring his later Gettysburg Address and Emancipation Proclamation, which are much more polished speeches with more developed thought on the issues of slavery and national unity, ignoring them on the grounds that *the style and substance of the later speeches is more polished or more developed or both*. But surely, with a thinker as important as Paul was for the nascent Christian movement, it would be wise to take as much source material as possible into account to get an accurate assessment of Paul's thought world, even if, in the end, we have some doubts about some of the "later" Paulines and how the Paul of Acts comports with the Paul of the letters. In regard to that last issue, I would say that Luke is portraying Paul as a missionary and a church planter and does not focus on his work of discipling those already converted, whereas the letters are written to those who are already followers of Christ. These are not two different Pauls in Acts and the Epistles but rather Paul playing two different roles.

What about the issues that the new perspective(s) on Paul raised in the last twenty years? Well, if one starts with the *pistis Christou* controversy, one quickly discovers that there are a variety of views—only Wright and Richard Hays are strong advocates for the "faithfulness of Christ" view of the phrase, whereas Dunn and Barclay are completely unconvinced and it would appear Sanders is mostly unconvinced. Sometimes fresh readings of Paul open up new vistas on how we read the corpus of Paul's letters in general, but the rendering of this phrase at the end of the day doesn't change a lot theologically. Faith in Christ is still seen as affirmed and necessary for salvation by Paul, but perhaps one can argue that the subjective genitive reading of the phrase did open some new vistas in regard to Pauline ethics, namely, the imitation of Christ. Being faithful even unto death or martyrdom could be said to be undergirded or supported by that fresh way of rendering *pistis Christou*.

What should we think of the apocalyptic Paul, sometimes assumed to be a development of the Schweitzerian Paul? Part of the problem in that whole discussion is approaching the matter from an all too modern and post-Enlightenment perspective. What we mean by this is, if one starts with a naturalistic worldview and then sees God's action in this world as an invasion, much less seeing miracles as a violation or contravention of the natural order, one is approaching this whole matter in a way that would be unrecognizable to Paul and the other early Christians. From their worldview, God is an actor in the human drama just as much as any human being is, and one could hardly talk about God violating the laws of nature that he himself set up! The modern notions about miracles or "divine intervention" (as if God were normally AWOL, or only rarely and miraculously involved) do not suit the mindset or proper contextual discussion of ancient texts.

On the other hand, it is true to say that Paul did not see the present, or the recent past since the Christ event, as simply a matter of business as usual. Paul was a visionary; he believed God kept on working and acting in and through human beings, and sometimes directly as well, for Christ came to bring in God's final divine saving activity, and Paul believed that the present was not simply a continuation of the story of God's people in the past. No, God was doing something new, and it was good news for both Jews and Gentiles. This is precisely why Paul does not see the new covenant as a continuation of the Mosaic covenant but rather connects it with the Abrahamic covenant, bearing in mind that Abraham started out as a pagan, came to trust in the biblical God, and is accordingly the forefather of both Jews and Gentiles, even "according to the flesh."[2]

Advocates of the apocalyptic Paul are pointing to something important, namely, that the traditional Reformed perspective, which sees God's actions as an example of "covenantal faithfulness," as though the Mosaic covenant were still in play in Paul's view, is simply incorrect. God had no obligation to keep a covenant egregiously broken by his people. But God, quite apart from covenantal obligations, is a God of grace and mercy, and indeed a promise keeper, keeping his promises to Abraham. This brings us quite appropriately to the most important work done on God's grace in Paul's thought in living memory.

---

[2]That is, though Abraham was born a pagan and was Gentile by ethnic extraction, he not only came to trust in Yahweh alone but also got circumcised and can be said to be the forefather of the chosen people, the Hebrews.

The most recent groundbreaking work that could really *change* the understanding of some aspects of Pauline thought is that of John Barclay on grace in Paul's letters. Here we have a careful parsing out of the six different ways the language of grace has been and could be used when interpreting Paul's letters, and Barclay rightly points out the anachronism of reading modern notions of grace (anonymous givers or giving with no thought of return, giving without regard to merit or worth of the recipient) into the Pauline discussion. Barclay shows in detail how, while Paul affirms incongruous grace (grace given even to the ungodly, even to sinners, even to enemies), at the same time he does not affirm the perfecting of grace in such a way that it prevents a saved person from committing apostasy (denying the irresistible efficacy of grace too often assumed in more Reformed analyses of Paul). Paul is also clear enough that God's grace is meant to set up a relationship where there is a return, at least in the form of thanksgiving and love. We may expect a good deal more from Barclay's pen when he deals with the horizontal or intrahuman aspects or dimensions of grace in Paul's thought, which will be explored in a second study.

PAUL THE MISSIONARY

Because these studies do not much deal with the Paul of Acts but rather concentrate on Paul's letters and therefore what he says about theology, ethics, and praxis in those letters, there is not much discussion of Paul the missionary in these recent studies. After all, all of Paul's letters are addressed to those who are already "in Christ" and so can be said to be exercises in discipleship, not evangelism. Missing from these discussions is assessment of the work of, for instance, Paul Trebilco, or Rodney Stark, or Edwin Judge, or Eckhard Schnabel, or the older work of Wayne Meeks. There is a little of this sort of discussion in Sanders, and more in Dunn's Beginnings series, and a little in Wright's work as well, but not nearly enough. More integration is needed, more understanding required of the interface between Paul's identity, Paul's thought world, and Paul's evangelistic work. How exactly did early Christianity become such a

Gentile-dominated enterprise with a life of its own, even before the end of the first century AD? The temptation, of course, is to dwell on Paul's thought world and ideas, and not do the hard work of assessing the social history and impact of Pauline communities in the Greco-Roman world.

All indications are that Paul converted a cross-section of society, including some Jewish and Gentile elites who could provide venues for the Christian meetings that needed to be held each week (notice 1 Cor 16:2, "On the first day of every week, each one of you should set aside . . ."). Paul himself was educationally elite in various ways, and in a highly stratified society it is noteworthy that he was able to integrate both men and women, both Jews and Gentiles, both slaves and free persons, both married and single persons, both ordinary people and more elite people, into the same communities. Pauline communities were not like trade guild meetings or symposiums for the elite only. The later polemic that Christians chiefly were "women, slaves, and minors" was indeed a polemic, but with a strong element of truth. These people had the most to gain socially and spiritually, in some ways, by becoming followers of Christ.

In other words, though all of these studies of the last twenty years have advanced our understanding of Paul as a thinker and as a rather radical Jew, not enough has been done to help us understand Paul's role in helping the faith of Jesus Christ spread up and down the social hierarchy, geographically from Jerusalem to Rome, and into the hearts of men, women, and children throughout the empire. We may hope that the next twenty years may shed more light on these things, even while it is inevitable that we will still be talking about Paul the talking head, the shaper of Christian thought, and perhaps as well Paul the first great Christian theologian.

BIBLIOGRAPHY

Anderson, Garwood. *Paul's New Perspective: Charting a Soteriological Journey*. Downers Grove, IL: IVP Academic, 2016.

Bailey, Kenneth. *Paul Through Mediterranean Eyes: Cultural Studies in 1 Corinthians*. Downers Grove, IL: InterVarsity Press, 2011.

Barclay, John M. G. *Paul and the Gift*. Grand Rapids: Eerdmans, 2017.

———. "Why the Roman Empire Was Insignificant to Paul." In *Pauline Churches and Diaspora Jews*, 363-87. Tubingen: Mohr, 2011.

Barclay, John M. G., and Simon Gathercole, eds. *Divine and Human Agency in Paul and His Cultural Environment*. Edinburgh: T&T Clark, 2006.

Bauckham, Richard. *Jesus and the God of Israel*. Grand Rapids: Eerdmans, 2008.

Beker, J. Christaan. *Paul the Apostle: The Triumph of God in Life and Thought*. Philadelphia: Fortress, 1980.

———. *Paul's Apocalyptic Gospel: The Coming Triumph of God*. Philadelphia: Fortress, 1982.

———. *The Triumph of God: The Essence of Paul's Thought*. Philadelphia: Fortress, 1990.

Blackwell, Ben C., John K. Goodrich, and Jason Matson, eds. *Paul and the Apocalyptic Imagination*. Minneapolis: Fortress, 2016.

Boer, Martinus C. de. "Apocalyptic as God's Eschatological Activity." In *Paul and the Apocalyptic Imagination*, edited by Ben C. Blackwell, John K. Goodrich, and Jason Maston, 45-64. Minneapolis: Fortress, 2016.

———. *The Defeat of Death: Apocalyptic Eschatology in Romans 5 and 1 Corinthians 15*. Sheffield: Sheffield Academic Press, 1988.

———. *Galatians*. Louisville, KY: Westminster John Knox, 2011.

———. "Paul and Apocalyptic Eschatology." In *The Origins of Apocalypticism in Judaism and Christianity*, vol. 1 of *The Encyclopedia of Apocalypticism*, edited by John J. Collins, 345-83. New York: Continuum, 2000.

———. "Paul and Jewish Apocalyptic Eschatology." In *Apocalyptic and the New Testament: Essays in Honor of J. Louis Martyn*, edited by Joel Marcus and Marion L. Soards, 174-84. Sheffield: JSOT Press, 1989.

Bryan, Christopher. *Render to Caesar: Jesus, the Early Church, and the Roman Superpower*. Oxford: Oxford University Press, 2005.

Campbell, Constantine R. *Paul and Union with Christ: An Exegetical and Theological Study.* Grand Rapids: Zondervan, 2012.

Campbell, Douglas. *The Deliverance of God: An Apocalyptic Rereading of Justification in Paul.* Grand Rapids: Eerdmans, 2009.

Carson, D. A., Peter T. O'Brien, and Mark A. Seifrid, eds. *Justification and Variegated Nomism.* 2 vols. Grand Rapids: Baker, 2001–2004.

Chester, Stephen. *Conversion at Corinth.* Edinburgh: T&T Clark, 2003.

———. "Faith Working Through Love (Gal 5:6): The Role of Human Deeds in Salvation in Luther and Calvin's Exegesis." In *Doing Theology for the Church: Essays in Honor of Klyne Snodgrass,* 41-54. Eugene, OR: Wipf & Stock, 2014.

———. *Perspectives on Our Struggle with Sin: 3 Views of Romans 7.* Nashville: Broadman & Holman, 2011.

———. *Reading Paul with the Reformers: Reconciling Old and New Perspectives.* Grand Rapids: Eerdmans, 2017.

Collins, John J. "The Apocalyptic Genre." In *The Apocalyptic Imagination: An Introduction to Jewish Apocalyptic Literature,* 1-52. 3rd ed. Grand Rapids: Eerdmans, 2016.

———. "Introduction: Toward the Morphology of a Genre." *Semeia* 14 (1979): 1-20.

———. "What Is Apocalyptic Literature?" In *The Oxford Handbook of Apocalyptic Literature,* ed. John J. Collins, 1-18. New York: Oxford University Press, 2014.

Congdon, David W. *The Mission of Demythologizing: Rudolf Bultmann's Dialectical Theology.* Eugene, OR: Cascade Books, 2015.

———. *Rudolf Bultmann: A Companion to His Theology.* Eugene, OR: Cascade Books, 2015.

Cranfield, C. E. B. "'The Works of the Law' in the Epistle to the Romans." *Journal for the Study of the New Testament* 43 (1991): 89-101.

Davies, J. P. *Paul Among the Apocalypses?: An Evaluation of the "Apocalyptic Paul" in the Context of Jewish and Christian Apocalyptic Literature.* New York: T&T Clark, 2016.

Davies, W. D. *Paul and Rabbinic Judaism: Some Rabbinic Elements in Pauline Theology.* Minneapolis: Fortress, 1980.

Donaldson, Terence L. *Judaism and the Gentiles: Jewish Patterns of Universalism (to 135 CE).* Waco, TX: Baylor University Press, 2007.

Dunn, James D. G. "In Search of Common Ground." In *Paul and the Mosaic Law,* edited by James D. G. Dunn, 309-44. Grand Rapids, Eerdmans 2001.

———. "The New Perspective on Paul." In *NPP,* 99-120.

———. "A New Perspective on the New Perspective on Paul." *Early Christianity* 4 (2013): 157-82.

Fee, Gordon D. *God's Empowering Presence.* Grand Rapids: Baker, 2009.

———. *Paul, the Spirit, and the People of God.* Grand Rapids: Baker, 1996.

Fredriksen, Paula. *Paul: The Pagan's Apostle.* New Haven, CT: Yale University Press, 2017.

Frey, J. "Demythologizing Apocalyptic?" In *God and the Faithfulness of Paul,* edited by Christoph Helig, J. Thomas Hewitt, and Michael Bird, 489-531. Minneapolis: Fortress, 2017.

Friesen, S. J. *Imperial Cult and the Apocalypse of John: Reading Revelation in the Ruins*. Oxford: Oxford University Press, 2001.

Gaventa, Beverly Roberts, ed. *Apocalyptic Paul: Cosmos and Anthropos in Romans 5–8*. Waco, TX: Baylor University Press, 2013.

———. "Thinking from Christ to Israel: Romans 9–11 in Apocalyptic Context." In *Paul and the Apocalyptic Imagination*, edited by Ben C. Blackwell, John K. Goodrich, and Jason Maston, 239-56. Minneapolis: Fortress, 2016.

———. *When in Romans: An Invitation to Linger with the Gospel According to Paul*. Grand Rapids: Baker, 2016.

Hanson, Paul D. *The Dawn of Apocalyptic: The Historical and Sociological Roots of Jewish Apocalyptic Eschatology*. Philadelphia: Fortress, 1979.

Harrington, Hannah K. "Sin." In *The Eerdmans Dictionary of Early Judaism*, edited by John J. Collins and Daniel C. Harlow, 1230. Grand Rapids: Eerdmans, 2010.

Hays, Richard B. *Echoes of Scripture in the Letters of Paul*. New Haven, CT: Yale University Press, 1993.

———. *The Faith of Jesus Christ*. Peabody, MA: Hendrickson, 2009.

———. *The Faith of Jesus Christ: The Narrative Substructure of Galatians 3:1–4:11*. 2nd ed. Grand Rapids: Eerdmans, 2002.

———. "Humanity Prior to the Revelation of Faith." In *Beyond Bultmann: Reckoning a New Testament Theology*, edited by Bruce W. Longenecker and Mikeal C. Parsons, 61-78. Waco, TX: Baylor University Press, 2014.

Heiser, Michael S. *Angels: What the Bible Really Says About God's Heavenly Host*. Bellingham, WA: Lexham, 2018.

Helig, Christoph, J. Thomas Hewitt, and Michael F. Bird, eds. *God and the Faithfulness of Paul*. Minneapolis: Fortress, 2017.

Hengel, Martin. *Judaism and Hellenism*. Philadelphia: Fortress, 1981.

———. *Paul Between Damascus and Antioch*. Louisville, KY: Westminster John Knox, 1997.

Hurtado, L. "YHWH'S Return to Zion." In *God and the Faithfulness of Paul*, edited by Christoph Helig, J. Thomas Hewitt, and Michael F. Bird, 417-38. Minneapolis: Fortress, 2017.

Käsemann, Ernst. "The Beginnings of Christian Theology." In *New Testament Questions of Today*, translated by W. J. Montague. Philadelphia: Fortress, 1969.

———. *Perspectives on Paul*. Philadelphia: Fortress, 1971.

Kim, Seyoon. "Paul and the Roman Empire." In *God and the Faithfulness of Paul*, edited by Christoph Hellig, Michael F. Bird, and J. Thomas Hewitt, 277-308. Minneapolis: Fortress, 2017.

Lee, Max. "Greek Words and Roman Meanings Part 1: (Re)mapping Righteousness Language in Graeco-Roman Discourse." In *Fire in My Soul: Essays on Pauline Soteriology and the Gospels in Honor of Seyoon Kim*, 3-28. Eugene, OR: Wipf & Stock, 2014.

———. "Greek Words and Roman Meanings Part 2: A Prolegomenon to Paul's Use of Righteousness Language in His Letters. In *Fire in My Soul: Essays on Pauline Soteriology and the Gospels in Honor of Seyoon Kim*, 29-52. Eugene, OR: Wipf & Stock, 2014.

Longenecker, Bruce W., ed. *Narrative Dynamics in Paul: A Critical Assessment*. Louisville: Westminster John Knox, 2002.

Longenecker, Bruce W., and Mikeal C. Parsons, eds. *Beyond Bultmann: Reckoning a New Testament Theology*. Waco, TX: Baylor University Press, 2014.

Luther, Martin. *Word and Sacrament I*. Edited by E. Theodore Bachmann. Luther's Works 35. Philadelphia: Fortress, 1960.

Marcus, Joel, and Marion L. Soards. Foreword to *Apocalyptic and the New Testament: Essays in Honor of J. Louis Martyn*, edited by Joel Marcus and Marion L. Soards, 7-8. Sheffield: JSOT Press, 1989.

Martyn, J. Louis. *Theological Issues in the Letters of Paul*. Edinburgh: T&T Clark, 1997.

Matlock, R. Barry. *Unveiling the Apocalyptic Paul: Paul's Interpreters and the Rhetoric of Criticism*. Sheffield: Sheffield Academic Press, 1996.

McKnight, Scot. "Exiled in the Land." In *Exile: A Conversation with N. T. Wright*, edited by James M. Scott, 201-16. Downers Grove, IL: InterVarsity Press, 2017.

McKnight, Scot, and Joseph B. Modica, eds. *Jesus Is Lord, Caesar Is Not: Evaluating Empire in New Testament Studies*. Downers Grove, IL: InterVarsity Press, 2012.

Meeks, Wayne. *The First Urban Christians*. New Haven, CT: Yale University Press, 1983.

Moore, G. F. "Christian Writers on Judaism." *Harvard Theological Review* 14 (1921): 174-254.

Munck, Johannes. *Paul and the Salvation of Mankind*. Louisville: John Knox, 1954.

Nanos, Mark, and Magnus Zetterholm, eds. *Paul Within Judaism: Restoring the First-Century Context to the Apostle*. Minneapolis: Fortress, 2015.

Price, S. R. F. "The Place of Religion: Rome in the Early Empire." In vol. 10 of *Cambridge Ancient History*, edited by A. K. Bowman, E. Champlin, and A. Lintott, 812-47. Cambridge: Cambridge University Press, 1996.

Rad, Gerhard von. *Old Testament Theology*. Vol. 2. New York: Harper & Row, 1965.

Räisänen, Heikki. *Paul and the Law*. 2nd ed. Eugene, OR: Wipf & Stock, 2010.

Rowland, Christopher. "Apocalypticism." In *Eerdmans Dictionary of Early Judaism*, edited by John J. Collins and Daniel C. Harlow, 345-48. Grand Rapids: Eerdmans, 2010.

Schweitzer, Albert. *The Mysticism of Paul the Apostle*. New York: Seabury, 1968.

Scott, James M., ed. *Exile: A Conversation with N. T. Wright*. Downers Grove, IL: InterVarsity Press, 2017.

Segal, Alan. *Paul the Convert: The Apostolate and Apostasy of Saul the Pharisee*. New Haven, CT: Yale University Press, 1992.

Standhartinger, Angela. "Bultmann's *Theology of the New Testament* in Context." In *Beyond Bultmann: Reckoning a New Testament Theology*, edited by Bruce W. Longenecker and Mikeal C. Parsons, 233-55. Waco, TX: Baylor University Press, 2014.

Stendahl, Krister. *Paul Among Jews and Gentiles*. Minneapolis: Fortress, 1976.

Sturm, Richard E. "Defining the Word 'Apocalyptic': A Problem in Biblical Criticism." In *Apocalyptic and the New Testament: Essays in Honor of J. Louis Martyn*, edited by Joel Marcus and Marion L. Soards, 17-48. Sheffield: JSOT Press, 1989.

Sumney, Jerry L. *Identifying Paul's Opponents: The Question of Method in 2 Corinthians*. London: Bloomsbury, 2015.

Thornhill, A. Chadwick. *The Chosen People: Election, Paul and Second Temple Judaism*. Downers Grove, IL: InterVarsity Press, 2015.

Tilling, Chris. *Paul's Divine Christology*. Tübingen: Mohr, 2012.

Vielhauer, Philipp. "Apocalypses and Related Subjects." In vol. 2 of *New Testament Apocrypha*, 542-68. Louisville, KY: Westminster John Knox, 2003.

Witherington, Ben, III. *Biblical Theology: The Convergence of the Canon*. Cambridge: Cambridge University Press, 2019.

———. *Grace in Galatia*. Grand Rapids: Eerdmans, 1998.

———. *The Indelible Image*. 2 vols. Downers Grove, IL: InterVarsity Press, 2009–2010.

———. *Isaiah Old and New: Exegesis, Intertextuality, and Hermeneutics*. Minneapolis: Fortress, 2017.

———. *Letters and Homilies for Hellenized Christians*. Vol. 1. Downers Grove, IL: InterVarsity Press, 2014.

———. *The Paul Quest: The Renewed Search for the Jew of Tarsus*. Downers Grove, IL: InterVarsity Press, 1998.

———. *Paul's Letter to the Philippians*. Grand Rapids: Eerdmans, 2011.

———. *Paul's Narrative Thought World: The Tapestry of Tragedy and Triumph*. Louisville: Westminster John Knox, 1994.

———. *Psalms Old and New: Exegesis, Intertextuality, and Hermeneutics*. Minneapolis: Fortress, 2017.

———. "Reading Paul with the Reformers—Part One." The Bible and Culture, November 15, 2017. www.patheos.com/blogs/bibleandculture/2017/11/15/reading-paul-reformers-part-one/.

———. *Torah Old and New: Exegesis, Intertextuality, and Hermeneutics*. Minneapolis: Fortress, 2018.

———. "Wright's Paul and the Faithfulness of God—Part Eighteen." The Bible and Culture, March 8, 2014. www.patheos.com/blogs/bibleandculture/2014/03/08/wrights-paul-and-the-faithfulness-of-god-part-eighteen/.

———. "Wright's Paul and the Faithfulness of God—Part Eleven." The Bible and Culture, February 24, 2014. www.patheos.com/blogs/bibleandculture/2014/02/24/wrights-paul-and-the-faithfulness-of-god-part-eleven/.

———. "Wright's Paul and the Faithfulness of God—Part Fifteen." The Bible and Culture, March 5, 2014. www.patheos.com/blogs/bibleandculture/2014/03/05/wrights-paul-and-the-faithfulness-of-god-part-fifteen/.

———. "Wright's Paul and the Faithfulness of God—Part Fourteen." The Bible and Culture, March 2, 2014. www.patheos.com/blogs/bibleandculture/2014/03/02/wrights-paul-and-the-faithfulness-of-god-part-fourteen/.

———. "Wright's Paul and the Faithfulness of God—Part Nineteen." The Bible and Culture, March 9, 2014. www.patheos.com/blogs/bibleandculture/2014/03/09/wrights-paul-and-the-faithfulness-of-god-part-sixteen/.

———. "Wright's Paul and the Faithfulness of God—Part Seventeen." The Bible and Culture, March 7, 2014. www.patheos.com/blogs/bibleandculture/2014/03/07/wrights-paul-and-the-faithfulness-of-god-part-seventeen/.

———. "Wright's Paul and the Faithfulness of God—Part Thirty." The Bible and Culture, April 3, 2014. www.patheos.com/blogs/bibleandculture/2014/04/03/wrights-paul-and-the-faithfulness-of-god-part-thirty/.

———. "Wright's Paul and the Faithfulness of God—Part Thirty-One." The Bible and Culture, April 4, 2014. www.patheos.com/blogs/bibleandculture/2014/04/04/wrights-paul-and-the-faithfulness-of-god-part-thirty-one/.

———. "Wright's Paul and the Faithfulness of God—Part Thirty-Two." The Bible and Culture, April 5, 2014. www.patheos.com/blogs/bibleandculture/2014/04/05/wrights-paul-and-the-faithfulness-of-god-part-thirty-two/.

———. "Wright's Paul and the Faithfulness of God—Part Twelve." The Bible and Culture, February 25, 2014. www.patheos.com/blogs/bibleandculture/2014/02/25/wrights-paul-and-the-faithfulness-of-god-part-twelve/.

———. "Wright's Paul and the Faithfulness of God—Part Twenty." The Bible and Culture, March 10, 2014. www.patheos.com/blogs/bibleandculture/2014/03/10/wrights-paul-and-the-faithfulness-of-god-part-twenty/.

———. "Wright's Paul and the Faithfulness of God—Part Twenty-Eight." The Bible and Culture, March 27, 2014. www.patheos.com/blogs/bibleandculture/2014/03/27/wrights-paul-and-the-faithfulness-of-god-part-twenty-eight/.

———. "Wright's Paul and the Faithfulness of God—Part Twenty-Five." The Bible and Culture, March 18, 2014. www.patheos.com/blogs/bibleandculture/2014/03/18/wrights-paul-and-the-faithfulness-of-god-part-twenty-five/.

———. "Wright's Paul and the Faithfulness of God—Part Twenty-Four." The Bible and Culture, March 15, 2014. www.patheos.com/blogs/bibleandculture/2014/03/15/wrights-paul-and-the-faithfulness-of-god-part-twenty-four/.

———. "Wright's Paul and the Faithfulness of God—Part Twenty-Nine." The Bible and Culture, April 1, 2014. www.patheos.com/blogs/bibleandculture/2014/04/01/wrights-paul-and-the-faithfulness-of-god-part-twenty-nine/.

———. "Wright's Paul and the Faithfulness of God—Part Twenty-One." The Bible and Culture, March 11, 2014. www.patheos.com/blogs/bibleandculture/2014/03/11/wrights-paul-and-the-faithfulness-of-god-part-twenty-one/.

———. "Wright's Paul and the Faithfulness of God—Part Twenty-Six." The Bible and Culture, March 24, 2014. www.patheos.com/blogs/bibleandculture/2014/03/24/wrights-paul-and-the-faithfulness-of-god-part-twenty-six/.

———. "Wright's Paul and the Faithfulness of God—Part Twenty-Three." The Bible and Culture, March 14, 2014. www.patheos.com/blogs/bibleandculture/2014/03/14/wrights-paul-and-the-faithfulness-of-god-part-twenty-three/.

———. "Wright's Paul and the Faithfulness of God—Part Twenty-Two." The Bible and Culture, March 12, 2014. www.patheos.com/blogs/bibleandculture/2014/03/12/wrights-paul-and-the-faithfulness-of-god-part-twenty-two/.

Wright, N. T. *The Climax of the Covenant: Christ and the Law in Pauline Theology*. Minneapolis: Fortress, 1991.

———. *Justification: God's Plan and Paul's Vision*. Downers Grove, IL: InterVarsity Press, 2009.

———. *Paul: A Biography*. New York: HarperOne, 2018.

———. *Paul and His Recent Interpreters*. Minneapolis: Fortress, 2013.

———. *Pauline Perspectives: Essays on Paul from 1978–2013*. Minneapolis: Fortress, 2013.

Zetterholm, Magnus. *Approaches to Paul: A Student's Guide to Recent Scholarship*. Minneapolis: Fortress, 2009.

SCRIPTURE INDEX